LIFE AFTER LIFE

A GUILDFORD FOUR MEMOIR

PADDY ARMSTRONG

with Mary-Elaine Tynan

Gill Books

Gill Books
Hume Avenue
Park West
Dublin 12
www.gillbooks.ie

Gill Books is an imprint of M.H. Gill & Co.

978 07171 7247 4

Print origination by O'K Graphic Design, Dublin
Printed by CPI Group (UK) Ltd, Croydon, CRO 4YY

This book is typeset in 11/16.5 pt Minion with titles in Frutiger Light.

The paper used in this book comes from the wood pulp of managed forests. For every tree felled, at least one tree is planted, thereby renewing natural resources.

A CIP catalogue record for this book is available from the British Library.

5 4 3 2 1

This book is dedicated to Alastair Logan, who fought for 15 years to ensure our lives were given back to us.

I wish to also honour the memory of two amazing people whose lives after their life sentences were far too short: Carole Richardson and Gerry Conlon.

Above all, I dedicate this book to the three people who have made my life after 'life' so precious: Caroline, John and Sophie.

PROLOGUE

As a boy from the Lower Falls Road in Belfast, I never expected to go further than the end of my street. Looking back over the last six, almost seven decades, the images that flash through my mind are hardly believable – sometimes, it feels like I'm remembering someone else's life.

The truth is, I've lived three very different lives: the one before prison; the one in prison; and my life since then. It has taken years, and the help of a very strong woman, to make sense of it all. I'm a man who hates confrontation, likes a good party, a tall tale, a bit of craic. I'm not someone who ever wanted to stand up and talk about stuff like this – I never wanted to live it in the first place. But I have, and even though it's taken a long time, now I've found a voice to speak about it.

Again and again I'm asked the same questions. *Are you angry? What's it like to be one of the Guildford Four? Is there anything that can compensate for all you lost?* There are no easy answers. I've spent almost three decades trying to figure it out – my fears, my losses, my loves, my fights – but I feel I've reached an understanding now. What I know is that my life has been many things, but whatever it's been, I remain unbroken. It's been a long, winding and at times very rocky road, but I have a life after life.

CHAPTER ONE

On the street where you live …
(My Fair Lady)

There's all these people outside my house. People of all ages – adults, children, neighbours, friends and others from streets nearby. They don't seem to be doing anything. Just standing there. They're talking, but in hushed tones. It doesn't look right.

Just a few minutes ago I was playing football with some boys from another street. *There's been an accident on the Falls. It's your wee sister, Paddy.* Gertie? What would Gertie be doing up on the Falls? She's only two years old. It doesn't sound right.

So I kept playing. I was goalie, as usual. They needed me. But then a few minutes later I heard some other boys talking about an accident on the Falls. *A wee girl from Milton Street.* Oh, Gertie, for God's sake. *I have to go. Think my sister's fallen or something.*

And now I'm walking towards the house and everyone's gone quiet. Why are they looking at me? What are they whispering? *That wee lad – that's the brother. He's her only boy.* A few of them are smiling in a funny way. Smiling without smiling. One woman reaches out to pat me on the shoulder as I go past.

~

My early life is marked by women. I'm surrounded by them. There's Mammy, my two grannies and then there's my sisters, Harriet, Eileen, Gertie and, later on, Josephine. And my daddy and me. The only two men in an alpha-female household.

A typical Catholic family, we arrive in quick succession. Harriet's born in 1949, me in 1950 and then Eileen (named after Mammy) in 1951. There's a break then as my parents catch their breath and then wee Gertie comes along when I'm four. Josephine, my eternal baby sister, arrives when I'm almost nine and she completes our family. There are five Armstrong children, four of whom will survive one millennium and grow old in the next.

Mammy, Daddy, Harriet, myself and Eileen spend our first few years living with Granny and Grandad Maxwell in their house down on the Short Strand, beside the Belfast docks. When Gertie comes along that makes six of us living with them, all crammed into a tiny house. It's too much, so we move a mile or two down the road, to live with Granny Mullins. She's Mammy's mammy – the Omagh Woman. So now the six of us are living with her in a two-bedroom terraced house on Milton Street, just off the Falls Road, in West Belfast.

The buses and cars roar up and down the Falls, coming and going to and from the town. There's more traffic every year as motor cars become popular. My first memory is the roar of bus engines, the acrid taste of fumes and the trembling of the pavement as they chug past.

Behind the Falls is a confusing labyrinth of narrow streets and lanes, for those who don't know the area, but we know every bend in every alley. Me and my friends have to know every inch of every laneway as we flee the local grocer, our pockets filled with apples or oranges. We know which neighbours will come and shout at us if we kick a ball against their wall. And I'm quite familiar with the bigger boys who'll push and chase me for the only shilling in my pocket. Those boys are the only bad thing I have to deal with, though, because the Falls in the 1950s is a peaceful community. Those streets and lanes of my childhood are one big playground where we spend our weekends, the short afternoons in winter and the warm, endless summer evenings, chasing, hiding, and then later on getting up to mischief with drink and girls.

When I'm a boy on the Falls the biggest social problem is poverty. Large families, many far bigger than ours, live in these wee poky houses. Getting by, just about. Getting nothing from the government. Passed over for good jobs and bigger houses in favour of Protestant families. The invisible majority.

So the people of the Falls have to just do their best. We help one another. Passing a bit of dinner over the fence when there's some left over. Sending outgrown clothes in to the neighbours when they're almost threadbare but not quite. *There's a few more months in that there skirt, Maisie. Do your Margaret rightly.* We're wearing shoes with holes in them and saying nothing in case we get a clip around the ear or the wallop of a wooden spoon until there's enough money for a new pair. We're cutting up newspaper and threading string through it, to hang up in the outside toilet in the garden. Toilet paper is a luxury none of us can afford.

And even though most of us have very little, this is a community in the truest sense. Doors are left unlocked and people walk in and out of each other's houses. I might be in a house eating some boy's dinner and he might be in my house eating mine – nothing strange about that. Women talking to each other on the doorsteps, washing the doorstep, sweeping their wee patch of space so it almost shines. In the evenings, as the sun glows before it drops down behind the Divis Mountains, young men are playing cards, smoking and trying to get the attention of the local girls lucky enough to have a job in the mills.

The landscape of my early childhood isn't burnt-out buildings. It's chippies and bookies, pubs and pet shops, drapery shops and tiny corner shops. It's the pounding of small feet through the lanes and the drumming sound of a ball against a wall or a kerb. It's children squealing, shouting and the smoke rising from the factory chimneys in the near distance. And it's the women and men pouring out of the linen mills and factories at the end of the day. Once a country lane leading from the city centre, the Falls is now a hub of industry. Walking along Milton Street, Lemon Street, Mary Street, Peel Street, you can smell flour and chocolate and bus fumes – the smells of a busy manufacturing area. Catholics and Protestants work together in the mills, all getting along, all making a few bob, all glad when the bell rings and the work day ends and they stream out together, heading home.

~

That wee lad – that's the brother. He's her only boy.

I walk past the whispering crowd. Another woman pats me, this time on the arm. I walk by her and through the front door and find everyone inside. My whole family standing around, all in the kitchen, Mammy, Daddy, Granny, Harriet and Eileen. Everyone except Gertie. All quiet-looking. Mammy sitting down, holding a cup of tea in her hand. Not drinking it. Daddy looking out the window. Biting his lip. Eileen and Josephine just standing there. Pale and silent.

I'm looking at them, from one to another, but nobody's speaking. I don't want to ask. I'm only six, but I already know that I don't want to know the answer. I can hear my voice, but it sounds like it's coming from someone far away, speaking from the other end of a tunnel.

What's wrong?

Silence.

Finally, someone speaks.

It's Gertie, Paddy. She was hit.

Silence.

Gertie's dead, Paddy. She's was killed. On the Falls.

Dead?

I don't really understand dead. I know what it means. They talk about it in school all the time. Hell and Purgatory if you're bad. Heaven if you're good. It's to do with your soul and God and that kind of thing. There's a boy in my class and his mammy died, but she was old. Our Gertie's not even three yet. And besides, I only saw her half an hour ago, asking Mammy for money for a penny poke (ice cream).

She's probably out playing somewhere, I say. *Gertie's fine,* I assure them.

But they're shaking their heads. *She's not. She was hit, Paddy. Wasn't she, Mammy?*

Yes.

I'm shaking my head. She can't be dead. If she was, they'd have her here now.

Where is she? I ask.

She's gone to the hospital in the ambulance. That's where we're going now, your daddy and me. You stay here with your granny.

You're wrong. I know you are. There's nothing wrong with Gertie. She's probably upstairs. You'll see. That's what I want to shout, but you don't say that to adults.

~

Our house, like every other on our street, is full of noise. Clanging pots and banging doors and children running in and out. Somewhere in the background is the sound of my mammy's voice, humming or singing some song. You never have to look for her, just follow the sound of her voice. She loves the songs from the old films, like *My Fair Lady*. The soundtrack of my childhood.

These girls will be the death of me. For now I sleep downstairs, in the living room, but when my granny gets too old to go upstairs I'll have to share a room with the girls. It's just as well I have always been able to pack my life into a tiny bag, because there'll be precious little space for any personal belongings when I'm sharing a room with three girls. But even though we're all crammed in, we manage very well with what we have. A happy house.

The worst part is not having a bathroom. We have a toilet in an outhouse in the back garden. The ceramic toilet bowl and the wooden seat are built into the outhouse, so it's all one solid piece. And that's it. In the early hours of a winter's morning, before the sun has risen, we stumble barefoot through the house, half asleep, in search of the back door. With the gas streetlight barely illuminating the wet ground of the concrete back yard, we feel our way along the wall, no torch to guide us, groping our way towards the creaky, broken door of the toilet, praying there's some newspaper squares left.

We're scrubbed to within an inch of our lives once a week in a big basin, one by one. As the only boy I always go first and then the girls are washed, Gertie last. Once we are old enough we'll be given sixpence every week to go down to the local swimming pool on the Falls. No shower – just a chlorine-filled pool that we jump into, have a swim and come out clean. Ready for a night out.

Sometimes I think the girls believe I'm a wee doll for them to play with. They want to dress me up and tell me what to do. I'm a softie. They know how to boss me around and make me play their games. Skipping. Dolls. I don't let on, but I'm very happy. I like it when someone ties a rope to a lamp-post and we swing around it. *Your turn, Paddy.* I get a few spins about the post and then they're poking me again. *Off now, Harriet's turn.*

Even when I've reached my late teens and I'm off out to a local dance, nothing has changed. I'm inspected, and at least one of them checks my neck and invariably sends me back inside to wash it. Even Eileen, who's a year younger than me, loves to boss me around. This sister of mine, the one who'll visit me in prison like a surrogate mother when Mammy can't afford to travel over, really knows how to wind me up. She teases me, calls me *a big girl*, once again sending me running to Mammy, who, we all know very well, has a soft spot for her only boy.

Amidst all these women, I'm very grateful for my daddy's company. We share a love of football and the races. His brother is a greyhound trainer so he prefers the dogs, while I like the horses, but we can talk about anything. Even after he's gone I can hear his voice for many years. See his gentle smile. When he's gone it gets a bit claustrophobic, all these women. But I get on so well with my mammy and granny and sisters, and everything they do is out of love, so I never get too annoyed. There's no point, I always say. They tell me I'm so laid-back I could be dead, and I laugh.

My earliest and clearest memory of my father is tied up with my first experience of music. I'm about five years old and Daddy and I have taken the bus into town. Just the two of us. The boys. It's a wee surprise, something very special – I've no idea what to expect. Nothing in my short life could have prepared me for the operatic tones of Gilbert and Sullivan's *The Mikado*, but even more memorable is my father. Watching him watch the opera: his eyes wide, his mouth slackened in awe and, when he eventually turns to me, his smile. This is the moment. I know from then on that music has a special quality; it can take you out of yourself, to somewhere magical. I will need it one day, though my five-year-old self doesn't know it yet.

~

Granny shoos us out of the house when my parents leave for the hospital. What do we do now? Can you play when your sister is dead, or do you stand with your hands in your pockets? Go back and save a few more goals? It doesn't seem like the right thing to do, but there's nobody to ask. The adults don't seem to know and I certainly don't.

I still don't know how Gertie died. I'm trying to listen to a few people talking, see if I can work it out. But all I can hear is that she was knocked down on the Falls.

Later, Eileen tells me exactly what happened. She and her friends from the street wanted to go to the local pet shop. It's on the other side of the Falls, in a little row of shops, just where the road curves around. There's a real, live monkey in the window and it draws small groups of children every day. They tap on the glass, wave, want to hold and feed it. We've all done it. Wishing you could bring it home.

As she's leaving the house, Eileen tells Mammy she's away to the pet shop to see the monkey in the window. Now she's waving goodbye to Gertie, who's sitting on the front step eating a penny poke. Eileen and her group of wee girls, all around five years old, are walking down to the Falls. They're talking about the monkey. Dying to see it. And now they're crossing over the busy road. Buses and cars pass by regularly, but the girls are careful. They've reached the other side and are getting closer to the pet shop when one of Eileen's friends calls her. *Eileen. Your Gertie's followed us – look, she's behind us.*

Gertie is running across the road. Eileen is sighing. Gertie follows her everywhere. She'll have to wait a moment while Gertie crosses. Then she'll take her to the window before bringing her home. *How did the wee one get away without anyone seeing her? Mammy will be so angry.*

Gertie's almost made it across the road when one of her shoes slips off. It's lying on the road, and when she realises she turns back. She's bending down to get it and Eileen's shouting now. *Leave it.* Gertie doesn't see the bus coming around the bend on the Falls. Eileen sees it. It's getting closer. *Leave the shoe, Gertie, leave it – come on!* Gertie is standing up and looking. Eileen doesn't know if she's heard her voice or the sound of the driver slamming on the brakes, but either way it's too late.

~

As a young boy in the mid-1950s, one of my favourite smells when I walk in the door of our house is my father's mince stew. Everyone hates Mammy's stew so Daddy has to make it, and it's the best of a weekly menu that rarely changes: stew on Monday, cabbage and potatoes on Tuesday, fish on Friday, soup on Sunday with boiled potatoes and a brisket of cheap meat.

Apart from the stew, most of the cooking is done by our mammy or Granny Mullins. She's a formidable woman, our granny, very kind and generous, but she's a plain-speaking country woman from Omagh who doesn't suffer fools gladly. She's not educated. No-one is in our house. But she's a hard worker. Every morning she leaves early and walks the couple of miles up to the Ormeau Road where she cleans big fancy houses. She often brings our Eileen with her and lets her play with the toys in the house while she works. A very good-looking child, Eileen is her favourite.

Our one ongoing battle is over my name. I just want to be called Paddy. My friends call me Paddy, my sisters do and even my parents are fine with it, but Granny Mullins insists on calling me Patrick. She shrieks my name in her Omagh accent. *Paaaaaaaatrick!*

In my teenage years I find out there's another lad called Patrick Armstrong living locally. Apparently a bit of a hell-raiser, this other fella gets into a lot of trouble, so on the fairly regular occasions when I'm stopped on the street or in a pub for random questioning, the police will pounce on me when they hear my name. *Patrick Armstrong, we've been looking for you. Into the van!* Each time they drag me out before I have the chance to tell them they have the wrong one, that I'm called Paddy. Sometimes they'll only listen when we get to the barracks.

My mammy is a softer version of my granny. They're both hard working, but Mammy is very affectionate. She bears her burdens silently, and she never asks for anything in return.

I'm very like my father, Johnny, everyone says. A quiet person who likes a quiet life. Everybody likes my dad. When I was young he worked hard, as a scaffolder. Then he had a bad fall and hurt his leg and his head. That fall saw him plagued with pain and health problems for the rest of his life.

My daddy is a man of routine, just as I will be when I'm grown. The highlight of his week is his Friday-evening trip to the pub along with all the other men who work in the local mills, factories and building sites. He only ever drinks pints of Guinness, just as I'll do when I'm old enough. He might take an hour over a pint and savour it. Other times he'll suck it down like a starving child, in one hungry gulp.

As kids, sometimes we try to sneak into the pub and hope that someone will buy us a drink or a packet of crisps. More often than not, though, they chase us out. As a young boy, I want to be one of those men sitting on a bar stool beside my dad, having a pint of Guinness with him. Chatting and laughing with the other men; having a laugh, as we say. I'll only get to do it a few times before he's taken from us.

Fridays are my favourite day, too. Like all good Catholics, we only eat fish on a Friday. When he's feeling generous or had one too many, Daddy sends me down to Sylvia's, the local chippie, for two fish suppers between the seven of us. Wrapped in a newspaper is the biggest piece of greasy, battered fish and a huge portion of thick, home-cut chips – real potatoes that they soak in salt and vinegar. You might wait an hour in a queue snaking down the road, but there's always a bit of banter among all the hungry people waiting to get in the door and order.

Sometimes we go down to another chippie. It's a bit further away, but it's worth it just to see the man with one arm who works there. We joke that he's like the one-armed character in the TV series *The Fugitive*. Anyone who's off to get the fish suppers there says, *Right, I'm off to see the Fugitive*. It's the funniest thing we've ever heard.

Every Friday evening, after dinner, Granny makes a big pot of soup from lentils and vegetables for Saturday's dinner. She leaves it to simmer gently in the pot and it sits there overnight, cooling down, before she serves it for dinner the next day. Lying in bed upstairs I can smell the starchy potatoes and sweet carrots as I fall asleep.

Some Fridays, Daddy stays in the pub all evening and eventually slinks home in the early hours with a few friends in tow. The next morning, when she comes down to make the breakfast, Granny Mullins will find a kitchen filled with beer bottles, dirty plates and an empty pot of soup – and then the war will start!

As money is always very tight there's never a holiday, but sometimes Mammy packs us onto the bus to Omagh to see her family for a weekend or maybe longer. More often, though, we take the bus to Bangor or other beaches for a day trip. We spend a few hours in Bangor, running along the sand, and if we're lucky we get a penny poke too. At the end of a day out we take the bus back to Belfast. Our family never owned a car, so none of us can drive. It's not until later in life that Harriet will learn, and then me even later again. When I'm growing up there's no money for cars so we get around on buses. It suits me fine – you can't miss what you've never had.

~

Eileen sees the bus striking Gertie's tiny body. *Thud.* Sending her sailing into the air. The two-year-old body is moving slowly through empty space. Travelling forwards and upwards. Surrounded by silence.

Eileen is standing there. Looking at this unbelievable scene in front of her. The bus has stopped. Everything has stopped. Gertie's tiny body went up into the air and so it must have come back down, but Eileen can't see her. Where is she? Eileen's dumbstruck. Like any other witness who suddenly comes face to face with horror. What should she do? Run over there? Shout?

The Falls traffic has come to a standstill. No roar from car or bus engines now. Just the gentle chugging of engines idling. And a low hum of shocked voices. People standing on the road. Pointing. Shaking their heads. Blessing themselves. Offering up a prayer.

The traffic is gradually building up, snaking back along the Falls. Buses. Cars. Taxis. All stopped. Filled with people wondering what's happened. My daddy's on one of those buses. He's wondering too.

And now Eileen's running home to our mammy. Not sure what she'll say, but home is the best option. Mammy will know what to do. Back across the Falls. Through the streets. Fast as her little legs will take her. Up Milton Street to our house. In the open door. To Mammy.

Gertie's been hit, Mammy.

What!

She's been hit. She followed me to the pet shop and then she lost her shoe and then a bus hit her. On the Falls.

But she was on the doorstep a minute ago. Mammy is shaking her head. *Don't be silly. Gertie's fine. She'll be back in a wee minute. She's probably playing on the street.*

Eileen doesn't know what to do, so she listens to Mammy. And now she's outside, still not knowing what to do.

Daddy's bus has finally let the passengers off and he's walking home. He can see there's been an accident. People talking. *A wee child was hit. She's not moving.* He's coming down the road now, thinking of the poor family whose child has been knocked down. Into the house. Telling Mammy. *A child was just hit on the Falls. God love that family.*

Mammy's looking at him. The realisation. She tells Daddy what Eileen said. The colour drains from both their faces as they take it in.

But she'll be okay, surely. She might have broken a leg, or an arm, maybe. We'll have to see if she's gone to the hospital.

When a policeman knocks on the door, Mammy knows.

Sorry for your troubles, Missus. She died on the way to hospital.

They have to catch her as her legs give way beneath her.

∼

School, for me, has good days and bad days. My primary school, St Comgall's, is a large mixed school. I keep my head down and rarely come to the attention of teachers but I do attract the notice of a few bigger lads, both at school and in our street. I never say anything at home when they give me a hard time.

I'm an easy target. I know this. Something gets broken, a window maybe. *It was Paddy Armstrong, Missus. From Milton Street.* They know I won't stand up to them or fight back. I don't like confrontation.

It's a funny thing when people single you out for no reason at all and pick on you. When I write it down it looks funny, but I always seem to immediately assume a position of guilt. When that group of lads decides that I will be their target for a few years in school and on the streets of Belfast, I don't run to my sisters. I could tell Eileen and Harriet. They'd stand up for me. But I feel weak and embarrassed. In my head I wonder, Have I done something to provoke this? Do I deserve it? Can they see something in me that makes them want to hurt me, that makes them confident they can go ahead and do that without it backfiring on them? What is it they see? It's painful, but as I get older, stockier and a little braver, it will come to an end. One day I'll suddenly retaliate and, blinded by rage, push one of them to the ground and pound him until he begs for mercy. It's too big a reaction, but then, after holding it all in for so long, it's inevitable. That's part of the pattern that's set down now, too: a submissive, fearful and acquiescent person who gives in quickly, but who can also eventually explode when pushed too far over the line. Not often, mind you. But these early traits will colour the rest of my life.

~

When Gertie's laid out in the casket, she's only visible from the waist up. They've cleaned her little face. No ice-cream, no jam. A clean, pale child. No marks on her face. You'd never know.

She's dressed in a blue silk dress adorned with a picture of the Sacred Heart, just above her heart. They tell us it's called a shroud. She looks like she's asleep. We have a wake for her in our house. She's laid out in our living room for a night. We sit beside her and pray, looking down on her tiny body in her blue shroud.

Years later, Eileen tells me something about that night and I wish I'd never known. Eileen is standing there, looking at our little sister laid out in the living room, and she finds herself wondering, *What happened to the bottom part of her body? The part that was hit by the bus?* When there's nobody else around, Eileen decides to take a wee look. Under the blanket. To see for herself. Never imagining for a moment what she'll see.

When she lifts up the soft blanket covering my sister, she finds herself gazing at empty space where Gertie's lower body should be. It takes a moment for the full force of this to hit her, and she drops the blanket. Shocked. Her baby sister, my baby sister, was hit with such force that her entire lower body was separated from her. Now there's just nothing. Nothing at all. It's an image that will haunt Eileen for the rest of her life – and then me.

I don't know the last time I saw Gertie. That afternoon before running off to play with my friends? Or maybe at breakfast time? I don't know what I said to her, whether I smiled at her or made fun of her, or if she was annoying me. I'll never know now. It shouldn't really matter, but it does.

After spending a night in our house Gertie is taken to the local church for a night and then buried the next day. I don't remember the burial and nobody can remember who she's buried with. Many years later my sisters try to find her grave, but they can't. It's a mystery. She isn't buried with my parents and she doesn't appear in any records. It's like she disappeared into thin air.

~

Despite my shyness and even though I play with girls, I'm just a Belfast boy. Love the company of other boys. Love my football. Playing football with a ball made from an old woolen jumper stuffed with wet newspaper. Using the busy Falls Road as our pitch, we spend entire afternoons and evenings playing fierce and long matches against boys from other streets, stopping only to eat. We go home only when the man comes around with his ladder to light the gas lamps that glow around Belfast.

In the late 1950s and early 1960s I cross paths with another local boy. Gerry Conlon. Sometimes we end up on opposing teams. Our street against his. He's younger than me and goes to a different primary school. And although we're not good friends, our paths will continue to cross on the streets of Belfast through football and hanging around on corners.

In our teens and early twenties I still see Gerry occasionally. Although we both love music, football, a few pints, touching for a girl and going to the bookies, we're also very different. I keep my head down; Gerry is a wild child. He's known around the Falls for always being in trouble, an answer for everything. Later he'll describe me as *a meek and mild kid, afraid of his own shadow.* When I think back on it, I suppose I was like that with people I didn't know. We end up in the same workshop for a few brief months in Mackie's, one of the biggest factories in Northern Ireland, but apart from that we move in different circles, just bumping into each other every now and then.

That's how my life was back then. I was a typical boy in hard-working, poor and peaceful 1950s Belfast. I never strayed more than a mile or so from my home in Milton Street, mostly content in a world of family, friends and narrow streets and laneways. A timid, fair-haired boy, tearing through the streets behind my sisters Eileen and Harriet, often with wee Gertie trailing behind, crying. *Wait for me.* We've been waiting for our poor wee Gertie ever since.

CHAPTER TWO

I suppose I can't be choosy, when there's not too many choices ...
(The Blades)

F ather McKinley is talking and talking, telling me that England might be
the best place to go. *You'll get a job there, Paddy. Help your mammy out.*
He's sitting comfortably in our kitchen, drinking the tea that Mammy
made and eating the biscuits that she keeps for such occasions, although
she can't afford them. He leans back in his chair, his dog collar pristine, his
stomach protruding slightly, painting a picture of a beautiful city full of
possibilities. We've had a talk and I've agreed that I'll pay back the £22 she
borrowed from him so she could pay the bills and rent. *Whatever I have to
do, Father, you'll get it*, I assure him. Even if it means going to London. That's
how it is where I come from. People are very close to the Church, and if
you're in need they'll help you out.

~

After the loss of our Gertie, we learn to go on. We talk about her. We
comment on things she would have liked. She was only a little girl, but she
had a very definite personality. She was chatty and funny and friendly and
trusting. Children are good at adjusting, though. Within a couple of years,
my little sister feels a bit like an almost-remembered dream.

We have a new baby in the house now. Josephine. Our wee sister. She
comes along in 1959 when I'm almost nine, so I'm very protective of her.
A baby to maybe heal a tiny part of the heartbreak. We don't know it
but Josephine will be Mammy's saviour, caring for her after Daddy and
Granny are gone and the rest of us have been forced to emigrate, fleeing the
Troubles. Wee Josephine, my darling baby sister.

Life as a teenager in Belfast is more boring. Too old to be out playing, too young to be working, it's that awful in-between stage. I still love football, but when I tell my dad one day that's what I want to be, he just looks at me. I'll have to wise up soon enough, he knows. I'll have to accept that I'll never be a professional player.

I've two new interests at least – gambling and girls. These take up most of my time and they'll play a big role in my life, positive and negative. They'll lead me to some of my darkest hours and some of my greatest highs.

All the younger boys play marbles for a penny. I often don't even have a penny, but if I can scrounge one I'm in there. The biggest thrill, though, is watching the big lads gambling. They won't let you gamble in the pubs, so we spend our evenings on street corners. I love the craic and the banter. Hours spent down on your hunkers, playing poker, slagging each other and just having a laugh. Someone has to be on the lookout for the RUC because they'll arrest you if they catch you gambling on the street. That's often our job, as the younger ones. You have to give a whistle or call out a code-word to warn if they're coming. And if I'm lucky, everybody runs off and leaves a few half-crowns on the ground, which I can grab before I run too.

Whenever I get one of these half-crowns, or a rare shilling from my mammy or granny, I muscle my way into a game. Because I've had an unusually deep voice from a young age, the older lads let me in. I even win sometimes, and that's the best feeling. The way they all look at me. Sweeping away the money in a move I've practised on my own and then slamming it back down for another game. It never makes it into my pocket. What's the point? I'd rather play another game, get another rush of adrenaline. You can never get enough. And if you lose, there's always the next time.

I end up with a reputation for always being broke, for hanging around, hoping for a penny. My sisters and some of my friends tease me that I'd gamble on two flies going up a wall and, to be truthful, there will be times in my life when I'll actually consider it, if there is half a chance of winning and a bit of craic to be had. Over the coming years I'll lose thousands of pounds without even really realising it, until it's too late. It's my Achilles' heel, but there's worse things you could do.

I have a purer obsession: music. As a teenager in the 1960s I love the Belfast band Them. The lead singer, a young Van Morrison, lives nearby and I've seen him at practice sessions with his friends. Music is an escape, a solace, a friend – it means the world to me. I love dancing too. I fancy myself as a bit of a mover. When I'm 17 I win a trophy for doing the twist in a competition at the Plaza disco one Saturday night. A rare moment of confidence for me.

~

I'm leaving school. I'm 15 years old and I've had enough. Waste of time. I'll never go to university. I don't know anybody who does. Like all the big businesses around here, Queen's University is technically open to Catholics by now, but it wasn't in fact. The reality is that Catholics leave school and get an apprenticeship or try to get a job, which suits me fine. I want to make a bit of money. Sick of having nothing. Hanging around the streets – nothing to do and nowhere to go and no money to go out with. I want to be able to buy a pint, go down the bookies, go out to a dance, meet a girl and take her out.

I get a job in the local bookies. A board-marker, just like Patrick 'Giuseppe' Conlon, Gerry's dad. He works in a bookies further up the Falls. I can usually get in a wee bet, even though I'm not meant to given my age. Giuseppe's a good man – tall but feeble, and he knows his horses. Always gives a kind word and a wee tip on who might win. Now I'm a board-marker, too. It's not a hard job. I just have to write up the names of the horses running and the prices. I have to concen,trate, though. You don't want to write up the wrong horse or price. Giuseppe has lovely handwriting and I try to copy his, as mine leaves a bit to be desired, but it's fine.

I want to have a laugh and some banter with people, just like Giuseppe does. When the favourite loses, everyone gives the board-marker a hard time, but not in the way that teachers give out to you in school. This is all done for a bit of fun. I duck and laugh when they throw their dockets at me in mock disgust. Soon I know most of the men who come in by name and they know me. When I see them in the street, depending on whether they've won or lost recently, they might say, *There's my favourite board-marker* or *Keep away from him – he's bad luck!* I love it.

~

Things are changing in Belfast. It feels like it's getting more dangerous. I leave the bookies after it gets robbed by men in balaclavas. One morning I'm cleaning the board, about to put up the new prices for a morning race, when these fellas burst in and one of them hits me so hard on the elbow with his gun that I drop the bowl of water I'm holding. Heart is racing. Petrified. Have to stop myself from wetting myself. Tears in my eyes. There is a moment when I think he's going to shoot me, but he just continues on and ransacks the till and then runs off.

Everyone says it's an IRA job. I say nothing. Best to keep your mouth shut in these events. It puts me off working in a bookies, though. I don't sleep for nights afterwards. Wake up in a cold sweat, sitting upright in the pitch black.

I'm leaving. I've got a new job. Sorry about that. I don't really have a new job, but I know I'll find something. Anything. I can't take a gun to my head again. In fact, this has put me off guns for life. I'd never have been any use to the IRA.

A lad in the Catholic Young Men's Society (CYMS) says he can get me an apprenticeship. The CYMS looks after local boys. He's as good as his word. I get an apprenticeship. I'm a plumber's mate in a Protestant company in a Protestant area. It's all right for a while, but when things get too dangerous I can't walk to work safely. There's boys looking at me every morning. Eyeing me up. They know. It's only a matter of time. So I quit before I get a beating. Or worse. And now I have to find something else.

I find a job as a factory storeman in a clothing manufacturer. It's in a Catholic area even though it's owned by a Protestant man, but that doesn't bother me or them. I like this job because the group I work with are great fun. Occasionally, when they have buyers in from the shops, I'm asked to model suits or clothes. My family can't believe it when I tell them. *You, Paddy? Aye, why not me?* But I know what they mean. For a quiet lad, it might seem surprising. But I'm slim and a decent height, so I've learned to strut up and down the factory floor like one of them fellas you see in the films.

The boss is looking at me one day. *Have a job for you, Paddy. New suit. Would you like to model it? Aye, no problem.* I'm ready to show off. Getting the walk perfected. I might start trying to build up my muscles like some of the boys I know. That would look even better.

He's smiling, though. He's up to something. It's going to be horrible, I know it. I don't care. I can wear anything now. I'm not nervous like I used to be. Those buyers always take the stuff that I'm wearing. I can do this.

He goes into the back and comes back with it over his arm. *Right, then, put this on you, boy.* It's a strange colour. Several, in fact. Red, white and blue.

Is that … You want me to wear that? Aye, dead on. No, it can't be. Fuck off!
What are you talking about, Paddy? That there's a lovely suit. Just put it on.
You can get lost – that's a bloody Union Jack. You'll not get me wearing a Union Jack.
Jesus, Paddy, it's only a suit, for God's sake. Just go in and put it on.
There's no way I'm wearing that. Fire me if you want.
Sure we're not going to fire you, but would you not just put it on?
I told you. No. Would you wear a Tricolour?
I would surely if I was selling it.
But you're not, right?
Exactly.
Well I'm not putting this on.
Ah, Paddy, I'm disappointed now.

But he's got a smile on his face. He knows fine rightly. I've no problem whatsoever working with Protestants in a Protestant-owned company, but, mild as I am, there are times when I have to put my foot down. There's no way I would ever wear a Union Jack suit.

We joke about it, but it's one of those moments. I feel like we've just crossed an invisible line. It seems that religion is muscling its way into every part of our lives. After more than a year and a half working there I have to leave. It's 1968 and things are heating up in Belfast, and it's just too dangerous to work in a Protestant company. It's a shame, because I really like it there.

I find other bits of work – in a cash-and-carry and in bars. Enough to be self-sufficient, which is all a fella of 18 needs. I like not having to ask anyone for anything. I have my own money and I can spend it as I please. Eileen's always telling me that I should be giving some to my mammy, but she says it's okay. *Go and enjoy your money, Paddy. You earned it.*

That means I can go to the bookies. Stand around with the other fellas. Throw my docket at the board-marker when I lose. But I'm not bad at it. Giuseppe says I've a good eye for a winner. Lots of them say that. Some even ask me for tips. *You used to work in a bookies, Paddy, didn't you? I hear you're good at picking winners. Is that right?* I smile. Maybe.

I don't mind that sometimes I spend most of my pay packet before the weekend is over, but the girls get really angry with me. *For God's sake, Paddy, you can't have spent it all. How much did you give Mammy this week? With Daddy out of work she needs you to help her.*

I try to be responsible, but I don't earn much. And aren't I entitled to spend my own wages? If the girls are so worried, why can't they give her money? But they do. They keep reminding me about it. I won't admit it, but I feel bad. I won't go into the bookies next week. Not every day.

Eileen makes me feel really bad. *I don't believe you, Paddy. Telling Mammy you lost your pay packet. Sure didn't I see you in the bookies earlier? You better give her more next week, okay?* I say, *I will, no problem, honest.*

What I love about the bookies and the pub is the peace. With rarely a woman in sight to tell you what to do or think, it's a relief to be there. I love the smell of paper and cigarettes, the banter, the wins, the losses, the adrenaline and the exhaustion. It's like a small community within a community and, for a fairly self-conscious lad like me, I can wander in and instantly feel like I know what I'm doing – like I'm at home.

As I go from job to job, the local bookies is the one constant in my life. Everyone knows me and the bets I do. A placepot. Every time. I love sitting there with a pencil, studying the horses. The form. Looking at the odds. The smell of tobacco. Cheap cologne on those who can afford it. Men just standing around, talking. Everyone knows everyone. This is my place. Even if it's just for a few minutes a day, this is the one constant apart from home.

And as I'm writing on my docket, I'm calculating the winnings. This is a good one. And the odds on that horse mean I'll do well. Yes, this could be the one. If I win today, I'll give Mammy all of it. Most of it. Just keep a little back for myself. But she can have the rest. Buy whatever she wants. She'll be so happy. I can just see her face. Coming up to give me a kiss. Then Eileen will see that I know what I'm doing.

~

If the Belfast of my childhood is largely one of poverty and relative peace, my late teenage years and early twenties are marked by poverty and bloody conflict. Nobody could ever have foreseen how this part of Belfast would become a scene of riots, explosions and shoot-outs, of women running through the streets, seeking refuge with their children as smoke billows from cars and out of broken shop windows, the likes of which we have only ever seen in films. But instead of it being hat-wearing cowboys wielding guns with wooden handles and having a shoot-out before sunset, our world is turned upside-down by angry, scared young men killing other men, women and children.

In 1968, life changes. Almost overnight. There had always been underlying tensions between Catholics and Protestants when I was growing up, but it was never personal. And never this bad. Growing up, it was more about the government's failure to give equal rights to the poor Catholics. We always knew we were the underdog. There's not a day as a Catholic kid in Belfast when you don't learn you're a second-class citizen. We could see that the best houses and jobs went to Protestants, and that the voting areas were rigged during my childhood and before. We listened to our parents complaining about gerrymandering, and, though we didn't really understand them, jokes about Protestants were told and retold, with a bitter laugh. Now, though, it's Protestant against Catholic. Two very separate communities.

In fact, I was nearly a part of that other community; I could very easily have been a Protestant. My father was born and raised in a Protestant family, but after my grandfather died my grandmother remarried, and her new husband was a Catholic, so she and her youngest children (including my father, aged about 16) converted to Catholicism. Some of her older children remained in the Protestant faith, however, like my uncle Billy. My dad then met and married my mother, who was a Catholic, but Uncle Billy married a Protestant woman and they had two children, Harriet and Billy, who were around our age. They grew up near us, down in the docks, and we all played happily together. Although my parents never hid the fact that some of our cousins were Protestants, it never occurred to us to ask why.

Now, in the summer of 1968, Belfast is beginning to simmer with new tensions, threatening to bubble up and spill out over the edges. Being a fairly naïve and politically disengaged teenager, I'm not really aware of the Northern Ireland civil rights movement, which started the previous year. I know that there's inequality and discrimination, but then, who doesn't? Isn't that the way it's always been? But even with my poor understanding it will soon become impossible to ignore the growing chorus of voices demanding change. When Bernadette Devlin leads a civil rights march through Derry in October 1968, suddenly we all understand.

We watch it on the TV in a friend's house. What starts as a peaceful protest quickly descends into a violent battle between marchers and police. It's terrifying. Witnessing fellow-Catholics being brutally beaten by the people who are supposed to maintain order makes even me, the most laid-back person, infuriated. Communities are shocked. People are angry. It is a moment that changes everything. Life will never be the same again.

~

What's happening in Belfast isn't my biggest interest, though. I'm working and I have a bit of money, although it burns a hole in my pocket. I stay at home most nights during the week, spend my Saturday in the bookies and go out on Saturday night. Having three sisters is still annoying – they're always looking me up and down, telling me to change my shirt, tugging on my collars (and ironing them). But the good part of enduring their scrutiny is that I always look pretty smart.

And when I'm out, there's Margaret Hutchinson – this gorgeous girl who lives nearby in the newly built Divis flats. Half the boys on the Falls want to go out with Margaret, including me. She works in the local ice-cream parlour, Sylvester's. It's a real American-style place with tables and proper, tall glasses in which they serve ice cream. It's like being in one of those films, buying a cream soda – a tall glass of cold lemonade with a scoop of ice cream in it, fizzing up in a creamy froth until it almost spills over the sides, a long spoon just about peeking out the top.

On a Saturday evening, with whatever is left in my pay packet, if I haven't spent it all in the bookies, we all go down to Sylvester's. I've been hoping that Margaret will notice me. So has Ronnie McCartney, another boy from the area, although he won't admit that to me for years. He's younger than me and I'm a sharp dresser, so I have the edge on him. When I ask her out, she says yes.

Looking back on it, my time with Margaret is like a series of tiny moments, captured in my mind's eye, idyllic and perfect: going to see her in Sylvester's and smiling shyly at her from a table at the back with my friends; taking her to the local dance and holding her hand so everyone knows she's mine; kissing on a corner where the street light doesn't shine too strongly.

I can't put a word on these powerful feelings, but later on I'll realise I was in love for the first time. I want to spend the rest of my life with her. Marry her. Live in a house not too far away and get a good job to look after her and our children. We don't talk about it but we play surrogate parents to our Josephine, who is only nine. Josephine is mad about Margaret – she spoils my wee sister.

~

December is always cold, but this is worse than usual. It's also wet and
windy. The tension on the streets is exhausting. Everyone is holding out
for Christmas. The Americans are preparing to launch Apollo 8, the first
manned spacecraft to orbit the moon, but all anyone here is talking about is
the marches. While thousands are marching throughout Northern Ireland
demanding equality for Catholics and clashing heavily with the RUC,
just miles away in our house turmoil is taking place in my father's head,
preparing to wreak havoc in the coming weeks.

On Sunday 22 December, as gale-force winds tear through Northern
Ireland, leaving a trail of damage in their wake, and as Apollo 8 orbits the
moon, I'm caught up in a show that we're doing today with the CYMS for
some residents in a local old people's home. At first I find it difficult to sing
in front of people, but it's such a laugh and the old people love it so much
that I soon grow in confidence. That afternoon, as I'm singing from my
usual place near the back of the chorus, I am unaware that my father has
been taken ill and rushed to hospital. When I get home, I'm greeted by a
neighbour who tells me to go to the hospital immediately.

There's a brain tumour swelling inside my 51-year-old father. It's big, the
doctors tell us, so it's probably been there a long time. Maybe since his fall,
we all wonder. They have already operated on him when I arrive. Cut him
open in an attempt to relieve the pressure on his brain. But there's little they
can do. *We've sewn him back up again. Go and sit with him.* He wakes and
looks at me. *Can I have some tablets for the pain, doctor?* I say, *It's me, Dad –
Paddy.* He nods, but I know he doesn't know me. Hold his hand.

He wakes again a few hours later and looks at me. *Paddy. How are you,
son?* He knows me. For the very last time before we lose him, he recognises
me. And for that I'm grateful.

We're all ushered out of the room shortly afterwards, so the doctors can
do their work. The winds are raging and ravaging the country, and while
my father lies in a hospital bed surrounded by doctors and machines, we are
sitting outside, waiting to know his fate, even though it's quite obvious.

When the winds die down and the weak winter light is replaced by
the damp darkness, and as we sit outside, waiting to hear, my father slips

quietly away and our family is a little smaller. Years later I'll realise that I don't have a photo of him. I was only to get one of him and Mammy many years later. A camera isn't something we have access to until I'm in my teens. I'll hold his image in my mind for years, but eventually it will become frayed and faded. Like a photograph that's been exposed to the light for too long.

On Christmas Eve 1968, as the snowflakes fall on Ulster and as families prepare for one of the most special days in the year, we bury our father. The baby Jesus is being born and my daddy has died.

Josephine is holding my hand. At nine she understands, in theory, what is happening, but her eyes are wide and uncomprehending. Just as myself and Harriet and Eileen were the day we buried Gertie.

As we carry my father from our house to St Patrick's Cathedral, snowflakes land on his coffin. Normally we would have been so excited to see snow in December, dreaming of that elusive White Christmas, but today we barely notice it, except to flick it off our dark clothing.

Standing outside the church after the service, greeting mourners, accepting their condolences, we're numbed by grief and the icy cold. I'm reminded countless times that I'm the man of the house now. Apparently I am responsible for my granny, my mammy and my three sisters. I'm 18 years old, but I've never felt more like a child. It doesn't mean that I don't care, but this is not what I imagined for myself. The pressure weighs heavily on me.

~

The civil rights protests and outrage grow and swell around us in the months that follow my father's death, but I barely notice them as I have to learn to accept fate – his and ours. We have to adjust and recalibrate and go on living because, like the protests, nothing is in our control and there is nothing we can do.

This is never clearer than on Thursday 14 August 1969, the day when my home and community become a war zone. After violent clashes between the RUC and the nationalist community in Derry, the anger has reached Belfast. Amidst threats of loyalist gangs coming to burn down houses on Clonard Street, there's an air of determined fury. People are shouting in the streets all around ours. There is a grim sense of purpose on both sides. And sure enough, they do burn down entire Catholic streets near ours. It's terrifying.

As havoc unfolds around us, I'm holed up at home. I probably should be with the other men outside, protesting, but I can't face it. I'm scared. It's cowardly, I know, but I'm not a fighter. I suddenly hear an unfamiliar chopping sound outside – it's some people hacking down a telegraph pole. They'll use it as a barricade in a clash just a short distance away between local Catholics and the RUC. I decide I need to see Margaret, the girlfriend I am madly in love with. Make sure she's okay. She lives in the nearby Divis flats.

As I'm rushing to her place, I pass a lot of my neighbours and friends protesting. I duck through the back streets, avoiding the Falls Road where the police are charging with batons, CS gas and water cannons. Later on, from the safety of a Shorland armoured car with a specially mounted Browning gun on the roof, the police will fire indiscriminately at homes and at the Divis flats.

As the riot is escalating I'm finally in Margaret's flat, surrounded by her younger siblings and other children from nearby flats, all sheltering there from the chaos while their parents and older siblings are rioting on the Falls Road.

It's exciting in a dangerous way at first. But when we hear the shooting there's a sudden silence, followed by petrified howls from the younger children. It's the first time I've ever heard gunfire myself. Stay calm, Paddy. You're the man here. They need you to be strong.

Someone is shouting outside. *Get the women and children higher up.* Suddenly my feet are pounding on the concrete stairs, carrying a child under each arm, wondering will we reach the next floor before a bullet hits us.

The B Specials are shooting in our direction. They're a branch of the RUC, armed and ruthless, the ones everybody is terrified of. They miss us, but a bullet pierces the back window of a flat, hitting and killing Patrick Rooney, a nine-year-old boy sheltering in the back bedroom of his home. He's the same age as our Josephine. The first child victim of the Troubles and one of five or six people to be killed by stray RUC bullets that night.

The next morning, as we welcome the British troops to the Falls, the relief is palpable. *We'll be okay now. They'll sort them ones out, coming to burn down our streets and houses. It'll be okay now. We're safe, thanks be to God.* It takes a while before we realise that the opposite is true.

Things don't calm down and now we're regularly evacuated from our homes and taken to local churches for shelter. In years to come my sister Eileen will remind me that I accompanied the women and children to a church on a truck instead of fighting with the men, but I maintain that I was there to protect my granny, who by then was getting frailer. And, to be honest, I just can't handle it all. I'll get used to it in time, but as an 18-year-old boy who's just lost his father, the violence and anger give me knots in the pit of my stomach and no amount of teasing could convince me to do otherwise.

In the middle of all this, just months after that horrible first night of gunfire on the Falls, I walk in to Sylvester's to find Margaret there with another lad. And that's it. The girl I thought I would marry doesn't want me any more. I won't let on how hurt I am, but it's crushing. Losing Dad, watching Belfast crumble around me and now my girl is gone. I want to get away. Maybe I'll take a boat over to France, pick some grapes. Come back when Belfast is calm again, find a half-decent job, meet a nice girl and settle down. Maybe.

~

By the end of 1969 everyone is on edge because rumours are flying around that the Protestants are going to attack us and wipe out the Falls Road area. The streets aren't safe any more. The games of cards on the corners are rare now. People are afraid. Staying indoors. You can't stand around having a a laugh without getting hassle from the RUC. We call them *black bastards* because they wear a black uniform and they're total bastards to us Catholics. You don't need to do much. If you're playing football and kick it near them, they'll dig a knife into it; if you're gambling on the streets, they'll try to catch you and arrest you. Instead of going out, I go to the CYMS Snooker Hall. I'm not bad at snooker, and it beats hanging around the streets and getting arrested by some RUC fella trying to be a hard man.

Nights now, for most boys in Belfast, consist of launching various objects, including petrol bombs and glass bottles, at armoured cars. Even as a pacifist I can't stay on the margins for ever, so I've managed to join in occasionally, albeit from a safe distance. Like every boy of my age I've considered joining the IRA, but it just isn't for me. They wouldn't take me anyway. They like clean-living young men, not ones like me whose idea of a good afternoon is going between a betting office and a pub. Anyway, I hate guns and violence. We would never be a good match.

Everything we know is disappearing, and then one day I hear that Sylvester's has been burnt down. The place where my friends and I spent so many innocent afternoons devouring cream sodas and smiling shyly at girls has been reduced to a scalded block of concrete. I stand outside, peering through the front window, half boarded up, a black lump where just days ago was an immaculate counter we all sat at, watching reverently as cold drinks were served from a shiny tap. Singed remnants of the décor hang from the ceiling and only the steel shells of the tables remain. It will lie boarded up for years, before being replaced by a row of houses. With the careless flick of a match and a carefully launched petrol-filled bottle, boys of my own age have blasted the heart out of our community

In the summer of 1970 the tide starts to turn against the British army. Just a week before the Twelfth of July, after a raid on a house in a nearby street, a group of boys (many of whom I know) attack British soldiers with stones and petrol bombs. The army responds with CS gas, their weapon of choice when they aren't firing bullets. After that, it's war again.

From our house in Milton Street I can smell the burning and I know that trouble is brewing yet again. I've no intention of joining in and none of my family will be involved, so I'm not too worried for their safety or my own. Even still, I mouth an all too familiar prayer. *Our Father, who art in Heaven …*

On that summer's evening in early July I decide to go and see a friend who lives a couple of miles away. I can't deal with another day of hostility. Picking my way through the back streets and lanes, my only thought is to get as far away as possible from the shouting and the armoured trucks. If I'd known what I was abandoning my ailing grandmother, mammy and three sisters to face without me, I would have stayed.

Throughout the evening, as I sit in my friend's house just a couple of miles away, the army launch gas canisters into the streets around the Falls. Men, women and children are violently ill in the streets. Other families, like mine, are sitting inside, terrified. Others put rags wet with water and vinegar on their front steps, to help those affected by the sting of the gas.

It's just after 10.00pm and I'm about to leave my friend's house. I'm trying to work out a way home that will ensure I don't get caught up in another riot and probably arrested. I'm tired and I've had a few drinks. I just want to go to bed. In between the sounds of intermittent gunfire and exploding petrol bombs, there's a distant whirr of helicopter blades. A disembodied voice floats down from the safety of the helicopter. *We are imposing a curfew. Indefinitely. Any resident caught out of doors will be arrested.*

Around 50 streets, including Milton Street, are on lockdown. But I'm outside the curfew zone. I can't get home. I'll have to sleep in my clothes in my friend's house and go home in the morning.

I have no way to let Mammy know that I'm okay. She doesn't know where I am. I keep thinking they'll lift the curfew, but they don't. When I wake early on Saturday, nothing has changed. All day Saturday the curfew continues and Saturday quickly turns into Sunday. Once again I'm up early, hopeful it's been called off overnight, but it hasn't. Two nights now.

I'm scared now. There's not much food in our house. Normally Mammy would have gone shopping on the Saturday, but as they've been locked in all day she may not have been able to. I'm exhausted with worry. I'm supposed to be the man of the house and I'm stuck here.

And then on Sunday, after mass, the women of Andersonstown and other nearby neighbourhoods decide enough is enough. I watch as around 3,000 of them march onto the Falls Road, like an army of angry bees. Many wearing their Sunday best. They're carrying bags of groceries and pushing prams filled with bottles of milk, bread and other supplies. I follow them towards the curfew zone, towards the soldiers and barbed wire, and I join them. As we march through the barricades, women, children and some men, there's nothing that the army or anyone else can do. When I finally get home, Mammy hugs me. The curfew is over, but nobody can forgive or forget the feeling of being locked into and out of their homes. The honeymoon period with the British army is well and truly over.

~

Two months after the curfew and less than two years after my father's passing, our house is in mourning again. It's Granny. One morning, early in October 1970, just after my twentieth birthday, I come down to an empty kitchen. There's something wrong. No tell-tale signs of a kettle boiling or a pot simmering. I glance into Granny's bedroom and there she is, slouched on the side of the bed, her head hanging to one side, her arms floppy. We call the ambulance, but it's too late. We bury Granny Mullins beside our dad. Our family is crumbling at a frightening rate. With Gertie, Daddy and now Granny gone, we've been almost halved.

Not long after Granny's death we're told they have a flat for us in the Divis complex, just a few streets away. It's a type of flat they call a maisonette. Our new home is 3 Massereene Row. Although it's smaller than our house, it's new, has a bathroom and toilet and proper heating, and I'll have a bedroom again. Even though we don't want to leave our close-knit community, most of our neighbours are going too. So we pack up the contents of Milton Street, including some of Granny's and Daddy's possessions and a few memories of wee Gertie. A new year, a new home and hopefully a new start.

In fact, what's going to be new is a constant military presence. In this strangled atmosphere our brand-new council flats don't feel much like home. In the years to come, these flats with their indoor toilets will fall quickly into disrepair; they'll become damp and cold and rats will run wild while drug-pushers hang around downstairs.

In the space of two years our place is raided by soldiers four times. On one occasion, my mammy is next-door in a neighbour's flat when the door is kicked down by soldiers. Not for the first time I find myself staring at the barrel of a pistol held in the trembling hand of a young soldier. His friends are screaming at me. *Where's the guns? Show us the fucking guns!* I can barely talk. *I don't … I don't know what you mean. I don't … don't have any.*

They're turning the place over looking for one – tearing open cupboards and breaking anything that gets in their way. Apparently one of them saw someone pointing a gun out of a window in our flat, sufficient grounds for their uninvited visit. When my mother returns they're still there and when she tells them I've no gun and no involvement with the IRA, they call her an Irish bitch. She tells them to keep searching, which they do. Eventually they leave empty-handed, ready to wreak havoc in someone else's home.

Every other day my friends and I get stopped, questioned and arrested. Just standing on the street is enough for them to throw you into the back of a truck already filled with other lads who've been scooped up off the street for doing nothing. They take us to the local barracks, march us around in the courtyard outside, make us face a wall and then, after questioning us, throw us back out on the street.

I'm completely paranoid now. Ever since a night when I was walking home with a friend and, just after we'd passed the army post in Albert Street, we heard the wheeze of gunshots and an explosion as bullets hit the pavement just inches from our feet. There was no-one else around so we knew those bullets were intended for us. I can't sleep properly now and keep waking up in a cold sweat. If they had hit us, we'd have had nobody to stand up for us, nobody would have asked why or how it happened. Just another dead Catholic.

And now our family is being ripped apart at the seams. On the night of her wedding in May 1971, Eileen and her new husband, Jim, leave us. There's nothing here for them. They take the boat to England and they'll never return, except for holidays. Harriet will follow them a couple of months later, leaving just Mammy, Josephine and me in the Divis flats. No memories or echoes of Granny or Dad to keep us company there – just a hastily constructed flat where I've never felt at home.

In some ways I'm glad that my granny and dad went when they did. They missed 1969 when West Belfast was changed into an angry, bitter and paranoid place. In the two years since then the Falls has become unrecognisable – I know they'd both be heartbroken to see it like this, to see how they've razed to the ground the narrow streets and laneways that hosted my childhood games and friendships. Disappeared for ever. When they do eventually rebuild it, there will be just one entrance and one exit to the area, so that no matter which street you come from, you'll be greeted by the security forces. We're trapped, like wee mice running around a maze.

~

Looking at Father McKinley, weighing up his words, I know it makes sense.

There's nothing here for you. Good work over there in London. No future for a young boy here.

I know, Father. It's very hard.

Mammy is nodding with him, but her eyes look puffed and sad.

You'll keep getting picked up by the police here, Paddy. Or get yourself into trouble. Get in with the wrong crowd.

I wouldn't join the Provos, Father. I'm not interested in that.

I know that, but the RUC don't. Young Catholic men like you have no chance. No opportunities to get a start in life. But if you go to England. London. You will get a start. All you have to do is work hard and you'll be fine. Nobody cares where you're from, what school you went to and what religion you are.

Really, Father?

No, Paddy. They don't care at all. So you'll have to make sure to go to mass every Sunday.

Yes, I will, Father.

And stay away from people like that. Stay around boys from home.

I will, Father. So there are boys from here?

Oh, yes, lots of our boys are out there working. Sending money home every week. And you can come home soon. When it all dies down. And get a good job

Yes, Father.

He's right. I can get work out there. Make good money. Send some home. Keep a bit back for myself. And be back in a year or two. That's what I'll do.

Mammy finally looks at me. She gives me her blessing. I'm ready to go. It's 1972 and I'm going to England. Just for a wee while.

CHAPTER THREE

I'm trav'lin' alone …
(Tom Waits)

G o on, get off the bus! That kind of behaviour might be okay in Ireland, but it's not here. Bloody Irish idiots.

Gerry's laughing. I'm laughing. We all are. Laughing so hard that we can barely get off the bus without falling down the step. Stumble. There's only a few passengers. We wave. It's late enough. Maybe ten o'clock, or maybe about one in the morning. Who knows?

Gerry's laughing again. Saying to the other fella we're with, *Can't believe you were barking at the conductor. You lunatic! He was fucking raging with you. I thought he was going to punch you.*

Barking? Was I? Don't even remember.

But who cares. It was funny. Want to say, Yeah, that was funny. But the words won't come out.

~

Standing on the boat, looking at Belfast receding into the distance, I feel a bit guilty for not feeling sad. But I'm not. I'm nervous, but more than anything I'm excited. A new place. A fresh start. A job. Some money. A means to help Mammy and Josephine. I want to experience a bit of life. Something different. Feels like there's hope at last.

It broke my heart to leave Josephine earlier. Seeing the tears in her eyes as I packed my bag. My wee sister, only 13. It's been just the two of us since Harriet and Eileen went to London. She's been like my wee shadow. I'll miss her so much.

I couldn't have stayed any longer. So sick of looking over my shoulder. Sick of getting thrown into the back of a police van at any moment and dragged into a barracks just for standing on the street, for being a Catholic, for breathing. The last time they took us to Springfield Road barracks, they made us stand for four hours with our fingers against a wall. Four hours.

I'm sick of not being able to get any work, of seeing Mammy constantly crying, having to go to Gormanston, in the Republic, to a refugee camp with Josephine and the other women because she's so scared. Sick of us living from hand to mouth, week to week. Sick of being scared and, more than anything, sick of being bored. Bored of sitting around. Bored of doing nothing. Bored of being broke. Bored of the violence, the hard men, the fear, the intimidation, the anger. Bored, bored, bored.

~

I love London as soon as I see it. Walking around, staring at everything, I can't believe that just a day ago I was in Belfast – how does a place like this exist just a few hours away? Everywhere I look I'm surrounded by hippies, peace-lovers in bell-bottoms and afghans. And instead of constantly glancing over my shoulder, I can breathe for the first time in years. This feels like a place where I can fit in.

I'm living in a house with a few lads and I've got my first job, working as a night hotel porter in a big hotel just down from Euston Station. The pay isn't great, but I don't care. I just need to pay my rent, have enough for a few drinks and send some money home to Mammy and Josephine. Occasionally the bookies.

There's entire shops devoted to things I've never heard of, so many different skin colours, accents and languages. It's a melting pot, and even though it's new to me this feels like the kind of place that belongs to everyone and where anyone can belong.

And yet, even though there's so many accents, people have real problems understanding me here. At least everyone can understand a name like Paddy. Some think I'm joking when I tell them. *Wot? Another fucking paddy?*

I laugh and shrug. For the tenth time this week. Not really my decision to be called Paddy. *So, is everyone there called bloody Paddy?* I'm shaking my head and thinking that if I had a pound for everyone who said that, I wouldn't need to be a porter.

Standing in a local pub in Kilburn one night, someone calls my name. *Paddy?* I'm looking around to see who it is. *Yeah? Yeah? Yeah?* There's me and two others answering at once. All saying *yeah.* One's a white English fella and the other is also English and black. And then there's me. *Very funny,* I say. They're looking at me. Confused. *Aye, right, making fun of the paddy. You're funny.* There's a pause and then a dawning of realisation on the black fella's face. *No, really, our names are Paddy. He's Paddy and I'm Paddy. Are you Paddy too?*

I can't believe I've met an English Paddy, never mind two. If one of them was Scottish, we'd have a classic Paddy Englishman, Paddy Irishman, Paddy Scotsman joke. And so begins a most unexpected friendship. We joke about who will be Pat, who'll be Paddy and who'll be Patrick.

I'll be anything except Patrick. Reminds me of Granny. I can still hear her calling me. Paaaaaaaatrick!

Seeing other people's faces when they realise the three of us are called Paddy is always very funny. One of the Paddys passes a joint over to me. *Try a bit of that, my friend.* My first one. In the middle of a London pub. I'm a bit nervous, but I'm not letting on. I'm a smoker so I hope they won't notice. It's different from a cigarette, though. Cuts the back of my throat. I'm coughing at the unexpected burning sensation. The two Paddys laugh. *You get used to it, Paddy. Hold it in your mouth for a few seconds. You'll feel it soon.*

And just when I'm starting to think it's not worth all the fuss, maybe I'm immune to it, my legs and arms feel suddenly heavy. Head light. My hands … what … are they even attached to me? Paddy's grinning at me. I'm laughing. I think I am. Maybe it's him. *That's it, my boy. Just relax and enjoy.*

Feeling sick now. Tired. Want to sleep. Home to bed. Wake up the next morning with a dry mouth and heavy limbs. This isn't for me. I'll stick with a pint of Guinness.

Being away from the repression of Northern Ireland is unbelievable, but England's not without its problems. Most people like the Irish, but occasionally, somewhere between the *Peace and love, man* and the flared trousers, there's an anti-Irish dig that you couldn't miss. Anybody who knows me is fine, but occasionally I meet a hard man with a chip on his shoulder. *Oi, paddy. Fuck off back home. And take the rest of your friends with you.*

Work is up and down. The porter job is over. I was late a few times and they got annoyed. Now I'm laying pipes for the council. I spend actual hours and days with my entire body wedged into a narrow hole in the ground installing them. Fortunately I'm slim and fairly fit, and it pays well. I can go out every night if I want, down the bookies on a Saturday, bit of a smoke and send a bit of money home to Mammy and Josephine when I can. I like being stoned now. Took a few goes, but it doesn't make me feel sick these days. Cheaper than getting drunk. Funnier.

~

What'll we do now, Gerry?

What do you mean?

We're miles from the party. I can't walk there.

Me neither. Let's go up here and get some KFC instead. One of those big family buckets.

Great idea – I'm starving.

I'm salivating just thinking about it. Walk, walk, walk. Is this hill moving against us? Like walking in mud. Lift the leg up, Paddy. Harder. That's it. Now let it down. Let it sink in. Good. Now, leg up. Drag it, further, further. And down again …

~

I have to go home. I've only been here six months but I'm needed back home. Mammy's not well and Josephine's beaking (skipping) school. I feel bad for thinking it, but I don't want to go. For the first time I feel like I'm living my life. Working, partying, meeting people, new cultures. I don't want to go back to Belfast.

I'm shocked when I see her, but I say nothing. In the six months since I went away Mammy has shrunk. And she has a shake in her hands. She and Josephine look so relieved when I walk in the door of our flat that I feel selfish for not wanting to come back, for not wanting to leave my new life in London. And it's so good to see them. Good to be home because, warts and all, Belfast is a place I understand and that understands me. At least I won't have to repeat myself constantly here.

Mammy isn't able to handle Josephine. *She's at that age. With your granny and your daddy gone, she won't listen. She looks up to you, Paddy. See if you can talk some sense into her.*

It's not that simple. Josephine is a rebellious 14-year-old who knows everything. She has a smart mouth on her and a smarter brain, so no matter what I say she has an answer. In the end she promises to go to school, but a couple of weeks later she's up to her old tricks and beaking again. Mammy is terrified. *What if she ends up with the wrong people? Belfast is a dangerous place now, Paddy. I'm down on my knees up in Clonard Monastery doing novenas day and night. I'm at my wits' end.*

A friend of mine has a plan. *You just need to give her a wee scare, Paddy. Just a wee one, mind. Let her think the Provos are watching her. She'll be back in school in the morning.* A few of us talk about it. *Aye, that's a great plan. We can do that. Just you tell us when, Paddy.*

I'm sitting at home while a small group of my friends are driving down the Falls. *Wait until she says goodbye to her friends,* I tell them. *Grab her then.* They work it out. *We'll have the balaclavas ready to go, Paddy. Pull in the car just behind her as she's walking toward the Divis flats. Get her in.* So they do just that. Grab her off the street as she's walking home. No time to run. *You hold her there. Shut up, don't move and you'll be fine.*

For a few minutes she's quiet. Shaking and terrified, they tell me later. *We drove her around for a while, Paddy, and then one of us spoke and she recognised his voice. She started fucking laughing, Paddy. We're there in balaclavas and your wee sister is laughing.*

She says, *I know who you are. You're our Paddy's friend. You're not the Provos. I'm going home. Let me out.*

He looks at me. *Sorry about that. We tried.*

All I can do is laugh. Typical Josephine. She's angry with me at the time, but we'll laugh about it later. She agrees to go back to school and for a while she stays, even though she hates it.

Even though it's nice to see my friends, nothing has changed since I went away. In fact, it's worse. No work for Catholics now. Anywhere. And now internment has been introduced and people are getting lifted every day and held without trial. That's how internment works. Only for Catholics so far, mind you. Not a single Protestant yet. They charge in, usually in the middle of the night, scare you half to death, tear your place apart, pull up your floorboards and anything else they can destroy before charging out again. Mammy's a nervous wreck and it's getting to Josephine. I am too, but I can't say anything. I'm the man of the house.

There's a bit of work going in Mackie's textile machinery plant, one of the biggest factories in Belfast. I worked there before I went to London. It's on the Springfield Road, which is Catholic territory and very handy for me. It's Protestant-owned, of course, so most of the men working there are Protestant, but occasionally (because they have to) there's a few scraps thrown to Catholics and I'm happy to take whatever I can get.

When I worked here last time I had a good job. On a machine. The work itself was fine – working on a machine the size of a room that coated other machine parts in metal oxide to prevent them from rusting. Mind-numbing work, but there were a few nice fellas there and we kept each other sane by just having a laugh.

There were occasional tensions back then, but I always tried to ignore it. One day I went to the toilet and when I came back there was a Union Jack draped across my machine. It was that little bastard in the next room. I wanted to punch his head in. I went in, ready to punch him. *Fuck you and your Union Jack. I'll have you outside.* He was ready for me. *Fuck off back to the Divis, you dirty Teig.* I was ready to punch him, but my friends held me back. *You'll lose your job, Paddy. That's what he wants. He's trying to get to you.* Not long after, I was called in by the big boss. *Leave your religion at home.* I nodded. *No problem, boss.* But I was seething. I didn't bring my religion into it – he did. I couldn't work like that. So I quit.

Never thought I'd be back, but here I am. In the year since I last worked there the mood has soured a lot in Belfast, and it's very obvious in Mackie's. There's much less communication between us Catholics and our Protestant workmates and more frequent hostile incidents. My old football pal Gerry Conlon and I are working together these days, which is great. It always makes it much easier when you're near another Catholic. One day we're in the mouldings shop and go on our break. Chatting away, walking towards the canteen, and I'm thinking that it's nice to have someone I know working with me. Standing at the canteen counter I feel something hit the back of my head and then my back. *Ping!* I rub my head and I see Gerry's rubbing his. Something else hits the side of my face. My leg. My arm. My back again. And then something flashes by my eye. I follow as it falls to the ground, spins around and then settles beside the other nuts and bolts that have just been thrown. It's the last time we'll go to the canteen. Gerry can't handle it. He's leaving. I'm going to hang in there this time. Choose my battles. Stick it out. Can't lose this job, I'm thinking. I can do this.

Last weekend feels a long time ago now. Just last Friday night everything was fine. We got paid and I went to the bookies and then met up with John Huddleston, a lovely fella I met in Mackie's, a Catholic from nearby Durham Street. I didn't know him before, as he's a few years older than me. After the bookies we went drinking down the Falls and had a great time, laughing about some of the things the boys in work got up to. He'll be a good friend to me, I was thinking as I came home.

I was out the next night too – the Saturday. With my mate Marty. I said goodbye to him and walked home. Heard shots fired a few streets away. Gunfire always makes me jump. I dived into a doorway, waited a few minutes and then ran home.

The next morning I could hear Mammy talking to me but I was hungover. *Paddy! I said, Did you see this?* I answer, *What is it, Mammy?* She's looking at the paper. *There's a young lad called John Huddleston – he was murdered. Isn't that your friend from work?* I'm listening now. Stunned. Sick. It can't be. *What does it say?* She reads the article aloud to me. He'd been out and gone to the chippie to get something for his mammy. On his way back, two men riddled him with bullets, from the safety of a car. On his own doorstep. The bullets also managed to go through the door and hit one of his brothers. I can't believe it. This man. My new friend. Gone. Just like that.

And now, just a few days after John and I stood cradling our pints in the local, I'm standing at his funeral. Our foreman, a decent Protestant man, is beside me. I'll take him to a Catholic pub later, at his request. *Are you sure? Absolutely. Out of respect to John. I've no problem if you don't. No, no. Of course not.* So I take him to this pub and introduce him around. My friends welcome him, this man who liked John and wants to pay his respects to him. Just as we all did. A rare moment of humanity and unity in our otherwise divided city. A moment I will always remember.

When I go back to work on Monday, even though nobody says a word, it's different. The atmosphere has soured even more. A few weeks later it's another fella. He gets a few belts from someone and ends up with stitches. A group of Catholic workers go to the big boss. *This isn't on – something has to be done.* He nods, but nothing happens. And then another Catholic fella is stabbed by a Protestant fella who also works in Mackie's. And even though there's no doubt that he did it, he keeps his job.

So for the second time in two years I've had to quit a good job in Mackie's. My foreman's trying to persuade me to stay and I'm shaking my head. *I'm sorry, but I have to go. I know you've done your best for us. You treated us with respect, came to John's funeral, but I can't take this any more. Next time it could be me.*

And now there's nothing. No income. No money to pay the rent or bills. Mammy is stressed and barely able to work herself. So I'm going back to London. I'm not going to stay long. A year, maybe two. Just enough time to save a bit of money. *I'll be back again soon, Mammy. Sorry, Josephine. See you soon, love.*

~

The hill is so steep. We're walking and walking up it. Never-ending. Don't seem to be moving. Must be broken, the hill. Or getting higher. *Gerry, are your feet moving? What do you mean, Paddy? Well, I'm trying to walk up this here hill but nothing is happening. How long have we been here? I don't know. Maybe an hour or two?* He's laughing and I'm laughing and people are looking at us curiously. *Look, there's the KFC. Where? Across the road. See? Oh, yeah, that's the one. Right, let's cross. Here, wait for a break in the traffic.*

Walk, walk, walk. Come on, legs, you can do it.

My legs are gone again, Paddy. Forget that, Gerry – look, there's tigers coming. What? Look, that one there is coming for you. Look at his teeth. Do you see them, Gerry. And that one has stopped. He's just looking at me. Roar back, will we? No. It might bite. Okay. Let's just keep going.

Horns beeping. Some fella yelling. *What's his problem? Maybe he's beeping at the tigers. To get them off the road. I can't see the tigers, Paddy. You must. Look! That's a car. No, it's not. Look again. It's roaring. It's definitely a tiger.*

~

I'll miss Josephine. She looked so sad and so did Mammy, but then Roy Clarke, who I'm travelling with, had to leave his wife and kids behind to come and look for work, so I shouldn't be complaining.

Despite the worry about Mammy and Josephine, I'm excited. It's 1973 and I'm in London and freedom-bound. I don't feel like a 50-year-old man in a 23-year-old's body any more. I can be young again. I'm looking forward to being back in north London.

We spend our first night in a bed-and-breakfast in Cricklewood and then about a week sleeping in an old car in Kilburn. When we find a place it's a flat-share in Chichele Road, Kilburn, with a few other fellas. The landlord is nice, he's an ex-policeman.

Finding work isn't as easy as I remember, though. Since I left London, only six months ago, England's been suffering its own IRA terror campaign. There's bombs going off all over London, including one outside the Old

Bailey a few months ago. And just weeks after my arrival, two bombs go off in King's Cross and Euston Stations. There's a lot of people injured.

If it wasn't bad enough being a poor Catholic living in West Belfast, targeted by every law enforcer from the RUC to the B Specials and the British army, here I am in England as a Belfast Catholic – one of the most loathed and feared people, because my fellow-Catholics are trying to bomb the arses off my fellow-Londoners. To say that we are unwelcome by some is a gross understatement.

There's work here and there on building sites and finally we get a start. It's not easy – you have to sit outside a café in Kilburn with some other boys every morning, drinking tea and waiting. A van pulls up and they look at everyone. It's like getting picked for a team in school. Some days I get something and other days I don't. Sending money home to Mammy isn't as easy as I'd hoped. The guilt is always there in the back of my mind, but what can I do?

Apart from that, life is good. I would never have been described as a party animal in Belfast; my sisters were far more sociable than I was. London is a different story. For starters, nobody knows me. No longer am I the Paddy who was too scared to stand up to the hard men in school; Paddy who hid when the doorbell rang in case it was the RUC; Paddy who went with the women and children instead of fighting with the men. I'm not quiet Paddy, the brother of one of the best-looking girls on the Falls, or Paddy whose poor wee sister was hit by the bus all those years ago. I'm just Paddy, plain and simple.

I dabbled in the drug scene during my first stay in London, but this time I dive in head-first. Cannabis, LSD, morphine, cocaine and a whole host of amphetamines are all on the menu. If you're not too choosy, you can be off your head every night and often into the following day.

Our nights usually start off in a pub down in Kilburn, followed by a gig, and eventually we end up at some party, smoking or taking something and spending the night dancing to Pink Floyd, Tom Waits, Eric Clapton, Elton John or David Bowie until we crawl home. Occasionally we go to the Galtymore, a dance hall in Cricklewood that's always packed to the rafters with young Irish men and women. But I'm more at home at a gig or a party. It sounds like a terrible existence when I write it down, especially with hindsight, but it's the time we're living in. I wouldn't recommend it, but it suits us for the moment.

Roy's gone back to Belfast, to his wife and kids, but I'm staying here. I'm okay now I know a few people and have a flat with some other Irish boys. Life is good. Go to work whenever there's a bit going, down the pub for a few drinks or a game of poker, across to the betting office to win or lose a few pounds on the horses or dogs when I'm off. Have a pint, a bit of craic. I'm enjoying myself.

~

I look at the judge with relief. *Case dismissed.* After two months of sitting in Brixton Prison, being held for a stolen TV that we didn't know anything about, my friend and I are out. Whether it was because we were Irish or because we had come to the attention of the neighbours with our party lifestyle I don't know, but they must have been given our names by someone. Now, thanks to our landlord – who vouched for us because we were helping him fix his car at the time of the robbery – we're out. They knew about this witness soon after they arrested us. They could have released us the day after we were lifted, when he came forward. But they decided to hold us while it went to court. Two months for a TV that we never stole.

I'm still shaking as I walk up the road to get the bus from Brixton. It'll take days for me to stop shaking. I'll have nightmares about it afterwards. The prison cells. The men in there. The noises. The smells. Crying myself to sleep almost every night. And even though I did nothing wrong, I feel so ashamed to have been in prison.

And now, after two months locked away, I've no money, no job and nowhere to live. And no prospects of any of that. People in the Irish community have heard I've been in jail, so now there's a question mark over my head. Who wants to share a flat with or get a job for someone who might get into trouble? I was cleared of the charge. I have an alibi. But that's not what they'll remember. So now I'm in real trouble.

The only place I can think of going is back to Kilburn. It's all I really know of London. Wandering up Kilburn High Street toward the Memphis Belle pub, I bump into some Irish boys I know. I'm mortified. I don't want them to know I was in prison, but I'm sure they do. None of us mentions it. *Where are you staying, Paddy?* Shrug. *There's a squat up in West End Lane. It's basic but might do you until you get a job and a flat.*

And now here I am, lying on a mattress in the West End Lane squat. It's not as bad as I'd expected, but it's a far cry from the nice flat on Chichele Road I was in two months ago, before I was arrested. Everyone here has been very welcoming, though. *There's a mattress in that room – make yourself at home.* From my mattress I can see a fireplace at the end of the room, a cracked wardrobe in the corner and a couple of tables stacked on top of each other. If there's wallpaper, I can't see it – whoever was here last obviously liked Jimi Hendrix, Deep Purple and Pink Floyd so much that they decided to paper the walls with their posters.

Not having to worry about bills is great. No rent. We have to pay for electricity or it would get cut off. But apart from that, it's a cheap way of life. There's so many different people here, some passing through and some here all the time. We cook together sometimes – sharing recipes and jokes. An Indian fella made me my first curry and I'll never forget the moment when the explosion happened in my mouth and the horror that must have been on my face as I ran for the water. Another night I made a Belfast stew. I threw everything into it and everyone loved it. I feel like I've travelled much further than London just through the people I've met.

There's a cash-and-carry nearby, they tell me, that's easy to rob. *You can walk out with a trolley full of stuff and they don't notice if they're busy.* My mammy would kill me if she knew what I was doing, but what choice do I have? As a Catholic from Belfast who has spent two months in an English prison, getting a job and earning any money is turning out be almost impossible.

The best thing about squatting is how many people you meet. There's a party almost every night. Two fellas I know, Patrick and Danny, took me to a party in a flat in Rondu Road in Cricklewood and I met some Irish boys who are very decent – John McGuinness and Sean Mullin. They all work and have a proper flat, not a squat. Whenever I've had enough of the craziness here, I go and stay there.

There's a bigger squat in Linstead Street, in Kilburn. I visit it and decide to move in there. It's a beautiful, big old building that's been vacant for a long time. Normally there's about six of us living there on a regular basis, but then there's people who just stay over for a night, so most nights there's about ten or fifteen people. There's wild parties sometimes, but often it's just a relaxed session with everyone lying back, having a joint and listening to music – someone playing a guitar or singing, or maybe a radio or record player if someone has one. Other nights, when we've taken something a bit more hallucinogenic, things get a bit trippier.

What I like about living in a squat is that it's not about the rich and poor, the educated and the people like me who left school at 15. It's just about people living together, sharing their thoughts and food and anything else they want. It's not about judging each other. I've got more of an education in squats than anywhere else.

This squat, Linstead Street, will be my home for a few happy, albeit impoverished, months. Bright, worldly people will wander into my world, and once the trauma of two months in Brixton Prison has abated I feel interested in the world again. It makes me realise how sheltered my life has been and how much I want to know and see of the world. With my long hair tied up in a ponytail, a thin moustache, patchy beard, sideburns, bell-bottoms and a hairy afghan, I've reinvented myself. The sharp Belfast lad in trendy cut suits has been reborn as a 1970s hippie, and I'm loving it.

~

The man behind the counter in KFC is staring at Gerry and me. *Oh, sorry there. Just a minute. We're. Just. Sorting. Out. Money. Empty your pockets there, Paddy. How much have you got? Eh, a pound maybe. Yeah, that's good. Here, give it to me and we'll get one of those family buckets.*

We're eating it with our fingers. Nearly eating our fingers, too. *Keep walking, Gerry, or we'll never get home. It's miles away. Hours. Is it? I thought it was near. How long were we on the bus? I don't know. I thought it was near. So did I. Someone's stretched the road, so it must be a fair way now. Here, eat that while you walk, Paddy. Mmm, this is unbelievable.*

~

I walk into a party on a summer's night in 1974 and I meet a girl. She will change my life. A beautiful 17-year-old English girl. Carole. So young, but already an old soul. She has long, thick brown hair, a big smile and the most beautiful eyes. In the years to come I'll wonder, if I could rewind my life and choose to have never met her, would I walk away and avoid the next 15 years of torment? What would I have done if I'd known? I've thought about it a lot. I think I'd have met her anyway.

I've actually met Carole before, at a party in another squat in July. She knows Frank Egan, one of a group of boys from Athlone. I felt an instant attraction to her. When I see her again, a few weeks later in the Memphis Belle, I remember our brief conversation at the party, the hint of a flirtation. As I'm collecting glasses and working at the bar, trying to earn a bit of money, I make it my business to talk to her again. She's underage and shouldn't be in the pub ordering drinks, but I turn a blind eye. I don't know yet that her friend Lisa, a petite girl, is only 15 and living in a local care hostel.

The more I talk to Carole, the more I'm drawn to her. It's not just that she's gorgeous, although she definitely is that, with her slim body, clear, bright eyes and long hair swinging loose around her shoulders. It's her energy, her outlook, her warmth. She's a great laugh to be with and loves partying. She's also very chatty and I could sit and listen to her for ages. She's sincere and kind and she cares about people and things. Loves animals, loves the Earth. A true hippie. She just wants to be free. Her eyes are shining when she tells me about her love of horses. She's the first person I've ever met who really doesn't care about material things or money, and this suits me because I don't have much of either and I'm quite happy that way. And of course she loves to party. We have a lot in common.

There's also something about her that's very different from me. She's a bit of a tearaway. I was living at home at her age, by and large doing what my parents told me, apart from beaking school. Carole, on the other hand, spent her teenage years rebelling after her mother started a relationship with a man Carole doesn't get on with, so she lives in a squat now and meets her mammy in cafés or at her mammy's work. We don't talk much about it. She just wants to be free and happy, so I don't press her on the matter.

And then she's everywhere – at parties, in the launderette, at the local café and the Memphis Belle. It's not serious at first – a few jokes, a bit of banter and flirting and a few stolen kisses, all very innocent. We go to pubs and gigs and parties together, me, Carole and her friend Lisa. They are inseparable. Lisa wears a big hippie crucifix around her neck and fits right into Carole's world. They share the same dark sense of humour, a giddiness and talkativeness that only girls can have.

Lisa's turning 16 on 6 September and she's asked if she can have her birthday party in our squat in Linstead Street. I've asked the people I live with and they've agreed. It's an open house and everyone loves a party. Carole and Lisa decorate the place with candles and incense and posters. Lisa likes to draw these psychedelic pictures when she's stoned or tripping – they have mushrooms or eyes in them. She writes messages on them sometimes, like the one with a massive eye in the centre that says *You are Being Watched* below it. It's creepy enough when you're straight and sober, but when I'm high it makes me completely paranoid, like that eye is following me all around the room.

Lisa's birthday party is a wild affair with plenty of drugs and dancing. It takes us days to recover. The one thing I will always remember is that it's the night Carole and I become official. And, suddenly, it's like she's always been in my life. She's moved into my room, downstairs at the front of the house, and brought her dog, Leb. A stray mongrel, he is named after Lebanese Gold hashish. A gorgeous thing who loves to cuddle into Carole at night.

Our room is pretty basic, just a couple of mattresses on the ground with sleeping bags that we throw over us that autumn when the weather gets colder. Carole and I stay together in Linstead Street most nights, often with Lisa curled asleep on the floor beside us. The three of us quickly become a tight little unit. They remind me of my own sisters. Having a female friend like Lisa is also a great comfort, and for our few short but intense months of friendship I call Lisa *little sister*, while I'm her *big bruvver*.

One day Carole and Lisa come home and they're holding a man's jacket. *Look what we got you, Paddy.* It's great. Just my size. *Where did you get it?* I know they've no money. They're giggling now. *We broke into a house. Didn't take anything except a few clothes. Got you this.* I'm laughing. It's a nice jacket. *We cooked a meal there too. It was gorgeous, Paddy. And we had a bath. I feel so clean.* I can't believe how brave they are. I could never do it.

They love teasing me. Lately they've noticed I'm putting on weight on my face and gut, but I just laugh at them. They make fun of my messy sideburns and long, greasy hair, which Carole says I should wash more often. Being ganged up on is weirdly comforting – it's like being inspected by Eileen and Harriet before going out on a Saturday night. Carole calls me her Piggy – *Silly Piggy* – but it's never nasty. I'm her older, worldly man, even though I'm probably less worldly than her.

Like me, Carole doesn't stay in any job for very long. Some days we just sit around eating stolen food, getting stoned and listening to whichever musician we're obsessed with for whole days on end, going out briefly to stock up on food, cigarettes and whatever we're taking at the moment. But as mature as Carole seems, there's also a girlish innocence about her that you can see without digging very far below the surface. It's there in the brown diary she fills with words, writing down every detail, however mundane.

We talk a lot about seeing the world together – leaving London, going to France and working on farms. I can't wait. My once-tiny world is expanding before my eyes and I am hungry to explore it. Now that I have someone to do it with, everything seems possible.

~

My own birthday is approaching now. Twenty-four. I'm going to have a party, but I don't want too many people there. Just a few friends. Lisa and Carole are getting excited planning it. They want it to be a great night.

Late in the afternoon of a warm September day in London, a few days before my birthday, I'm standing just inside the door of the Memphis Belle when my eye is drawn to a very familiar-looking, skinny, curly-haired creature. I do a double-take and realise it's Gerry Conlon. My childhood pal from Belfast. *Gerry! Gerry!* He walks over and smiles when he recognises me. *Jesus, Paddy, what are you doing here?* He introduces me to his friend. *Do you know Benny Hill?* Gerry asks. I nod. I don't know him very well, except to see, but we used to go into the same betting office on the Falls Road.

They're an unlikely pair. Gerry is a total wild card who was always known for his antics in West Belfast. Always involved in some racket or other – breaking into houses or shops to steal a few bits and pieces that he'd sell for a bit of profit. He's your run-of-the-mill, harmless hooligan whose idea of a good time, like mine, is to get drunk and lose a few quid on the horses. A very likeable fella. Benny, on the other hand, seems a bit more educated and serious. He was in the good class in school. And though he's hanging around with Gerry, he's not the kind who'd be into breaking into houses or living in a squat.

And now the three of us are sitting in the Memphis Belle. The two of them have just arrived in London after leaving their Irish girlfriends in Southampton. *We've come down for a wee bit of craic in London.* They're living in Hope House, a Catholic place in Kilburn that doesn't sound like my type of place at all. It's full of very serious Irish country lads, Gerry tells me. I tell them about life in the melting pot of communal living and Gerry's quite interested; Benny looks quietly appalled. I tell them about the smoking parties I go to and he's nudging Benny. Gerry explains he's been getting stoned a lot in Southampton. *I'll come along to one of the parties,* he says. I tell them I'm having a birthday party and they say they'll try to come along.

Everyone agrees to meet in the Memphis Belle on the night of my party. There's a good crowd of us there – Carole, Lisa, John McGuinness, Sean Mullin, Brian Anderson, Gerry Conlon, Benny Hill and a few others. I introduce Gerry and Benny to everyone and that's the start of my birthday night. We finish up in the Rondu Road flat for an all-night party in the early hours and Gerry comes with us. Benny's disappeared.

Over the next few weeks we go to a few parties together. Get stoned. Then one night we take a few pills. Acid. *Let's go to this party, Paddy. It's going to be wild.* I'm up for anything. *We can get the bus.* So Gerry and me and another Irish fella get on a bus. Sit looking out the window, trying to look straight. It's all going fine until the conductor comes up to us. *Tickets?* I don't know what possesses him, but the other fella who's with us starts to bark at the conductor. Down on all fours. Growling. Yapping. Barking. Like he's actually a dog. Gerry and I are watching and what starts out as giggling ends up in proper belly laughing. And suddenly the bus has stopped.

Go on, get off the bus! That kind of behaviour might be okay in Ireland, but it's not here. Bloody Irish idiots.

∼

While I'm walking down the road, this interminable road, my teeth are sinking into this chicken. Trying to pull the drumstick away. Can't seem to bite through it. Must be a special stretch recipe.

Look, Gerry, see how it's stretching between my hand and the chicken bone. Can't bite it.

Mmm.

Look – it's like elastic. It's so long.

Mmm. Wiping his mouth in ecstasy. *That's your squat there?*

Yeah, come on in. Let's get some smoke from one of the boys or Carole.

Good man, Paddy.

∼

I meet up with Gerry and Benny a few times. We have a few wild nights out, go to the Memphis Belle, but nothing too frequent. I like being around

Gerry, but Benny and I don't really hit it off. And then suddenly they're gone again. Vanished like the smoke that Carole blows into my mouth. *Makes you more stoned, Paddy.* I'll hear later that Gerry has gone home to Belfast, but we're not close enough that he'd get in touch to let me know where he is. I don't bother to enquire about Benny.

It's October now and the leaves are falling from the trees. Work is impossible to find, so our days are spent in a haze of smoke. Most days I couldn't tell you what I did the day before. That's why, when the policemen hack through our door on 3 December and point a handgun at my head, I won't be able to remember where I was on that morning, never mind a night seven weeks earlier. Had I been cunning enough to have done what they accuse me of, you'd assume I'd have also worked out an alibi. Have it ready on the tip of my tongue. But I didn't do it and I'm smoking too much and too often, so I'll be left completely dumbstruck, unable to explain where I was on a Saturday night two months earlier.

They ask me where I was when two Guildford pubs exploded on a Saturday night in October 1974. I can't remember because it's all a haze. What I do know is that, without fail, I spend my Saturday afternoons going between the pub and the bookies until I'm broke. Saturday nights are often spent at home or at the occasional party, in our squat or another one. Sometimes I get a bit of work clearing glasses in the Memphis Belle, to earn a few quid. Few events stand out for me from that time, as we're taking a lot of acid, hash and whatever else we can get our hands on.

Even though they all melt into one big session, when I think back on it later two Saturday nights stand out from that month.

On one of them I'm lying in bed at night but jump up when I hear the screech of brakes outside. I think that there's going to be a raid on our place and am ready to flush anything I have down the toilet. It turns out the police are chasing a car and they've cornered their suspects at the bottom of our street. All the fellas and I watch the scene unfold from my bedroom window – Pearse, Lenno, Rusty, Gatsy, Brian and me. We laugh a bit when one fella makes a run for it – mostly because we're thankful they're not raiding our house.

The other Saturday night, while Carole and Lisa are dancing their hippie backsides off at a gig in Elephant and Castle, I'm at home babysitting Leb, the dog. Carole's very devoted to Leb and made me promise to look after him, much to the amusement of my fellow-squatters. And so I watch a bit of TV, have a bit of smoke and then pass out in bed listening to music. Carole and Lisa will sneak in after their gig, but I won't remember them coming home, as I'm a heavy sleeper when I'm stoned. The next day they tell me about the gig and their friend Frank, who got them back-stage passes to hang out with the band.

The one thing I do know for absolute certain is that on 5 October 1974 I'm not in Guildford. Nowhere near it. Never been there. Don't know where it is. Have no reason to go.

I read about the bombings in a newspaper the following day and feel my heart sink. It's sad and I feel awful for the victims, the families. But, to be honest, I'm a bit anaesthetised, after everything I've lived through in the last few years. I'm thinking about me and every other Irishman here. This is never going to end, I'm thinking, looking at the headline. And now people like me, all over England, will have to bear the brunt of it, take the jibes, pretend we didn't hear the insults and duck the occasional punches, because we're the easiest targets. That's what it means to me, nothing more.

~

A week or two after the bombing, Carole and I decide to get out of London for a while. I have a few reasons, the most immediate being to avoid a fella I owe money to. He's come looking for me a few times, but on the last occasion he waved an axe around in front of Carole, demanding she tell me he wants his money. It's left her petrified, so we've decided to just go. I've always liked the idea of travelling around, working outside on farms. Carole and I have talked about it a lot and by the time we leave we have about £100 in our pockets. I've been doing some odd jobs for different people, and her mammy has given her money.

It all happens very quickly. Within hours of the axe-brandishing visitor we're giving the dog to a friend, saying our goodbyes and walking up the road, hand in hand, our lives packed into two small bags.

I'm so excited to be travelling. I want to go across Europe and work our way around. Maybe a year away from the city. In the countryside it will be easier. No fellas coming around looking for their money with axes. I can see the two of us working on a farm for a while and then moving on, to another place, a new farm. I want a pure life with fresh country air and the girl I love.

The plan is to make our way to Dover, hitching along the way. We've heard about well-paying jobs on building sites and, although the jobs are nowhere to be found when we get there, we're not put off. Just being out of London and away from the insanity of the squat and our usual lifestyle is good for us.

As we make our away through the southern English countryside, walking, hitching, cuddling up at night-time, we talk and laugh all the time. I'm falling more and more in love with this way of life and with this girl. We talk about our dreams of marriage, children and having a good life together. I can see it all ahead of us, once we've done our travelling and are ready to settle down.

We find B&Bs for a few nights, but when our money runs out we sleep rough. Under the cover of the thick October darkness we creep into a barn, find a comfortable spot and cuddle up there in our sleeping bag. It's no colder than any squat I've been in. Before the dew has evaporated we sneak out and are gone again before anyone notices. And on a milder night, under the cover of a black cloudless sky, we cuddle up together under a country hedge.

One night we're sitting on a hill overlooking a town as the sun is going down. It's so quiet. I feel like we're the only people in the world. She's leaning on me. My arms around her. I kiss her head. *We'll get married.* A question that sounds like a statement. Holding my breath. She nods. *Yes. Let's go to Belfast and do it there. That would be nice.* She has no ties to London except her mum and her grandparents, so she's happy with that. *Maybe they can come.* She nods. It's official and I'm so happy. In a few days, when we arrive in Newcastle, I'll write to Mammy to tell her. She'll be over the moon.

There's no work to be found so we decide to cut our losses while we still have enough money in our pockets to get to Dover and take the boat to France. Our last hitch has left us in a sleepy little port town with a couple of beaches, called Folkestone, less than 10 miles from Dover, where a boat is waiting for us. We could be in France by the morning, ready to start our new life. I can't wait.

By the time we buy something to eat we don't have enough for the boat tickets, so we make a plan.

I'm sitting on a wall while Carole rings her mother. *I shouldn't be too long. She'll have to call me back though,* she explains. *She'll send us a few pounds. No problem.* I nod. *I'm just going to sit here and have a smoke.* She disappears into the phone box and I hope that she can get us enough even just to get the boat. We can find barns to sleep in if we have to, just let us get there.

There's voices. Someone's shouting. And now someone else is shouting back. The voice is familiar. It's Carole. There's a man and he's leaning into the phone box and trying to pull Carole out by the hair. While she was talking, he got impatient and tried to pull her out.

Before I can even jump up he's grabbed her hair again and is banging her head against the door. Carole is whimpering like a frightened animal. I run over to defend her, but before I get there she's recovered and is punching him in the face. He looks stunned. By the time I reach them, all I have to do is drag him out of the phone box and push him up the road. It looks like he's had a few drinks and is pretty well on, so there's no point in hitting him.

Carole has rung the police and they're on their way. While we're waiting, four workmen on a nearby building site who saw the drama have offered to sort out the man, but I don't want anyone to get hurt so I tell them we'll wait for the police. The man has disappeared by the time the police arrive, so all we can do is make a statement at the police station. After that the police ask us to go with them in a car to see if we can identify the man who hit Carole. We see him, point him out and he's arrested.

Sitting in the police station waiting room, there's very little in the way of interesting reading material, so I'm looking at the WANTED posters. There's one poster of two long-haired people wanted for the Guildford bombing. Carole is looking at it too, but there's been a couple of bombings since then. It's too difficult to get upset about every bombing. I try to explain it to Carole. *When you've seen so much death and pain, you get used to it. If you cried for all of them, you'd just be crying all the time with the way things are going ... I'm glad to be away from Belfast and all that pain.*

The incident in the phone box has changed the mood completely. Gone is Carole's excitement and determination to explore Europe. She wants to go back to London. I don't. I'd rather press on, but I'm not going without her. I'm marrying this girl.

Just 10 days after we set off, we find ourselves back in London. Our plans to travel postponed. Something has changed in us, between us. We never expected to be coming back. We're both a bit deflated.

I don't want to go back to Linstead Street after the axe-wielding lunatic incident, so I go to the Rondu Road flat and stay with the boys there for a couple of weeks. Carole goes to see her mammy. Eventually I have to leave the Rondu flat, so I end up in Algernon Road, Kilburn, in a squat where Carole is staying. She hasn't mentioned marriage and children recently, but I'm hoping we can get back to that place soon.

~

December 1974, and we're living back in London. Carole has a bit of work in a hotel while I'm clearing glasses whenever there's a bit of work. Mostly, though, I'm shoplifting here and there, borrowing money and just trying to live on next to nothing. She doesn't come around every night. We were arguing a lot for a while there, but I think we're getting back on track now.

It's a mild December night. A couple of the lads from the Algernon Road squat have decided they're going to raid a chemist. *Do you want to come, Paddy? It'll be a laugh.* I shake my head. I don't mind robbing a trolley of food from a cash-and-carry, but not a chemist's. Not drugs.

Mind you, when they come back with tablets and syringes I can't help joining the party. They've got half the chemist's by the looks of it, mostly speed and Tuinal, a barbiturate. It's a proper drugs party. Out of control. Every few hours, when it starts to wear off, we take more. More speed. More Tuinal. More. More. More.

I can't sleep and keep walking around all night long. Will morning ever come? Will I ever sleep? Take more and that might get me to sleep. Most other people have conked out on any bit of space they can find. I'm lying here, staring up at the ceiling, then staring at Carole, who is out of it. My reflexes feel speeded up. I get up again.

It's day two and the party is still going. Carole went out and has come back with Lisa, but I'm completely bombed. Haven't slept in two days now. I've taken a lot of speed and several shots of Tuinal in the last 12 hours. No matter what I do, I can't rest. Another night passes. I'm going into my third consecutive day without sleep, but I feel okay. Past exhaustion now.

As long as there's drugs left over from the chemist raid I can keep going. Eat a bit of the food we stole from the cash-and-carry and here comes another day. The sun is rising.

I can't honestly say what would have happened six or 12 months down the line had I continued to live that life. I can only guess that I probably would have died, if not then, certainly down the line. There's no way I could have continued living the life I was living. The game of what-ifs would be never-ending if I let myself go down that road.

Later in the evening, around 9.30pm, a few of us are spaced out in front of the television watching a documentary about Lady Randolph Churchill. Carole and Lisa have gone out. To see Carole's mammy, I think. One of the lads, Pearce, stands up to leave. I head out with him. Get a bit of fresh air into my lungs.

And there I am. Walking out towards the front door with him. Not saying anything of great consequence. How could I? It's been a three-day speed and Tuinal party. I'm beyond tired. We're standing there in front of the glass front door and suddenly it's crashing down in front of my eyes. Glass shattering and a crowbar just behind it. These are powerful drugs, because this can't be real. It's not possible.

CHAPTER FOUR

It's a rat trap and you've been caught …
(The Boomtown Rats)

L ying on a flimsy prison mattress, contemplating the brown marks on the cold concrete walls, wondering what they might be: barely scrubbed brain-matter, vomit, blood or faeces perhaps? I hear a sound. It's the flap in the cell door clanking open. Another tormentor, no doubt. Jump up, Paddy. Before they scream.

A large, leering mouth has appeared in the flap's place, opening and closing like a hungry fish. But instead of roaring at me, it's speaking very quietly. Hissing almost. Soft and slowly. Saying each word with great care.

Armstrong?

Maybe this one is different. Could this be my salvation, at last, that it's all been cleared up? That this mouth is going to say: *You'll be out in no time. Sorry about that. Wrong man. On your way …*

Please, God, wake me up from this nightmare. Oh, Jesus, please.

~

It's frightening enough having policemen batter down your door when you're in good form, full of energy and completely sober. But after three days with no sleep, very little food and industrial amounts of hallucinogenic drugs, it's a whole other scene.

There's nothing fake about the gun in my face or the brute of a man holding it. I jump back automatically. The one holding the gun roars at me. *Don't move or I will empty this chamber into you.* I stop moving instantly, though I can feel my leg shaking. He's serious. He stares at me very briefly, as if examining a piece of shit on the bottom of his shoe, and then roars again, *Patrick Joseph Armstrong?* The sound seems to come from the very pit of his stomach. Detective-Constable Vernon Attwell – who'll become Dirty Harry to me, in time. It turns out Attwell was recruited shortly after the British police force lowered its educational requirements. He's less protector of the peace, more intimidating guard dog.

Are you Patrick Joseph Armstrong?

They don't call me Patrick Joseph. I'm just Paddy. Paddy Armstrong.

This doesn't seem to register with him.

You're the one we're looking for.

His breath is warm and stale in my face. I'd step further back except there's another one behind me, and he's holding a crowbar. *That's him,* he's screaming. And before I can even form the words in my head, let alone say them out loud, to protest or ask what it's about, I feel at least two sets of arms seize me from behind and drag me out the front door.

Hands on the top of the car.

Dirty Harry puts his foot between my feet, pushes them apart, and one of them searches me. There's nothing but a few coins and a betting slip in my pocket. Bit of tobacco. Amazingly enough, I've no drugs on me – I took them all.

Get in.

A hand on my head. Shove. I'm in the back seat with a constable each side and we're gunning down the road. The door of the house is still open, with the police dragging the others out.

We're driving around. Going to a police station, from their conversation.

What's this about? I wonder aloud.

Do you know about the Guildford bombing?

I heard about it on the TV.

Well, you're nicked for it.

The Tuinal is making me feel so heavy. My mind feels like it's been slowed right down. I think they're saying I've been nicked for doing a pub in Guildford. Wasn't that a pub? Did people die? I can barely remember it. But that can't be right. I don't even know where Guildford is, or how to get there.

I don't know what you're talking about. I had nothing to do with them bombings, is all I can manage. I try to move my hands slightly but one of them pushes my hands roughly in front of me, onto the back of the driver's seat.

Put your hands up on the seat in front of you, where we can see them. If you move, I'll empty this chamber into that thick Irish head of yours.

The gun's inches away from me. Pointed straight at me. He's going to use it on me. Please, no. Oh, God. What's happening? I can't think straight. Now they're talking about me as if I'm not there. What they'd like to do to me. Calling me every name under the sun. Need to sleep. Close my eyes. Slowing down. That looks like Carole in another car. Can't be right. What's going on? What's happening to us?

They have to drag me from the car. Can't walk properly. My wrist attached to one of theirs. There's others waiting for me just inside the station. How do they know who I am? Spitting at me and kicking me. *Is this one of them? You fucking murdering bastard. You're not fit to walk the streets.* Haven't yet learned to curl into a ball with my hands over my head – always protect your head, Paddy.

Hands against that wall. Legs open. I said, Open your fucking legs. Kick. *See. Open your legs!*

Empty his pockets. They're going through everything I have. Betting slip. Coins. Taking everything.

Sign this. For my property, they're saying, but it's got *Murder* written on the top. The fella's looking at me. Such hatred in his eyes.

There's balls of saliva clinging to the side of my jaw when they throw me into a cell. Maybe it'll be like back in Belfast. Get arrested. Get thrown in a cell and then let out a few hours later. The toilet in the corner is filthy. There's a bed on the other side and a small window. What do I do here? If I lie down, will they come back and get me? My arms and ankles are still throbbing from the pushes and kicks. Have to lie down. So heavy now. Just for a minute. Where am I? Where's Carole?

Bed's so hard. It's just a board with a blanket on top. Light's so strong. Feel so heavy. Don't sleep, Paddy. Just a few minutes. Have to rest. Wake up and this will be over.

There's crying outside. Is that Lisa? Why would they have her here? She's a 16-year-old runaway. Where's Carole? Is she here too? I think I saw her in another police car earlier, but now I'm not sure. Feel like I'm going crazy. Oh, Jesus, Carole.

Through the nights I manage to sleep for a few minutes and then wake again, terrified. Feels like I've been crying for hours. My whole body's shaking. Can't stop it. My hands. My legs. Just can't stop. And then there's the voices. Where are they? Who are they? Jumping up, searching for disembodied voices screaming through a flap in the door.

Wake up, you piece of shit.

Oi – you, fucking wake up. Get up, you paddy bastard.

So that's what a murderer looks like. Just you wait till I get my hands on you.

~

The mouth at the flap has been momentarily replaced with a wide, unblinking eye, but all I can see is an off-white piece of jelly flesh with a tiny hole in the middle that's focused on me. I look at it. Still unblinking. And then it pulls away and the fish mouth is back.

Armstrong? We know you didn't do it …

It's paused, the mouth, and in that moment I know I'm getting out. They're going to open the door. I'll forgive them for the punches, the intimidation, the threats, the humiliation. Everything they've put me through over the last couple of days. Anything just to get out of here and never have to come back. I'll say nothing. Just get me away from them. I'll never do anything that risks getting me arrested again. Not drugs, not stealing from the cash-and-carry, nothing. Just let me out …

~

The light is filling the cell window. I've been here all night. Slept maybe an hour. Body feels less drugged, more terrified. My brain is still working so slowly, but even so the reality of this is dawning on me.

Out. Let's go. He pushes me out the door. Outside, Lisa's sitting on a bench, wild-eyed. *Paddy, what's going on?* But they're pushing me too fast and too hard. My brain is only forming the words as I'm near the end of the corridor. There's others here from the squat, including one of the Irish girls. She's screaming at me. *Look at all this trouble you've got us into, Paddy.* I'm trying to shout back at her as we round the corner. *I haven't got nobody into trouble.* But I don't know if she can hear me.

We're back in the car. Dizzy now. Hungry. Tired. Need more Tuinal. Keep me awake.

Taking you back to Guildford. You remember Guildford, don't you, Armstrong?

Course he fucking does.

I don't know where Guildford is – I've never been there. I swear.

More of them are waiting when we get to Guildford police station. Block out the hatred. Fury in their eyes. *Strip!* I don't know how I've managed to pull open the laces on my shoes or unbutton my flared jeans. Standing in just my underwear, faded and baggy, and they're leering at me. Wobbling, trying to pull down my underpants with my shaking fingers. Somehow I've stayed standing. And now I'm in here, in this room, completely naked, covered only by my long hair down past my shoulders. Glancing down at the slightly rounded stomach. Piggy, Carole calls me. But in a nice way.

There's two women come into the room now. Looking at me. Up and down. Commenting like they're watching a game of football. Stop shaking. Drown it out. Stare at the ground. Tears splashing on the concrete floor. Don't make eye contact. Don't collapse. Hold it together, Paddy. Come on. And finally they throw my underwear back at me and they leave me sitting in a freezing-cold room, in a pair of jeans and a light shirt.

There's diagrams and photos all over the wall of the room they've put me in. Big Xs marked on photos showing a bar with rubble everywhere. Like it's been bombed. What am I doing here? Have to stay awake. Don't fall asleep again. There's voices. Footsteps outside on the corridor. Deep, angry voices barking orders. Are they coming for me?

~

The voice is still talking through the flap, interrupting my thoughts. Just waiting for him to open the door now. Breathe a sigh of relief. What a nightmare. Nearly over.

Armstrong? We know you didn't do it … but we're gonna do you for it anyway … because we need bodies.

~

Sweat's pouring out of me now. Tablets are really wearing off. Been more than 12 hours since they lifted us all from the Algernon Street squat. Need some food. Even just some water. A fella gave me a smoke last night in the station, but it did nothing to take the edge off. It's freezing. When are they coming back?

But when they do come back, I'll wish they hadn't. The one who had the gun in the car last night is the scariest. Detective-Constable Attwell – Dirty Harry. Square, squat, unblinking. There's another two with him this time, Detective Chief Inspector Thomas Style and Detective-Sergeant John Donaldson, but Dirty Harry is still the worst.

Is your name Patrick Joseph Armstrong?

I told you before – you don't call me Patrick Joseph, just Patrick. Paddy.

Suddenly my head's ringing. He's just slammed his fist into my side of my face and I'm crying out.

Where were you on the fifth of October?

I don't know. What day was it?

What the fuck did you say, Armstrong?

What day was it – what day was the fifth of October?

What day? Is that what you said, Paddy?

Yeah. I'm nodding furiously, in case this isn't clear.

It was a fucking Saturday, as if you didn't know, you murdering paddy bastard.

I don't know where I was. I swear I didn't murder no-one.

What? What the fuck are you saying? Is that even fucking English? Speak properly or we'll bang your head off that wall.

Saturdays I go down to the Memphis Belle or the Old Bell and then to the betting office. In Kilburn.

You wot? Did you understand a word he said?

Who's Paul Hill, Paddy?

I don't know. I've never heard of him.

There's a police dog outside the room. Whenever I pause or try to think for a few minutes, they open the door and bring the snarling mutt just inside, straining on his lead like he could make a break for it at any moment. I normally like dogs and they're usually very friendly with me, but this one is different. It's absolutely terrifying.

They won't stop. *Who made the bomb, Paddy? Who's Aunt Annie? Who planted the bomb? How did you get there? Train? Car? Who drove? Did you drive? Was your girlfriend with you? Carole Richardson? What was her part? Who did you get your instructions from …* On and on …

I don't know. I've never heard of her. I was never there. Carole wasn't there. Neither of us were there.

Yes, you do. You're fucking lying. Tell us the fucking truth, Paddy. Just tell the truth and this will all be over.

Round and round in circles. They're all talking over each other. Questions. Like rapid fire. Can't keep up with them. Don't know who to look at. No breaks in between. Shaking uncontrollably now. Can barely keep my eyes open and my mouth's so dry I have to keep swallowing. Can't concentrate. So confused.

I keep repeating my answers. *I don't know. I wasn't there. I've never been to Guildford. I'm not in the IRA. I don't know. I don't know.* But they don't want to hear that. And they're asking the same things over and over again. Bending down to scream in my face. Whispering at times. Grabbing my ear. Pinching my arm. They're relentless.

When I fall asleep, one of them pulls my chair backwards towards the wall. The screeching of the chair legs against the cold concrete floor is like nails down a blackboard. My legs are heavy again. I've no power to stop them. They could do anything to me now and I couldn't stop them. With my back to the wall and no table to protect me, I'm surrounded on three sides. And they're screaming. For hours and hours. *You're fucking lying, you Irish cunt.*

They've told me they can keep me for a week. Some new law. *Prevention of Terrorism Act. Just came in. Especially for you and your murdering IRA friends. We'll break you, Armstrong. Just tell us the truth or it'll get much, much worse.*

~

The mouth has disappeared, and for a moment the eye reappears at the flap. My own mouth is probably flapping open and then closing. Did I hear him right? They know I didn't do it. But they're going to do me?

Can't think. Can't speak. Can't shout or shriek out the agony I'm feeling inside.

This is my fate. They know I'm innocent. They know I had nothing to do with them murders. Them bombings. They know and they don't care. They need someone and I'm that someone. Oh, Jesus, please, no. This can't be right.

~

Hours and hours, without a break, in this room up on the second floor, images of the interior of a bombed pub and debris staring me in the face. They take it in turns to shout, and sometimes they all shout together. They throw me against the wall. Hiss in my face. Dirty Harry is never far away. He stands at the door looking menacing. Like the police dog. I can't decide who is more feral or dangerous of the two.

Are you proud of yourself? Blowing a woman's legs off? Are you happy with yourself? A young woman who will spend her life in a wheelchair thanks to you.

I'm not a bomber, I swear.

Every time I try to protest, they just continue. Describing people with missing limbs. Arms and legs all over the pub. Graphic details.

How'd you like that to happen to you? That's what we'll fucking do to you if you don't tell us what happened. How would you like to lose an arm? Maybe a leg too, Armstrong?

I believe them, especially Dirty Harry.

It's been hours and hours since they started questioning me and they're getting angrier. They've lost their patience. I can see it. Dirty Harry has his face pressed up to mine. Stale breath. Mean eyes. *You better tell the fucking truth or we'll throw you out that window over there. You see it? We'll open it up and throw you fucking out. Is that what you want, you murdering bastard? We'll say you jumped. Suicide. Nobody will ever be able to prove it. Come and look.*

He drags me over to the window. Makes me look down the two floors to the ground. His friend is nodding. *Yeah, suicides happen in police custody all the time, Vernon, don't they? I know. We just went out to make him a cup of coffee, your honour, and when we came back he was gone.*

Who'd miss an Irish bomber anyway? Be doing the world a favour, we would. Probably get a medal for it. Want another look out the window, Armstrong? I hear a quiet and terrified *No.* It must have come from me. *Then fucking confess. Just say you did it and then this will all be over.*

From next-door I can hear the sounds of thumps and groans. I can imagine other people being knocked from wall to wall. My own face is still throbbing from the punch. Is Carole there? Lisa? The boys from Algernon Road? They've been asking about Gerry. Is he involved in all this? Can't take it all in.

As scared as I am, I can't say I did this. I didn't. I couldn't. I wouldn't. And they would never throw me out the window for telling the truth, surely? They'd not get away with it.

I look down.

When they see that I won't submit, they're even angrier. I'm so tired now. My head keeps rolling. Trying to focus, but it's not enough. And then from out of nowhere comes the heavy crunch of knuckles across my left cheek. Courtesy of Christopher Rowe, the Assistant Chief Constable of Surrey – the man in charge of the case. He'll later deny in court that he was even in the room, but he was.

You killed eight people, you bastard! Because of you, soldiers have had their legs and arms blown off. Another one kicks my leg angrily. My ears are still ringing and my leg's throbbing now. *I swear to God, I don't know nothing about no bombs. I don't agree with all that.* I'm pleading now. With my voice. My eyes. My shaking arms and legs.

Every time they leave, I think that's it. They must believe me now. And then they're back. Screaming again. *Gerry said this. Paul said that. Carole said you did it together. She was there. You were there. We fucking know. Just tell us, Paddy. Get it off your chest.*

One of them moves towards me. He's going to hit me again. I can't take another punch. They'll kill me. I draw myself into a ball in the chair. Whimpering. *Please, stop. Please. I'll confess. Say anything you want. Just leave me alone.*

I can't believe the words as they leave my lips. I give up. I can't take it any more. Maybe if I give them what they want, they'll finally leave me alone. If I die in police custody, they'll get away with it. At least if I sign whatever they want it will be over. Theyll leave me alone.

∼

As quick as it appears, the fleshy gob has disappeared, the white eyeball gone and the flap clanked shut. *We're going to do you for it anyway.* Words that I know I'll never forget.

∼

It takes less than a day to break me, according to the police reports, although who knows how accurate they are in light of everything else that they wrote. At the time it feels like days, but I've lost all sense of time. All I know is there's been at least five of them around me. Hours on end. Screaming. Whispering. Kicking. Punching. Dragging. Sneering. Can't take it any more. They'll kill me. Just want to be left alone. Need to lie down. Just want to get away from this.

Okay, okay. Just tell me what you want me to say. I'll say anything you want. Where do I sign?

Now they're smiling. The relief at this point is impossible for anyone to understand. *That's it, Armstrong. Get it off your conscience. You'll feel much, much better.* They're offering me coffee now. Cigarettes. Smiling. Thank God. I'll get it sorted out later. Just want them to stop. I'll sign and they'll stop.

I'm crying uncontrollably. They tell me I've done the right thing. They march me down the corridor and into another interview room and suddenly I'm standing in front of Benny Hill. He's writing something. *Is this Armstrong? The man you've named? The one who did the bombings with you? Tell us, Paul.*

Why are they calling him Paul? Isn't his name Benny? And why's he nodding? What the hell is going on?

Benny looks up, but he avoids looking me in the eye. *No, that's not Paul,* I'm trying to tell them. *That's Benny Hill. We call him Benny Hill. That's why I said I didn't know him.* But they're not listening. The penny drops. Benny Hill is a nickname – after the fella on the TV. His real name must be Paul. This is the Paul Hill they keep asking me about. Why the fuck would they think I did some bombing with him?

Back down the corridor and back into the incident room. Around me again. *You haven't a leg to stand on, Armstrong. One of your own has said you did it. You'll go down for life, so tell us all the details.* I nod dumbly. Why the hell would Benny Hill say that about me? Paul Hill.

They want details, so they're asking me to tell them all about the bombing. All the details. Which I don't know. I try to guess, but it's wrong. They've stopped smiling. Jim Nevill snarls at me. *You may be telling part of the truth, but you're not telling it all. You're a fucking bastard and an Irish cunt.*

Round and round it goes. I keep guessing. Anything to make this stop. Finally they start asking the questions in such a way that all I have to do is agree or disagree. Mostly, I agree.

So you were a member of the Official IRA, is that right?

Yes.

And you joined the Provos later?

Yeah.

When?

I'm not sure what they want here ...

In 1969? they suggest.

Yeah, 1969.

And what kind of activities did that involve?

I stare at them.

Handling and firing guns? Taking part in raids?

Yeah, that's it – guns and raids.

You raided betting shops?

Aye, betting shops. Yeah, all of that.

I'm not even listening really. Just agreeing. Is the Queen friends with the Pope? Oh, aye, definitely.

Who was your lieutenant, Paddy?

What do I say here? I make up a name, but they don't like that. They're frowning.

No, that's not it. I don't remember his name.

Was it Connolly?

Yeah, that's him. Connolly.

On and on it goes. I agree and sometimes add to details they suggest. Just make up names, places, think about things I've heard about the IRA. Anything I gleaned from conversations at home or in the pub is thrown in. Just give them what they want, Paddy.

Yes, I was in the Official IRA. And the Provos. They're talking about betting shops and I tell them, *Yes, I've done raids on them.* Describe the one I was working in in Belfast. *And you did some in London, too?* Oh, definitely, aye, that's why I was living in a squat, I'm thinking, because I'm busy raking in the cash raiding betting shops. But I don't say that.

They ask me about the boys from Algernon Road and I say everyone was involved. Car thieves, drivers, bomb-makers, whatever the hell they suggest, I'm agreeing. They'll never make it stick. It's ridiculous. Doesn't even make sense. Connolly, I confirm, was the 'lieutenant'. *Yeah, I took my orders from him.*

Your lieutenant, Connolly – is that really Conlon?

Huh?

Your fucking lieutenant. When you said Connolly, did you mean Conlon?

I don't like their aggressive tones. When they stand right over me. Staring. Scares the hell out of me. Makes me shake even more. Haven't stopped shaking in hours. Gerry, a lieutenant. Seriously?

Aye, Conlon was the lieutenant.

And he contacted you in London, is that right?

Aye, that's right.

And he introduced you to Hill, didn't he?

Yeah, he did. He introduced us.

And when you met, he showed you photos of the pub you were going to bomb?

Yeah, loads of photos.

Whatever they say, just agree. Be over soon.

Whenever I think they've finished, there's always more. They're asking about the cars now. Makes, models. Where they came from. I make up colours but they go back to suggesting things to me, so I just have to agree. It's easy and in a way it's nice. When I tell them the things they want to hear, they fawn all over me. Pat my back, smile, offer me coffee, cigarettes, whatever I want. Makes me want to please them. I don't realise it then, but it doesn't help that I've taken so much Tuinal in recent days – it's a drug that makes you highly suggestible. It definitely makes me that way.

And finally, when they mention Carole's name again, I don't think I even try to object. *We know she was there,* they say. *She's told us. She admitted it. No point in lying. Just tell us the truth. You'll feel better.*

Carole admitted this? She must be as terrified as me. How could they even think that a 17-year-old English girl, who was going to school up until a year ago, could do this? Especially a girl like Carole, an innocent hippie whose idea of a good time is getting stoned and dancing around lit candles and incense; who loves animals and draws pictures with *Peace and Love* on them. This girl is supposed to have been recruited by the IRA, to have planned and planted bombs? Jesus Christ, nobody would ever buy it.

Aye, Carole was there, I'm agreeing.

And what kind of a bag did she have?

Trying to remember the kind of wee bags Carole used to carry about with her.

I don't know. A small one maybe? I'm guessing.

Was it a hippie shoulder bag?

Yes, that's it.

They're nodding and smiling again. And I'm happy. Has to be nearly over.

Different policemen keep coming in and out, with some detail that someone else has written down. *Gerry said this. Is that right? Paul's told us you did this …* I'm beyond caring. Just agree. And finally, after hours, they have my first statement. So far I haven't lifted a pen, just agreed and agreed and agreed.

Sign here.

I sign. Don't bother to re-read it. All rubbish anyway. Just sign it. Please, now leave me alone.

But they won't. After a short break I'm back in that room with the images of the interior of a bombed pub and debris. I can barely lift my head. Keeps slumping against the table. They throw me against a wall now. Hiss threats in my face again until I start shaking convulsively and tell them I'll tell them whatever they want.

After another sleepless night, no food, little exercise and still no solicitor, I'm back here again. Day three of this nightmare. Now they're quizzing me again about the bombs. I recognise a term they mention. I've heard boys at home talking about magnesium timers. I tell them and they get excited.

Where did you make it?

Did you carry it?

Who held it in the car?

Who drove?

Where did you put it in the pub?

There's a big X on one side of the diagram of the pub, so I point at it. That must be what they mean. I'm right. They look at each other triumphantly. It's like guessing the right answer in school. Thank God I'm getting them right. *There was a courting couple in the pub,* they tell me. They show me a photo of two people with long hair. *A man and a woman,* they say. *That was you and your girlfriend, wasn't it? Before you left the bomb there. Under the chair.* They actually believe that me and Carole are the people in this picture? I look at it again. The man is clearly a lot older than me, in his forties I'd say, with a receding hairline. Girl looks nothing like Carole. She's very attractive, but her hair is far shorter than Carole's and it's curly. Carole has long, straight hair. And yet they've managed to convince themselves that this pair could be us.

Some time on the third day, after yet another unending session during which one of them takes copious notes that they later translate into my statement, they present me with the revised statement and I sign it. I don't care now. I'll sign anything. It'll never stand up in court. It's not even in my handwriting or my words. These are words I would never use. It's not the way I speak. But they don't seem to care, so why should I?

And now, after hours of questioning, I'm back in the cell. Getting used to the stench of urine. The filthy walls. The crying from other cells and rooms. Just trying to block it out. Need just a few minutes' rest before they come and drag me out again. And then the hissing voice whispers through the flap. *Armstrong? We know you didn't do it … but we're going to do you for it anyway … because we need bodies.*

The voice is moving away. The heavy pound of footsteps moving further down the corridor is accompanied by a deep, chuckling sound. Off, no doubt, to find someone else to torment. And now I'm not tired. And the hollowness in my stomach isn't hunger. Just emptiness. And terror. And in spite of the piercing light taunting me from the corner of the cell, everything has gone dark. Inside me. And it's blacker than I could ever have imagined.

~

We're taking you for a drive, Armstrong. You can show us how you did it. We're nearing the centre of Guildford, though I don't know that until they explain to me where we are. I only saw it briefly, on the drive here the first night, but I was still so out of it I didn't register any of it. Now it's been several days of hell and I'm a bit more alert. And very compliant. I've stopped telling them I don't know how to drive.

Which way did you leave Guildford, after you put the bomb in the pub?
This way.

They're following my directions and suddenly we're back where we started and they're not happy.

Maybe I'm wrong. Maybe it's this way. Go down there.
It's a one-way street.
Maybe you went this way?
Yeah. This way.
They're happy now.

They're quizzing me about where we parked. I can't remember what I said before, in a statement. Later I'll realise I told them a load of different things. Like we'd parked outside a café. We'd parked outside the Horse and Groom, the pub that was bombed. This time I'll guess differently again. *We parked just outside the Wimpy Bar. Yeah, that's where we parked the car.*

They told me yesterday that we met at the Wimpy beforehand, so I reason they'll like this. They'll leave me alone now. But it's not making them happy at all because, as I'll learn later, you can't get into that part of Guildford by car and you certainly can't park there on a Saturday, as it would be closed to traffic.

They ask me again about where we parked the car, and as we drive slowly down a street I point out a narrow side-street. This is where we parked, close up to the wall there. I'm gesturing. The other car was just in front of us, just there. Not being a getaway driver, or even a driver, I don't stop to consider the fact that the place I have pointed at, Mill Lane, is narrow and winding. Also, parking is forbidden on that street during the daytime, even on Saturdays, so no decent bomber would park there. I won't find this out until later, though.

If they realise that I have absolutely no idea where I'm going, they don't care. So we all play the game. They make their suggestions and I nod vigorously. *Yes, that way. Aye, we parked there. Yeah, that's the way out.*

~

And now I'm signing another statement. Writing my name. Patrick Armstrong. December 1974. I did it. All of it. Whatever you say. Again I don't read it. Because even though I've never been to Guildford until they took me here, even though I can't drive and even though I know nothing at all about bombs and these explosions, what's the point? Surrey Police don't want to know.

And now I'm sitting in front of Paul Colman. My mate from the squat. I have to confirm his participation in the same way that Benny Hill said that I did it with him. The look of confusion in Paul Colman's eyes is horrific. *Why are you doing this?* he's saying. *You know it wasn't me. We didn't even know each other until three weeks ago.* Doesn't he realise I have no choice? Doesn't he know?

On and on. Day in, day out, through the night. Little food. Snatched minutes of sleep before they drag me out again or scream through the flap. In a freezing-cold police station in the middle of December. No solicitor. Threats and kicks and punches and big men standing over me.

After seven days of this we're all charged with murder. Myself, Carole, Paul Hill, Gerry Conlon, Annie Maguire, John McGuinness, Brian Anderson and Paul Colman are charged with the five deaths resulting from the Guildford bombings. Paul Hill and I are also charged with the two deaths resulting from the Woolwich bombings in November. They've also charged the family of Gerry's auntie, Annie Maguire, a family friend who was visiting Annie's house, and Giuseppe Conlon, Gerry's father, who was in London to visit his son's solicitor. And, finally, my friend Sean Mullin is charged with conspiracy to cause explosions. When I read the charge sheet later it says there are 11 counts against me: one for conspiracy to cause explosion;

seven for murder; one for causing an explosion likely to endanger life; one for conspiracy to murder; and one for doing an act with intent to cause an explosion. Eleven.

I'm numb. No fight left. They know I'm innocent. The guy who whispered through the door said so, but still they're doing this to me. And I've seen how they can throw you in a prison like Brixton for two months with no evidence whatsoever, keep you there until a trial and then let you go. So I'm going to say nothing and just wait for it to be sorted out. They'll realise we didn't do it and we'll be let go.

After seven days, I barely know my own name. Nobody in my family knows where I am. Nobody in the world will know I'm missing except the people arrested with me. My face is cut and bruised and unshaven. My clothes filthy. It's been about 10 days since I washed. But now I'm in a room with a serious-looking man with a British accent and glasses. My legal aid solicitor. Alastair Logan shakes my hand. I don't know it, but he only agreed to take me on after they rang him twice, because nobody else would take the case. *Can you represent one of the bombers?* I'll find out later that he's more experienced in divorce proceedings than criminal cases. But I don't ask anything like that today. Right now, as far as I'm concerned, he's just another person who wants to make me look guilty. Trust nobody, Paddy.

Alastair will later tell me how shocked he was to meet the man he was asked to represent. From what he can see of my face and neck, I'm bruised and swollen – a week after they beat me. *He fell down the stairs*, they explain. *Whilst he was going for a wash.* A wash? Look at me. And in a cell complex that has no stairs?

Alastair asks me for my mother's address and phone number. I'm trying to tell him, *Massereene Row, Divis flats, there's no phone there.* But I can't stop shaking long enough to speak properly and he can't understand me. He'll eventually work it out, but by that time Mammy will have heard it on the news. He has to go now. He says he'll see me again, in court. We'll talk properly. He shakes my hand again. I'm not holding out much hope for him.

On the way out, the constable who brought him in asks him if he wants to use the facilities.

No, thank you, Alastair replies.

I think you'll find that you do want to wash your hands. You see, you shook his hand twice and he has scabies.

The cop is wearing clear plastic gloves.

Alastair washes his hands.

Now that the questioning is finally over and they've charged me, I'm being transferred to a prison. Never thought I'd be so relieved to go to one after my recent experience in Brixton. There's a thin grey blanket over my head as they're transferring me from the station to the police van. I'm staggering along blindly, trying to yield to whichever direction my escorts push and pull me in. I can't place the direction of the shouts or their proximity, so I'm putting my hands over my head in case a blow should come from any direction.

For the second time in a year, as an innocent man, I'm going to a remand prison. Awaiting a date for trial. Innocent again. But this time, on a grey December day just a couple of weeks before Christmas 1974, it's not just petty theft they want to do me for – it's bombings and terrorist murders. I can only hope that when it does come to court, they'll see. The truth. They'll know I had no part in this. They have to.

CHAPTER FIVE

I offered up my innocence and got repaid with scorn ...
(Bob Dylan)

Early morning, 22 October 1975: trial verdict

B reathe, Paddy, *breathe*. Today has to be the day. They've got to be close to a verdict. It's over a year since the bombing, a year that I never, ever could have imagined happening in my life. But this is it. Could all be over by tonight. You just need those two words. *Not guilty*. Just get through this and you could be free in a few hours.

Oh, God, that's not going to happen. We're not getting off.

It will, Paddy. Be positive. Just think how good it'll be to hear the words *Not guilty*. Never see this place again with its freezing floors, filthy cells and disgusting mattresses. Stinking from shaking hands while slopping out, dripping onto the filthy floors. Putrid from screws pissing in our food, sneaking bits of glass into it, to make our lips and cheeks bleed. We could all be out of this soon and the Linstead Street squat will look like Buckingham Palace by comparison.

Stop, can't get my hopes up. They're going to do us all. They need bodies. That's what that fella in Guildford said. Who's going to believe us – a bunch of long-haired hippie stoners in our Category A patches, handcuffs and Belfast accents – over a bunch of CID pigs in their expensive suits and English accents? We've no hope. Tried and convicted by the press and now the court. Just a matter of time until they convict us. *Guilty*.

Stop! They've no evidence. Nothing. Just those ridiculous confessions they tortured out of us. Not a shred of evidence. Everyone says it. Be strong. And stop bloody shaking, man. Focus on something else. Pray, do some push-ups, anything ...

Our Father who art in Heaven … Oh, God, please, help me, even just
stop this shaking. Makes me look weak. Guilty. Please. Our Father who art
in Heaven, hallowed be thy name. Thy kingdom come, thy will be done, on
Earth as it is in Heaven …

ARMSTRONG! Van's here. Move.

~

December 1974

It's only two weeks before Christmas and we've just been charged. I'm not
going back to Linstead Street. Doesn't look like I'll be out by Christmas.
Please God my mammy doesn't know yet. It'll break her heart.

The van tears up the road, away from Guildford Police Station. Thank
God. When they pull the grey blanket off, the world is Technicolor. It's only
been a week, but it feels strange to be outside again, colours so bright it's
almost blinding. It feels wrong that the world is going on around us.

Speeding out of Guildford in the police van, there's cafés, pubs and shops
flashing by. And people. Just ordinary people walking along, going about
their daily business. Men standing outside a pub, nextdoor to a bookies.
Women wheeling prams along the road as if nothing has happened. Relaxed
and happy. Like I was a week ago. Walking along, just like these people, in
my platforms and bell-bottoms, half stoned or tripping, thinking about
how to get the money for the bookies, going for a pint, maybe looking for a
bit of work. All the ordinary things. Where will I find the money to send to
Mammy and Josephine for Christmas this year?

When I catch a glimpse of myself in the rear-view mirror, I almost
jump back. It's bad. Face is all bruised and swollen from where that animal
hit me. Scraggly beard. Unwashed. Lank, oily, filthy hair. My underpants
are scratching me, my shirt is filthy. Them trousers are hanging down on
me a bit now. They never did that before. And my little Buddha belly feels
shrunken, but I don't even feel hungry any more. I don't feel nothing.

Wish I knew what prison they're about to take me to. I'll be killed in one
of those places. How could I survive?

You're away from Guildford, so just take it easy. It'll be better in this place. You might see the others from Linstead Street if they're still in custody.

Oh, Jesus, I hope they're not. They'll kill me.

Gerry and Benny Hill might be there.

I'll kill them.

But it turns out it's not Brixton. HMP Winchester is what it says on the gate. They're waiting for me.

Here's one of the bombers. He's all yours!

Oh, great, another murdering bastard.

Hang the bastards.

The shaking starts again. My legs. Arms. Everywhere.

Reception. Every prison has one. Nice choice of word. As if you're welcome. Like my mammy at the door of our flat to one of her friends: *Come in, won't you. A wee cup of tea?*

I hear them talking about the other men also arrested: Paul Colman, Sean McGuinness and Brian Anderson. They must be here. Oh, Jesus! They're going to kill me. I think of Paul Colman's face, contorted in confusion, when they dragged me in to him. Just like Benny Hill and Gerry named me and Carole, I named Paul Colman. A man's in prison because of me. I'd have done anything to get them off my back.

Patrick Joseph Armstrong?

It's Paddy Armstrong. I've no middle name. I'm not Patrick Joseph.

Shut up, you Irish piece of shit. Date of birth.

It's the … It's the … the twenty-fourth of September 1950.

What? Speak English.

I am. The twenty-fourth of September 1950.

Right … twenty-fourth September 1950. So you're what age?

Jesus, I barely know any more. Actually have to think about it. *I'm … I'm twenty-four.*

Finally. Fuck's sake. Another genius.

He's trying to fill in his form about me, but he can't understand a word I'm saying. I'm trying to spell words, just so he can understand me, but I'm so fucking tired and petrified, letters and words are just swirling around in my head. Feel like I'm going to faint. The more impatient he becomes, the more my voice shakes, and now he definitely can't understand me. This is never going to end. Trying not to cry again.

Strip!

I remember Guildford vividly so I pull my bell-bottoms and underpants off quick as lightning, dropping them on the floor. The screw looks down in disgust as they almost stick to the ground. He holds out a bag and I drop them in, along with my shirt and the rest of my clothes. I'm mortified.

I've never felt so worthless, so … nothing. Want to die with the shame of all this.

Naked. The pasty, sweaty skin of my pot belly is shaking and my quivering hand drops down as I try to cover myself. Anyone who comes in stares, openly hostile, makes a comment, loud enough for me to hear.

Another fucking murderer.

Sick bastards.

He'll wish he was dead soon.

I'm weighed. Measured. Photographed. Fingerprinted. I wince and he sneers. My fingertips are still aching from Guildford – the detective there jammed every single one into ink and then he mashed them down onto a piece of paper so hard I thought they were going to explode.

They hand me a pair of massive underpants and a uniform. Prison browns – the ugliest thing known to mankind and worn by the most despised prisoners. A heavy brown uniform, an unhealthy-looking colour of thick fabric, with trousers and a matching top with a yellow stripe down the side.

The shoes are massive too. No platforms. Imagine what Lisa and Carole would say if they could see me now.

∼

22 October 1975

It's taken a long time coming, this day. The verdict. Ten months and 18 days. That's a lot of nights, though very few involved sleeping. That's 322 nights spent turning over and over on damp, putrid, horse-hair prison mattresses.

Praying. Crying. Whimpering. Wishing I could end it all. They've taken nearly a year of my life now. Our lives.

322 nights

Two police stations

Two prisons

One Christmas

Anniversaries:

Gertie's

Daddy's

Granny's

And birthdays:

Gerry's

Carole's

Benny's

Mammy's

Josephine's

Eileen's

Harriet's

And right in the middle of the trial – my twenty-fifth birthday.

I spend it sitting in the dock, drawing silly pictures with the others, kicking each other, playing hangman and looking at them looking at us. Like monkeys in the zoo. Except most people actually like monkeys. They're not murdering IRA bastards. No pint. No LSD. No spliff. No pub. No bookies. You're not getting nothing. Happy birthday, Paddy, you murdering Irish bastard.

Mind you, the last five weeks, while we've been on trial, have been the easy part in many ways. We're together. We're warm. We get fed. And though we kind of do hate each other for all pointing the finger at each other, we're together.

It's the rest of the 322 days that have me pasty and pale. Stammering. Shaking. If we get a verdict today and if, by some miracle, it's a Not guilty, I'll appreciate every minute of my free life. Every. Single. Minute.

~

December 1974

It's official. I'm now a Category A remand prisoner in HMP Winchester while we wait for our committal hearing and then, maybe, a trial.

I look dangerous just wearing this uniform. All the other prisoners wear their normal clothes. Except Category A.

Category A – the most dangerous, scariest criminals of them all.

Category A – to be loathed, feared, spat on, mocked. Even by other criminals.

Category A – reserved for the lowest of the low, like us *fucking Irish bastards* - considered the *scum of the earth.*

Category A – terrorists who pose a threat to national security.

Category A – fucking murdering IRA Irish bastards.

We stand out. In our brown denim uniform we are clearly a scourge from whom the public must be protected.

Fucking murdering Irish bastard.

I soon learn that Murdering Irish Bastards get a number. I'm 462813. Like a telephone number. *You'll need to get used to it. You'll be here a very long fucking time*, one of them tells me, flashing his yellow teeth as he grins. Anyone who wants to write to me needs that number and I have to quote it on any letters I send out. *Though why anyone would write to a murdering IRA bastard is beyond me.*

That number is on the front of my file – the file that will follow me everywhere, through every prison reception and into their office until I move on again. And even though it's supposed to be *my* file, I'll never get to read it. Not even when I get out. Although in the next few months I'll see a couple of carefully chosen pictures that were placed inside it and learn about one particular comment. Both will nearly destroy me.

For now, though, all I know is that I have a file and an A book, which is a passport-size book with my number on the front. This must be taken with me wherever I go – the hospital, to court, down for visits. The only time it won't follow me is to the shower or to take a pee. Every time I do something they'll enter a summary of where I went, what time, when I returned. Like one of Carole's diaries, I think, wondering where she is.

As the doors open and my remand period begins, HMP Winchester swallows me whole. I follow the screw and shuffle forward in my prison browns and massive slip-on shoes. *One on*, the screw shouts. *One on*. That one is me, and now I'm on the wing. I'll hear that cry many, many times when I'm moved and ghosted to various prisons in England and Scotland. *One on*. And on and on and on …

And just like when I hear it, the other prisoners will wonder: who is he? What did he do? Is he dangerous? Is he above or below me? Will he try to kill me? And when they learn I'm meant to be IRA, it's game over. In the beginning anyway.

C Wing, HMP Winchester, is my home for the next couple of months. There's screws behind and in front of me. Passing through the main prison, I'm focusing on the screw's feet in front of mine. There's a few shouts, but nothing as bad as I was expecting. When I squint out of the corner of my eye I see that a few are staring, but most just look bored.

C Wing, it turns out, is also home to Benny Hill and Gerry. I don't know this yet and won't until I see them in court in a couple of days' time. Which is just as well. For now I'm slung into a cell and the gate slams behind me and I'm home. Home. An iron-frame bed concreted into the floor. A bare mattress with tufts of horse-hair sticking out. A cracked chair. A dirty, uneven table. A pot (to pee in and then slop out). A water jug. And utensils and cutlery – mug, plate, bowl, fork, knife, spoon. All plastic. Home … as if.

High up the freezing-cold walls, past the damp stains, beyond the splashes of red and brown and above the scribbles, there's a slot masquerading as a small glass window with rusty grey bars. If I strain and block out the bars, I can see the grey sky beyond it. My multicoloured world has disappeared again.

Christ, Paddy, would you stop pacing – you'll be exhausted in an hour.

I'm exhausted already.

So sit down.

Can't – what if they come back – send in screws or another prisoner to get me?

Right, then, sit against that there wall at the back and watch the door.

I'm never going to settle in. Just want to die.

Give it a rest. Do you want to break your mammy's heart, haven't you caused her enough worry?

My mammy will hear about it shortly. Later that day. Alone in the house when the lunchtime news comes on. They'll mention my name, and Carole's. She won't believe it, though. Nobody will at first. She'll check with Josephine as soon as she gets home.

What do you call that wee girl our Paddy goes out with?

Carole?

Aye, that's it.

Why?

Nothing.

Mammy will try to hide it from Josephine, thinking it'll blow over in a couple of days. But it won't. It'll be on the six o'clock news that evening and again on the next bulletin. It'll be the lead story in every newspaper, radio and television bulletin all over England and Ireland. Within a couple of hours it'll be all over the Falls, up in Andersonstown and all across Belfast. Anyone who's in the know, who's involved with the IRA, will know it's rubbish. They wouldn't have anything to do with me. Most people, though, those who aren't involved with the IRA, they'll believe it for a long time. They'll believe we did it – our own people.

Josephine will refuse to go to school the next day. And the day after. And every single day after that. She's only 15, but with most of the country talking about us who'd blame her? She and Mammy will visit me, although it will be nearly six months later, when Mammy finally gets the money together for a ticket to England.

You didn't do it, did you, son? You never killed those people?

No, ma. I'd never. I swear.

I know. I'm sorry. I just had to check. You were never even into that.

Sure I've never run about with the RA or the Provos. I don't know any of them boys.

I know that, son. Sorry.

It's all right. You had to ask.

I lean against the wall and jump back. Baltic. It may be December, but it's worse than the outhouse in Milton Street in the depths of winter, when your pee would almost freeze mid-air on its way to the ceramic pot. And even though they're massive and scratching the legs off me, I'm grateful that these prison browns are thick, heavy fabric. I could be here for a couple of months, until around February, while this gets sorted.

I'm sitting, my back to the wall, eyeing the door. A trick I'll use for many years after I get out. Waiting. Watching. I wish there was one of Lisa's weird psychedelic pictures on the wall. Wish I was lying on the mattress with Carole beside me. Pink Floyd or Bob Dylan in the background. A joint in one hand.

When I finally manage to block out the intoxicating fumes of God knows what body fluids, rat shit and damp, I focus on trying to control the shaking. Linstead Street, the Memphis Belle, the Kilburn Snack Bar, Camden Markets – only a week ago. So close I could touch it. What would I be doing now if I wasn't here? Probably be back at the squat after waiting outside the café, hoping for a bit of work. Scrape together a couple of quid for the bookies. Have a win maybe on some horse, home then and have a pipe or roll a joint. And then go and meet Carole and Lisa somewhere.

How could I have thought this godforsaken country would be better than Northern Ireland? I never stood a chance here. At least back home I was one of many Catholics – I had my own to look after me. And though they were evil bastards, at least you knew what to expect of the soldiers and the RUC. A smack around, a few hours in a cell or walking around a yard and then you'd be back out when they knew they had nothing on you.

Creak.

I'm standing up, my back to the wall, before I know it. Must have dozed off. I feel better. Less crazed. On the ground there's a tray. With food. A plastic knife and fork. I lift the plate and look at it. It must have been food once, but now it's just a grey, shiny lump of stewed or mashed pulp. Who knows what the hell it was at one stage, but suddenly my belly rumbles. I pick up the plastic fork and knife and I shovel it into me. The knife is useless, not least because it would break with any pressure at all, but also because you don't need a knife with this food. It's mush. Still, I eat it in minutes. I feel like crying with relief.

~

Approx. 9.00am, 22 October 1975

The police van is tearing through the streets from Brixton to the Old Bailey, sirens screaming around us. Verdict might be in today. Oh, God.

We've done this now every day for five weeks, so it should be normal by now, but this is different and we both know it. We don't talk, Gerry and me, from our separate cells in the van. There's a song in my head.

'Once upon a time you dressed so fine ...'

We're slowing down and I can hear them now, the protestors. They'd be close enough to touch if we weren't separated by the steel wall of the armoured van.

String them up!

Hang the murdering bastards!

The screw I'm handcuffed to sneers. *Hear that? Your life won't be worth living if you're found not guilty, Armstrong. They'll get you anyway. But you will be. You'll be sick and old before you get outside again.*

I focus on the song in my head instead of his voice. I always loved this song. Learned every word in my teens. Sang tunelessly along to the radio. Wanted to be that rolling stone, travelling around, seeing the world.

From Belfast to London to Belfast to London. Rolling. It was cool. I used to sing it in London. A rolling stone. The world was my home. Then suddenly to Brixton for those two months, until I was dumped back out of prison onto the streets of London. Without a home. The squats. Rolling along beside Carole and Lisa. And then Guildford. Rolling faster now. Stop it, I'm scared. In Winchester and then Brixton. Won't stop now. The Old Bailey. Back and forth in the prison bus every day, the last five weeks. No control any more. Waiting for the prosecution to end. Waiting to stand in that witness box. Faster and faster and faster. Concluding statements now. Let it end. Verdict has to be near, but I can't see it – completely out of control …

~

December 1974

After just a day in Winchester Prison the three of us are pulled back into the van. We're going to Guildford, we realise, after two hours in the prison van cuffed to two screws. One on each side. I'm terrified. What if they take us back to the police station? But no, thank God, we're at the magistrates' court. Alastair, my solicitor, told me to expect this, but I'd forgotten. They'll remand us for another week and then send us back to Winchester for another week. They'll have to do this every week until our committal hearing. A magistrate will then decide if the case should go to court and whether there's enough evidence against us. There won't be. There can't be, I decide. All they have is that bloody stupid false confession.

As the van carrying us roars into the centre of Guildford and down the lane to the small magistrates' court, many of the 57 people injured in the bombings are still in hospital, their bodies mourning a limb, healing from facial disfigurement or burst ear drums. Others are home, avoiding mirrors and the public – their facial scarring is so severe it will be a lifetime reminder of a quick drink they had in a pub in Guildford. And now, the *bombers* are back.

It starts as a dull roar. I can barely make out the words, but there's no mistaking the tone. The people who hate us are out there. Crowds of them. I've never felt such hatred until this moment. It's terrible. I understand. There are families mourning their children, husbands, wives. Their pain is real and I feel sick for them. But I didn't do it. Never would. Now the threat of being dangled and dropped from a second-floor window seems like a more attractive option than facing them and their cold, pure hatred.

Fortunately they've closed the street, so the one consolation is that I don't have to contend with coming face-to-face with any of the crowd, who have already convicted us. Instead they take us in the back and there's police everywhere. I look up. I must be tripping – there's snipers on the roof, their guns trained on us. Dying to shoot. Don't trip, Paddy. Don't make a wrong move. Oh, sacred heart of Jesus. I can barely breathe.

Half naked again. Gloved hands probing everywhere. No more dignity left anyway. As if I could have found anything lethal and illegal between my prison cell and here. The screws who don't throw insults at me just stare. You'd think I would be getting used to the hatred, but every time it gets me all over again.

And there she is. Carole. Handcuffed to the screw. Still beautiful. But pale. Tired. So confused-looking. She hasn't seen me yet. Gerry and Benny Hill are here too. The reason I'm here. Want to be sick again. Steady, Paddy.

They haven't seen me yet. Need to breathe and calm myself. Never felt so angry in my life. Why me and why the hell Carole? I don't know what I expect from them. An explanation, an apology, some kind of justification, something before I go insane.

I don't know it for certain yet, but I've a fair idea that it was Paul who named me first. I don't know if they are looking at me. I need to keep staring ahead so I don't get sick. I don't know yet that they were arrested first. Subjected to the same torture as I was, worse even, because I caved quickly, cowed into submission. They were forced to give names. They'll say that giving my name seemed okay because it was so ridiculous. Everyone knows Paddy Armstrong isn't in the Provos.

But right now I don't know any of this, so I look away from them. I look at Carole, pleading with my eyes. But she won't look at me. I hate them and she hates me. I know her. She's hurting. She's confused. Terrified. I see it and I look down, hiding my shame. I'm glad she won't talk to me, because I don't know what to say. I'll expose my fear. My weakness. My unmanliness.

Her hair is hanging about her face, her eyes sunken and wild. She looks as bad as I feel, but this seems worse. Just seeing her there makes me want to crawl under a rock.

The judge mutters a few things. As quick as it began, it's over. We're remanded for another week it seems. I see Alastair, my solicitor, briefly. I desperately want to talk to Carole, but she's vanished. So agonisingly brief. No matter how badly those cops hurt me, this is a million times worse. My girl hates me. Maybe as much as I hate myself.

~

Approx. 9.30am, 22 October 1975

The helicopters are circling the Old Bailey today. They're not normally here. Sounds like they're directly above us. Guns pointed straight at us, no doubt. The crowd has grown in the past few weeks. In the beginning there were probably a handful, but from the noise today it's reaching a frenzy. Light pierces the van window. The press. Waiting for their pound of flesh.

Out!

I follow Gerry. We know the drill. Blanket. Chain. Bridge. Cells. Wait. Sit. Stand. Shut up. Fucking Irish murderers.

The jury's been out of a full day now, since 11 yesterday morning, after Donaldson finished reading the last of the 126 pages of summing up. The jury are still going. Has to be good news.

It's Guilty, I know it is.

No they're not. They're not. You've come this far, Paddy. This is the end. Feel like I'm suffocating.

Blanket will be off any minute now. Think of something else.

They're gonna do us for this, we've no hope.

They won't, they can't. Now keep going. Just think, Carole's up there. She needs you to be strong.

Oh, Carole. Just let her get off. I'll go to prison a hundred times over if she can just get out.

~

Some time during my first week in Winchester I receive a letter from her. It's dated 10 December – the day she got sent to Brixton on remand, after being charged. Before I saw her in court and she wouldn't look at me. Her words tear the heart out of me.

290719   HM Prison
Richardson, C.   Jebb Avenue
                                                    Brixton
                                                    London SW2

10/12/1974

Dear Paddy,

I really wish you would pull yourself together and name the people who
were with you on the 5th – they wouldn't stop at putting you in it if in
fact someone did. How did they have your full name and everything else if
someone didn't talk? In Harlesden I thought it was a bit of a joke until they
showed me what was written underneath. I nearly broke down. It's only
hitting me now just how bloody serious this is and you had better realise it
pretty soon. Who are you afraid of? What can they do to you whoever and
whatever they are? Who knew my mum's address, did you give it to anyone
because the police were at my mum's just after we met you, they wouldn't
even tell us what it was about - all I got was could you come to the station
and have a look at a few pictures and see if you recognise anyone and then
they drop this on me. In Guildford they said I was probably at Woolwich as
well. Jesus Paddy what have you got me involved in. I wouldn't believe them
at first until they said you said I was there, which I don't believe now, at least
I hope you didn't say it. Tell Andy and John I'm sorry but the police said they
said I was there and there was nothing I could do then.

All I do is hope and pray that you'll have the sense to tell the truth in court
and the same with Paul Hill and whoever else was there, then if you and
Paul were, and nothing either of you have said or done has made me think
otherwise. I wouldn't mind but as far as I remember I have never seen Paul Hill
before in my life, how many times have I seen Gerry, once maybe twice. How
could you get involved in anything like this, you were always fairly quiet, oh
Paddy it's cracking me up locked up nearly 20 hours a day. I'm used to being
out all the time, never having to worry about anything. I keep crying for no
reason at all. I'll go mad if this doesn't end soon. I can't sleep at night. I have
dreams, bad ones, most of the time. I feel like killing myself at times.

Well I'll close for now, keep your chin up and please do all you can before I
crack up. Write soon.

All my love

Carole xxxxxx

Bob Hope for President

I put it down. Pick it up again. Re-read it. Turn it upside-down. Wipe my hands and forehead so the sweat doesn't blur the words. Bat away the tears. Read it again. The fact that this letter will survive for decades is a miracle.

She couldn't possibly believe I was involved with this, could she?

No, she couldn't. And they showed you her statement. They said she admitted to it first, didn't they?

Yeah, but I should have known better – lying bastards! They played us all off each other, scared her into it, like they did to me.

Exactly. Like they did to you.

But I'm a 24-year-old man from Belfast who should be used to getting abused by police, who understands how all this works. They lie, they bully. I should have been stronger.

But you were off your head. No sleep. No food. Paranoid. Coming down from a load of Tuinal– it's a very powerful drug, Paddy. Leaves you highly suggestible. You'd no chance against them. They were going to do you, no matter what.

Yeah. Yeah. But still, poor Carole.

I re-read her letter. Can't write like her. Just don't have the words to explain.

~

We manage quick conversations. Me, Benny and Gerry and the other boys in our one hour of exercise. We're trying to work out what the hell happened. Not blaming now. Not aloud anyway. Wondering why the hell we're here, why us, and when the hell we'll get out. Every day we wonder, through the three-month wait for our committal hearing.

Every Monday we go back to court. And I go back to Carole. Mondays are getting me through these three months. Through every meal that might have the sharp taste of urine, glass or God knows what. Through 23 hours a day in this freezing-cold cell, in my own head. Through Christmas 1974 and the nights when I'm worn down and wishing I had the balls to hang myself from the bars of this grey hell.

I can tolerate the hours we spend travelling to and from Guildford, trying to ignore the chafing handcuffs, the hatred in the eyes of the screw bolted to me, the wail of sirens, the skidding tyres signalling our arrival, the pounding on the windows. I can block it all out because I know at the end will be a few precious moments beside her, in that tiny room in the Guildford courthouse where we are the most hated people in the universe.

All through December she bristles. Barely looking at me. I'm shaking so much I can't even attempt to form a coherent sentence in the few seconds that we get together. Her eyes look crazed, her long hair lank. A shadow of my carefree hippie girl.

I don't know how she manages it, but in January 1975 Lisa, who is still just 16, travels to Winchester and gets in to see me. I'm trying to tell her what happened. I'm shaking, but she understands. She believes me. She's been in touch with Alastair and she's been able to put the pieces together.

She tells me how scared Carole is, scared and confused. *What happened? Why did you give her name, Paddy?* I answer, *I didn't, Lisa. I swear. I wouldn't. They said her name first. Someone else gave it to them. Paul or Gerry by the sounds of it. I'd never. Those cops said she'd already confessed. It was too late to deny it. I just had to confirm it. I said no first. No way. I wasn't there and she wasn't. I swear. I'd never do that. But in the end I was so scared, I just agreed to everything.* She nods. She was outside the room I was in. Heard them screaming at me. Chairs being dragged across the room. She told Carole this. They did it to us all – to Carole, to Lisa. Everyone.

I try to explain to Lisa. Tell her I can't write well. That no matter how many times I try, I don't have the words. *You need to help me.* She nods. She leaves me with the warmth of a human hug and promises that she'll explain it all to Carole.

Monday after Monday we all stand in the dock. Fifteen of us. Me and Paul Hill have been charged with carrying out the Woolwich bombing. They've charged nine of us with murder: me, Carole, Paul Hill, Gerry, four of the lads from Algernon Road and Gerry's auntie Annie. Then they're doing another seven for making the bombs in Annie's house, including Annie herself, a woman who is more British than Irish. A woman whose children were reared here and have only ever visited Belfast. Who has pictures of the Queen in her house. She's meant to have murdered people, to have had her whole family making the bombs. They even arrested her 13-year-old son, Patrick, and her brother Giuseppe. This poor slip of a man who'd snap in two with a strong wind, a man riddled with TB who could barely move from his chair, is being done for making explosives. It's a joke.

At the end of January, Sean Mullin and Brian Anderson are released. They're acquitted shortly afterwards. Paul Colman and John McGuinness also have their charges dropped and are set free. I am immensely relieved. One massive weight off my shoulders. Later on we'll learn that the cops can't keep them because they never confessed. They have nothing on them. And that's the difference between them and us. I'm happy for them, but so sick for us.

The murder charge against Gerry's auntie Annie has also been dropped. She never confessed either, so they couldn't do her. But she's still being done on charges of unlawful possession of nitro-glycerine, along with several members of her family, including her husband and two children. They apparently kept it in their house, now a 'bomb factory'. I don't know this woman, but it seems as far-fetched as us bombing Guildford.

That leaves four of us being done for murder: Benny, Gerry, Carole and me. We will eventually become known as the Guildford Four. A tag that will follow me, follow all of us, for the rest of our lives. Annie, her family and friends will become the Maguire Seven. A tag from which they will never be able to escape either.

Monday to Monday. Back and forth to that tiny room. All through December and January, Carole's not looking at me, and there's days when I can barely look at Benny and Gerry. We're all exhausted with anger, accusations, recriminations. Need Carole to just give me a sign that she understands. I think I'll crack up if I can't make her realise the truth. If I lose her …

And then one Monday, towards the end of January, just after we've been remanded for another week, she edges a little closer. Glances in my direction. And just before she's reattached to the screw, she nods at me, smiles a little and utters just one word in the soft voice that's been haunting my dreams.

Paddy.

A couple of days later I get a letter. The envelope has already been slit open. Already read by somebody else. But it's her writing, her words, so I don't care.

I can barely open it my hands are shaking so much.

HM Prison
Jebb Avenue
Brixton
London SW2

1 Feb 1975

Dearest Paddy

I have just seen Lisa and she told me what happened, of course I believe you weren't there. The way the police put it, it made me think I was there. But when it's all over we'll show them.

Lisa will be up again next Wednesday. I told her not to worry about me but to get to see you whenever she could. She won't take my advice I know, but I wish you all the luck in the world because I didn't think you would have done such a thing and I'm really glad I know for sure.

Put in an application for the ring because there's no reason you shouldn't have it in there. Anyway, I'll see you Monday I hope, if your solicitor doesn't mind that is.

Lisa said you heard from your sister, is it Eileen or Harriet – I can't remember which one lives in New Barnet. Well at least she wrote.

I've just seen my solicitor. Nothing good, nothing bad. Well one thing, there were photos from that night and the police have them. So it's all really good in a way.

Paddy just answer me one question: why did you make a statement against me? I don't think you did now and the way everything is going we'll be making statements to the press pretty soon.

It'll be good to walk down the road with you again though. Maybe we can go hitch-hiking again. I still can't wait to see the palm trees in Wales, if there are any that is.

It's done you some good though, you've lost weight and that can't be bad – all you need is a <u>shave</u> (HINT HINT). You could do with a haircut as well but you can't have one, so I can't tell you off about that.

Tell Gerry his letter must be going around the world because it still hasn't arrived. But he might not have written at all. You can't tell with some people, can you …

I'll close for now, it's teatime so off I go for a while, but see you Monday. Look after yourself and for the last time <u>have a blooming shave</u>.

All my love

Carole xx

Dearest Paddy. She wrote *Dearest.* Oh, thank you, God. Thank you. Less afraid now. Less alone. The cell feels less grey. The walls less cold. And although each of the 23 hours a day between now and when I'll see her next Monday feel like an eternity, I can deal with anything because I know she doesn't hate me.

What does she mean there were photos of that night? Does she mean photos of the bombings? Are there photos of me, too? Where were we? I wish I could remember.

Finally it's Monday again, and I'm here. And she's here. Standing beside her as they renew our remand for another week. She's so close I can smell her skin, her hair. I take her hand. She's squeezing it gently. I can feel my body relax just as the magistrate is shuffling his papers, ticking his boxes. Then suddenly she's gone – handcuffed to a screw and out the door and I'm attached to my screw and the van is taking off at high speed, like it had never stopped. The anticipation of this moment has got me through the last week and now it's over. Another week to while away.

Seeing Alastair is also keeping me sane. He's not what I expected. He's very posh and he has a very hard time understanding me, but I feel like he really believes me. We talk a lot about where I was. *You need an alibi,* he keeps stressing, but I just don't know. I must have been in Linstead Street, but how could I remember where I was, what I did on that one Saturday night? I honestly have no idea. I never went anywhere or did anything that would set it apart from any other weekend.

When he comes to me and tells me that they might know where I was, I can't imagine it can be true. He explains that an English acquaintance of Carole's, Frank Johnson, has come forward and said that Carole and Lisa were at a gig with him the night of the Guildford bombings. Even better, there are photos of Carole from that night to prove it – the ones she mentioned in her letter.

Most importantly for me, Carole says I was minding the dog while she went out. I'm nodding at him. *Yes, I was. That's where I was. I was minding the dog while she and Lisa went out to that gig.* I only remember it because of the slagging I got for staying home to look after a stray dog.

She has you wrapped round her finger, Paddy!

Yeah, you stay home and cuddle the dog, Paddy, while your girlfriend goes out!

Will you make my dinner while you're at it?

It went on for ages and everyone laughed. I did too, but I was a bit mortified. It's crystal clear now. After that I got stoned, watched TV and fell into bed before Carole and Lisa came home.

I'd never bothered to find out much details about what they did that day. Why would I? All I knew was that they got backstage passes from a fella called Frank and they had a great time. I was too busy in the Old Bell, drinking with Benny Hill, Gerry and a fella I knew called Ninty, to be thinking about what the girls were doing. When Benny went to get his train to Southampton to see his girlfriend, Gerry and I went back and forth to the bookies for the next couple of hours. By the time Gerry headed off around 4.00pm and I was settled in the bookies, Carole and Lisa had done the laundry and gone up to see Carole's friend, Maura Kelly, where she works. They'd gone there earlier in the day, borrowed some money, and then gone back again later on and hung around until closing time. They came back to Linstead Street then, which was when Carole asked me to mind Leb the dog while she and Lisa went to the concert. *She'd gone out in her bare feet,* Alastair tells me. *That sounds about right,* I agree. *Probably with her wee hippie bag.* Alastair writes it all down and I feel so relieved. Leb can't talk, but I know the others can and they must surely remember that night.

I'll learn from Lisa that she and Carole went off to meet this Frank Johnson early that evening. I might have met him, but I honestly can't remember. She met him in the Memphis Belle apparently. He's a Geordie and Carole's family come from there, so he offered them backstage tickets for this gig. I've never heard of the band – Jack the Lad. They'd met Frank before the concert in the Charlie Chaplin pub and then headed up to South Bank Polytechnic for the gig. The bouncer remembered them. They arrived around 7.45–8.00pm. Well, you couldn't forget them easily, could you? Barefoot Carole with her little hippie bag, the pair of them a bit stoned, giggling and delighted to have free tickets, backstage passes, to see a band. After the concert there was a small party in the dressing room; free Guinness and joints were shared. Carole took some speed, too. And at some point a relative of one of the band, visiting from Canada, took photos of them all. One of which included Carole with a member of the band.

Oh, thank God! Carole was at a concert and I was at home. Alastair and I talk about it. I will be able to work back and remember who was in Linstead Street because of the dog conversation. And even without that, we have the photo of Carole. Without her, the whole story will fall apart because she and I were allegedly the 'courting couple'. They have nothing. I can finally stop shaking now. I might even sleep better.

HM Prison
Brixton
SW2
290719
D Wing

10 Feb

Dearest Paddy,

It was good to see you looking so good … Why won't they let you have a shave? You don't look so cuddly with a beard …

I really miss you. At least they let me see you for a few minutes in court. It's so hard to put my feelings down on paper, but I'm sure you understand what I mean.

At least I know a bit more about Guildford now and what happened in the police station. I didn't know what or who to believe at first, but now I know I don't blame you if you went through the same ordeal as Paul and Gerry. I hope you didn't though, it didn't sound nice at all.

Do you see Gerry, Paul, Paddy, Sean and the rest of them in Winchester now or are you still separated?

I wrote to your ma just now. She must think we're mad – one minute getting married, the next trying to get bail.

Are you really locked up 23 hours a day? I thought it was bad here.

How come you're only remand prisoners yet you're not allowed writing paper and stuff like that? This place is a palace compared to where you are by the sound of things …

All I hope is that the truth is believed in court. Because I'm sure Anne and Paddy are innocent and I know you and me are, so we have nothing to worry about really. It's surprising how you get to know someone in a few weeks. Anne's a really nice person. I wonder if I'll ever get to see her when I get out, or should I say we get out.

Have you still got the cross? I meant to ask you today but I forgot all about it. I've a few other questions when I see you next time, but I'll probably have forgotten them by then.

When we get out do you fancy going picking flowers at midnight? I keep thinking back to Lisa's birthday party – it's really funny, but it seems so fresh in my memory …

Is Josephine coming with your ma? I'd really like to see her. You used to talk about her so much. I keep thinking back to that tour of England that lasted 9 days, the things we talked about, and do you remember that question sitting on the seat at the top of the Dover Road? It doesn't seem real now. I was so happy then.

I feel so fed-up now and depressed thinking about it. Why didn't they wait till this month to arrest us? It's not fair. I thought January was going to be a good month as well. Oh well, I suppose it's the way things go. I'm writing to Lisa now so I'll close. See you Monday. Keep your chin up.

All my love

Carole

PS I want a kiss next week.

She wants a kiss. Oh, Jesus, thank you. I want to see her again now. I want a kiss too. I want to cling on to her, on a mattress in Linstead Street, with the sleeping bag slipping off us as we sleep like babies. Jesus, I wish it was Monday.

Mondays – the day they renew our remand for another week.

Mondays – the day I get to see Carole for a brief period.

Mondays – the day I know I haven't imagined all this.

Mondays – the day I know I'm not on my own.

Mondays – the day I feel like someone cares if I live or die.

Thank God for Mondays.

The strangeness of the situation isn't lost on me. Wanting to get to a courtroom to be remanded on a murder charge just so I can see my girlfriend and maybe kiss her. It's perverse. But it's getting me through.

I rub my beard. Scraggly, scratchy and patchy. Driving me insane. How long are they going to keep this up for – insisting I keep the beard so I look like I did when I'm supposed to have bombed them pubs? Like their photofit picture, which obviously isn't me.

Sitting in my cell, reading her old letters. I can hear her voice all the way from Brixton to here. She's been writing to me more often the last few weeks. It's getting me through. Every time they hand me a new one with a sneer on their faces, I grab it and hide it like a child with a sweet. I turn the envelope over and over, hoping it's positive, hoping she's feeling happy, no recriminations. When I finally take it out I'll read it slowly, make it last. She makes me forget the taunts and the abuse. Her innocence is my antidote for their hatred. Between Monday remands, her letters, letters from my family and visits from Alastair or Lisa, I can get through this. And I feel least alone when I hold her letter and look at the curve of her familiar writing. The Xs that flow down the page at the end of each letter remind me how young she is, but I'm touched by her innocence.

Wednesday [probably 12 Feb]

Dearest Paddy

I know I only wrote the other day but I'm really bored. I've got flat batteries and a boring book. So I thought I'd bore you for a while.

Have you seen your solicitor? Because I don't remember if I put it in my statement or not but promise me you won't hit me if I have? I know you won't hit me because you never have, and never will because I move too fast. Bloody statements and bloody liars. The police will be having us up for writing statements we know to be false …

I keep thinking I'm going to die, silly really, but it's not a nice thought. I wonder what it would be like to die because I believe in reincarnation. I wonder what I'll be in my next life. Maybe I'll be the daughter or son of a rich ranch owner in Texas with plenty of horses. Or maybe I'll be a fly buzzing around and annoying people. I don't know which I'd prefer because I like buzzing and I like horses. Maybe he'll own a poppy field in Texas so then I can have the best of both …

I wonder if they'll let me have my kitten in here. Poor Smack, she hasn't got anyone to look after her, she's probably dead by now and she was loverly – all furry and cuddly.

I'm getting really morbid. I must think of something nice and unmorbid if you know what I mean. Blast, I can smoke that fag now. Egh it tastes rotten. I should have smoked it earlier …

I don't want to bore you too much so I'll close for now. See you Monday. God Bless

Love Carole xxx xxx

Don't forget I want a kiss

Sometimes her thoughts about death scare me. They're thoughts I can't entertain. Since Christmas I've resolved that I have to keep it together. For Mammy. For Josephine. For Eileen. For Harriet. For Dad. For Granny. For Carole. My future wife. Our babies. We'll be out soon. Keep it together, Paddy.

Friday 14th Feb

Dearest Paddy

Lisa came up to see me just now. She's got flu but she should be up Wednesday.

I'm getting silly Valium 10 g for my bloody nerves. It's not good, I can't go on for much longer …

There's some horrible coloured guy in here and he keeps shouting out 'you murdering cow'. Jesus, some people have no sense at all, they believe in Guilty before the trial. Well I know I wasn't there. But I suppose everyone to their own ideas.

What a Valentine's day. Well next one I'll be free, so who cares …

They played 'Stairway to Heaven' again today. It's getting a bit boring. Led Zep all the time. Why don't they use their brains and play some Floyd for a change?

I'm starting to break down now. When this gets committed I'll cry with joy. At least it won't be another 'remanded for 7 days in prison custody'.

I can check the date we were in Dover by the police in, I can't remember where, but it was for the two days after I got attacked in that telephone box. It seems so silly now. I've still got his address, bloody mad man. Make a phone call and get attacked – not bad going, eh? Well I always have had good luck!

I've just had a clear up in my cell, the junk I've collected is unbelievable. I have a clear up every day, but it doesn't help much and it's back to normal in an hour. Well at least it's not as bad as Linstead St. Remember my dog? It seems so silly now, me and Lisa off out leaving you dog-sitting, but poor little Leb couldn't be left on his own, and he never behaved for Brian. I don't blame him, though – Brian used to hit him all the time, the little sneak …

I've no straights left so I have a choice of menthol or roll-ups and neither are very nice. I suppose I could always pretend it was a joint, stoned on Memory's Chocolates and Flowers. I bet you felt a fool for carrying them home that night. I mustn't think like that or I'll start crying again. I really miss you at times like this – it's funny, missing a little pig like you. The sooner this is over, the better.

I'll be able to get a job in a pub or betting shop, anywhere because I'll be 18 by the time this is over so it has its rewards I suppose.

Anyway I'll close for now as I'm running out of space and I don't want to bore you too much.

So good night, sleep tight. God bless

All my love
Carole xxx

God Bless The Innocent
May The Guilty
Be Brought To Justice

I'm dreaming about her. Thrashing about on the horsehair mattress – stolen chocolates and flowers. We are wandering the streets of north London, eyeing up flowers in people's gardens. We're not quite flying high but we're not straight. Just me and her. She's wearing her cheesecloth shirt and a loose skirt. No shoes. Her fingers laced through mine.

Do ya want some flowers to go with the chocolates?

Aw, Paddy, you are sweet.

See, I told you I was romantic.

You really are, Piggy!

Those ones?

Nah, let's keep going.

How about those ones over there – in the big garden … Do you like them?

Oh, they're lovely, yeah.

Right, hold on … Here.

Flowers? For me? Where did you get them? I hope you didn't pay too much?

Anything for you! Now give us a kiss.

Carry them for me, Paddy, will you? I'm tired.

I've already got a big box of stolen chocolates and now you want me to carry flowers! I've a reputation, woman. Imagine someone saw me …

We're laughing and laughing. And now there are hands around my throat. Someone's behind me. Dirty Harry is strangling me. He's squeezing my neck. Can't breathe.

Murdering Irish bastard!

We're going to do you for this!

Drop him out the window!

Fucking murderer!

We're going to do you …

I wake up in a cold sweat. Squirming on the thin mattress. Tears in my eyes.

22 Feb (Saturday)

Dearest Paddy

I'll have seen you before you get this letter but so what …

I'm really starting to miss you bad. When we get committed, God only knows when I'll see you again. It's not fair. Why didn't they pick on Gerry's or Paul's girlfriends, why the heck me? It's not fair, but this bloody world isn't fair to anyone that does any good in it, is it? Anyway, why worry? We know the truth and that's all that matters. I know where I was and you know where you were, I think, so the truth's got to come out that we weren't there.

What's bugging me is how did they get to know mum's address? Even you didn't know that – it was a sort of secret, if you know what I mean. It just doesn't make sense …

What's the weather like up there? It's been nice and sunny down here most of the day. But they say it's gonna rain tomorrow. But it won't.

I'm psychic. Sounds silly, but it's true. Tomorrow will be a nice day and Monday will be bad weather-wise and court-wise. Tuesday I'm gonna get a surprise visit. Whether it will come true or not I don't know, but that's what's in my head and an accident, but that's all. I hope it's not you, but something tells me it will be.

I'm going to sleep now so sweet dreams.

God Bless

See you Monday

All my love

Carole

xxx

God Bless The Innocent And May The Guilty Be Brought To Justice.

The letters come every few days. I write back sometimes, but I just don't have her gift for words. Can't make something out of nothing like she can, so my letters to her are so much shorter and won't survive her prison days.

26 February 1975

Wednesday 7.45am

Dearest Paddy

Beware, I'm in a bad mood, so if you don't want to be driven mad don't read any further.

Why in hell's name did you pick on me to put in your blasted statement? I'm in a really bad mood with you at the moment, well not just you, but mainly you.

Why did you hold a party for Lisa's birthday and why did I meet Frank Egan [a Dublin fella who invited Carole to the party where I met her first]? If I hadn't met him, I wouldn't have been at Lisa's party and I wouldn't have met you and then I wouldn't be here – it's all his fault…

Did you get the radio or the ring? I'm really sick to death of this place – it's driving me insane. When we get out, if you want we'll get a flat and settle down and to hell with everyone else, but it's up to you, ok? Think you've probably got about 8 months or more still after the trial, so make sure you think really well and it is to you for better, for worse and all that.

I'm making a stuffed dog now because I'm finished my rug and I need something constructional to do. We used to play poker for match sticks and monopoly money, but the two wardens who used to play with us have gone back to their usual prisons so I haven't got anyone to play with anymore. I'll have to find someone who can play chess now because there's nothing else I can do really. I can't concentrate on my exams and I'm supposed to be learning German in about 3 weeks' time so I'll come out of here quite brainy, which I wasn't when I came in …

What I'd give for a steaming mug of coffee. You'd think I'd be sick of the stuff after the amount I drank in Guildford police station, horrible stuff. Imagine sitting in Kilburn Snack, chip butties and cups of coffee. It was boring then, but now I'd give the world for it, and a nice stew or curry with a bottle of slightly chilled Blue Nun. My imagination's running away with me but it would be lurvely. I didn't get my medicine again last night. I'll collapse through lack of sleep soon because when it does arrive it doesn't do much good, not for an hour or two anyway, so I was awake til gone 11.00 again last night.

I think I'll lay on the bed all day today and dream of what I'd be doing outside. I can't even cry anymore. Well I can, but I'm determined not to because then Guildford CID will sit back and laugh and little things like them ain't gonna laugh at me.

Did you hear about the bloke who got shot near the Divis Flats? He was from Andersonstown – poor bloke was only 25 … The ceasefire won't last much longer according to the radio, or something like that anyway. I can't remember what they said on the radio. They're bloody fools the lot of them. I wish they'd all blow themselves up so there'd be no more trouble because it's only innocent people who get hurt or blamed for it and them bastards don't give a damn.

Oh God, why did they have to pick on me? I can't stand it any longer, it's driving me mad. People don't seem to understand they can make mistakes, but God forgive them for what they have put me through. I'm just not strong enough to stand it anymore.

I'll close anyway. See you Monday I hope.

All my love

Carole

God Bless The Innocent And May the Guilty Be Brought to Justice.

I'm wishing I'd never read that letter. She hates me. I knew that was going to happen.

Why didn't they pick on Gerry's girlfriend? Or Benny's? And then I remember – they have Gerry's dad. A sick man who wasn't even in the country, for fuck's sake. And Benny told us they threatened to do Gina, his girlfriend, until he confessed to save her. They got us all good.

But the truth will come out and I hope it's soon. I'm worried about Mammy. Eileen came to see me and she said Mammy's out of her mind. She has nobody. Just Josephine. They're coming to see me in a few weeks. Have to keep it together for them.

Can't bear to think of the Divis flats and Mammy and Josephine sitting there, wondering what the hell is going on. Josephine has refused to go to school since I was arrested, Eileen told me so. I could kill her. After me going home from London to persuade her. After setting the lads on her. Don't blame her, though. What must they be saying about me? But nobody could believe this, could they? Surely anyone who knows me would know it's impossible. Eileen's not saying much about it in her letters, but I get the feeling it mightn't be that simple. Force myself to write another letter home to tell them I'm fine. *It's not that bad here and we'll be out soon.* Screws will read it, I know. Not giving them the satisfaction. Not worrying Mammy. Be over soon, please God. Please.

24 February 1975

Dearest Paddy

[...] You didn't look so well today, but I don't think anyone did. Paul Hill looks really cocky. I suppose he thinks he's it though ...

I'm really fed-up. This is starting to get me down. I'm cracking up. What you said about British Justice. It's Guildford CID that hasn't got their heads screwed the right way round, not BRITISH JUSTICE. That doesn't come into it until the trial. Sorry about the writing but my hands are shaking like a leaf and I can't concentrate properly ...

I can't sleep and they've stopped my medicine – the one night I need it most – now I'll lay awake all night thinking over what happened today. Why can't I just die in my sleep or fall down the stairs and break my bloody neck or something ...

I can't concentrate so I'll close for now and see you Monday. God Bless.

All my love

Carole xxx

God Bless The Innocent
And May The Guilty
Be Brought To Justice

Keep your chin up and don't worry as long as you know the truth it's alright. Keep going to mass.

All my love

Carole

xxxx

3/3/75

Monday

Dearest Paddy,

It was good to see you today …

I'm waiting for Lisa to come up. It's 3.00 at this moment and she still hasn't arrived. I just hope she comes up today because I want her to ask you some questions, like have you still got the cross because I've still got the watch and the ring and if you haven't I'll eat you next week, you little piggy, and I like pork even if it is a bit fatty.

My barrister thinks we might be committed next week if we go for a section 2, but Anne's going for a section 1 so I don't really know what's happening except it's driving me mad … I just feel like finishing it all … they don't care about humans. I know I'm innocent, but them bastards just keep pushing bloody CID – all they are are animals, the bloody lot of them.

How are you anyway? You didn't look too good. It's hit you harder than what you let on, hasn't it? I know you're innocent, but them animals don't know the truth. When I was making them statements, every time I lied they said it was the truth and when I told the truth they walloped me, bloody animals that's all they are.

Sorry about that outburst, but I keep getting the feeling no-one gives a damn whether I get out or not. I know it's not true but I can't help it. I'm so fed-up, it's just unbelievable. I must have read every book in the library twice and all my letters about 50 times at least. Oh blast, I've just dropped a bottle of orange on the floor, it's all blooming sticky … that's not concentrating but so what.

My blooming memory's terrible. I can't remember who I've written to and who I haven't. Everyone probably reads the same things 2 or 3 times.

I went to the dentist today and had another 5 fillings and ones fallen out - my bloody mouth's really sore now. Oh hell I'll close for now. See you Monday, look after yourself, keep cool and remember I love you.

All my love Carole

xxx

God Bless The Innocent
And May The Guilty
Be Brought To Justice

Wednesday 12/3/75

Dearest Paddy,

I really miss you. It's not fair, why can't they have double cells? And you're not being allowed an engagement ring is ridiculous. Just because you're not married, it's silly. What's the use of an engagement ring after you're married? Anyway, we would be by now if everything went according to plan and you had kept your job and we hadn't been arrested. Not that I can remember being placed under arrest. I suppose they took it for granted I was aware of the fact and they thought they needn't tell me. But still there's plenty of time to get married. I'm really fed-up. At least next week we will see some action I hope. I'm smoking myself to death as well, but so what, we've all got to die sometime, haven't we?

I suppose they'll want to go into why I went to Dublin as well. I don't know the answer to that myself except that Mag wanted to go. Oh well, we were searched at customs coming and going so they can't say much about that …

Can you get Radio Caroline on your radio? It's just above Radio 1. They play some really good sounds at the weekend and during the week at around midnight, but you're probably fast asleep by then. I usually am, but some nights I'm not. And play Capital in the daytime – it's more interesting. It's pretty good in the evening as well, especially around 9.00. Your mother wouldn't like it. And Nicky Horne, he plays fairly good sounds as well.

How's the lieutenant going? Your statements are unbelievable in some places. The names you called Gerry, I wouldn't be surprised if he didn't attack you when he gets his papers, and I wouldn't blame him. Mind if he did, I'd have a go at him the next time I saw him myself.

I had a flashback last night – really nasty it was, but it didn't last long, thank God. I'm wondering if you can stay up permanently after a flashback. I hope not. Because Martin hasn't come down for nearly 2 years and Lisa's boyfriend's brother was up for over 6 months and he had to drop a load of downers to come back to earth.

They're playing 'Jack of Hearts'. Bob Dylan. Off his new album, 'Blood on the Tracks'. It's brilliant. There are so many good albums coming out around now, and I'm missing them all. But I'll hear them when I get out, I hope. But that's one album I'm gonna get as a reminder of Brixton Prison, Guildford CID and the bloody IRA.

Oh I feel like screaming; in fact, I think I will – it'll clear my mind a bit. I'll ask Anne to join me though because I'll feel like a fool screaming on my own.

When do you think this will all be over? I ask myself but can't find a suitable answer, so you tell me.

I'll close now because I've got a visit, so see you soon. Love to all, especially you – chin up, look after yourself.

All my love
Carole

xxxxxx
xxxxx
xxxx
xxx
xx
x

God Bless The Innocent
And May The Guilty
Be Brought To Justice

Blood on the Tracks. An amazing album. With lines that break my heart every time I hear it. '*Now there's a wall between us, something there's been lost.*' I've lost so much already, and if it doesn't end soon I'll lose my girl. When will it end?

~

St Patrick's Day 1975. St Patrick – the patron saint of Ireland. The man I was named after. Catholic areas of Belfast will be draped in green, children waving flags, singing songs. And as soon as the men come out of work, it'll be straight to the pub. It's not a holiday like it is down south, in the Republic, but it's still a big day for Catholics. Kilburn and every other town in London where the Irish live will be the same.

This year St Patrick's Day is a cold, bright spring morning – a Monday. I've woken early, dizzy with nausea. Won't be able to eat again today. I won't be going to work or to the pub today, for the day that's in it. And instead of going to Guildford to be remanded for another week, our committal hearing will start in a few hours' time. It's like a joke. *Let's get the paddies into court on St Patrick's Day. Do them for this bombing they never did.*

This time it will take place in the Guildford Guildhall. A public hearing. The first one. None of my family can come. Some of the crowd will be baying for blood, we've been warned by our solicitors. There could be placards, spitting, men and women screaming abuse, pushing against the police barricades. Sharp-shooters on the roof. Police bikes. Cars. Vans. Cameras. *Click. Click.* Jesus, I can't go through this.

This is good, Paddy. The truth will come out at last.

It had better. Can't take much more of this.

They'll see how ridiculous this is. Those Guildford CID bastards will get what's coming to them.

They can rot in hell. I'd kill them with my teeth at this stage.

They'll be the ones in prison, Paddy, soon enough. So just go there and it'll be over very quickly. And you'll get a couple of days beside Carole.

Aye. That'll be nice. Out of this place for a few days. That'll be great.

I'm walking blindly towards a door. From under my blanket I can hear very little. There's a couple of hostile female voices in the distance, but nothing like what I've been preparing myself for. Before I know it I'm in the courtroom, beside Carole, Gerry and Benny. Apart from a couple of spectators in the courtroom, the only activity is from the solicitors, magistrates and official-looking people. This must be a good sign. People haven't bothered to come out because they know there's nothing to see here, because we done nothing. A very good sign.

Michael Hill, the prosecuting counsel for the Crown, is talking now and I don't really understand what he is going on about. Then he gets to a bit I do understand:

On the afternoon of 5 October last year a terrorist gang of some eight persons, in two cars, travelled down from London to Guildford arriving some time before 5.30 in the afternoon … These four defendants were members of that eight-strong gang … involved in the planning of and preparation for this attack for some time … There is a certain amount of evidence in the papers as to the background of these crimes. Part of it comes from what each of the defendants told the police, and part of it comes from direct evidence …

Direct evidence? The four of us look at each other. What direct evidence? Coerced confessions, yes, but nobody could take them seriously. So what is this fella talking about? They've nothing. *Nothing.* Because there *is* nothing. They can't have evidence. There is none. We weren't there.

I tune in and out, trying to make sense of what's going on. Statement after statement is read out. I recognise the names of various police officers. Liars.

Lisa and Frank will both be called to give evidence as alibis for Carole. Frank's statement is complicated. When he couldn't find Carole's solicitor to explain that he was with Carole and Lisa at a gig the night of the bombings, he eventually walked into a police station and told them. He had no reason to lie, he reasoned. He didn't know Carole that well. Nothing in it for him. No benefit. And then they'd arrested him. Kept him there. Intimidated him. Terrified him. Threatened to charge him with murder, saying that if he was with her, he must have done it too. Raided his mother's house while he was there. Backed him into a corner. Eventually he agreed to write a second statement, changing the time they got to the gig. Agreed to make it a bit later. Just late enough to make it possible for Carole to have gone to Guildford, planted the bomb, then been driven back to Elephant and Castle and dropped off near the gig.

Today, at the committal hearing, Frank is looking at three magistrates. He tells his original story. How they met at the Charlie Chaplin pub in the early evening, before going to the gig. Arrived there by 7.45pm. No later. Definitely not at the time he said in his second, coerced statement. His evidence makes it impossible for Carole to have been in Guildford at the time of the bombing.

Lisa speaks now. She's explaining that she was with Carole all day long. In the laundry. In the shop with Maura. How she and Carole had bought Maura a little present. Hung out there for a while. Went back to Linstead Street. Met me. Left me with the dog. Got ready. Went out. Carole barefoot. Met Frank. At the gig. Back to Linstead Street where they slept near me, already passed out. The dog in the corner. All of Lisa's evidence shows that it would have been impossible for Carole to have been sitting in a Wimpy Bar in Guildford finalising the details of the bombings, because she was still in London at that time with Lisa and Maura.

After three days, the hearing ends. The case is referred for trial. Guildford town has seen enough over the last few months, so the judge agrees to hold the trial in the Old Bailey. And then we're back to the mundane routine of prison; 23 hours a day alone in a cell.

After months of anticipation in the lead-up to the committal, wondering, waiting, hoping, it's crushing that it's over. Feels worse than it did before. After three days of being near Carole all day long, sitting close to her. After seeing Lisa. Seeing Alastair. Seeing people who know we didn't do it. People who believe us. After all this I can't believe it's over and now we have to wait months for a trial.

It will be six months before I'll see Carole again, at the trial. It's a good thing I don't know that at the time because I would have cracked up. Gerry and I will be moved up to Brixton, where she is, but she will be swiftly moved out – down to Risley Remand Centre. A place that will crush her spirit beyond recognition. For now, though, the committal hearing is over. I'm emotional and exhausted and hoping that the end is near.

19/ 3/ 75

Dearest Paddy,

Not long to go till freedom now. I hope it'll be great to get out again, straight to the pub for a drink, a lurvely scotch and lemonade. I haven't had one for ages, or a Guinness and Black. But in summer Guinness is a bit warm and heavy, so maybe go back to Brandy and Baby Sham? Oh I mustn't think of alcohol, it's bad for the blood …

There is a rumour going round about June 2nd for the trial. Maybe I'll be out for my birthday. I hope so, but I won't see you till then or whenever the trial is. Tell your ma not to come up on a Wednesday or Saturday because they are the only days my mum and Nan and Grandad can really get up. But ask her to write to me, will you, when you write to her. I've just found out the committal started on St Patrick's Day and ended on St Joseph's day. I learn new things every day. I'm getting to be full of useless information, but it all helps in training the mind. I'm doing yoga and I've just given myself a really stiff neck, pulled the vertebrae I think …

How are you feeling now anyway? You didn't seem so bad today as you did yesterday and the day before, but old Frank was the limit. He just doesn't know when to stop, poor guy. But as I've said before, the truth has to be told and he knows it.

They just played a couple of tracks of 'Quadrophenia' – who else but The Who. I don't like Led Zep's new album, 'Physical Graffiti', it's nothing like the usual them at all. They played 'Stairway to Heaven' about an hour ago but that is brilliant – it's off their 5th album. I don't know what's happened to my Musical Express this week. I hope it hurries up and arrives. Why don't they ever play Van Morrison? He's just brilliant. They play 'Warm Love' and 'It Stoned Me' a few times, but what about 'Madame George' or 'Tupelo Honey' or even 'The War Children'? I'll be hearing them soon enough though …

Tell Gerry if he writes not to put any obscene drawings on the letters because they are rather embarrassing to say the least …

It's Easter a week Sunday. Last Easter I was down in New Market. I wish I'd blooming well stayed there …

Oh I'm gonna close now, but I'll write as soon as I get some paper and stamps. Tell Gerry his letters still haven't arrived.

Good night. God Bless

All my love

Carole

xxxx

God Bless the Innocent
And May the Guilty
Be Brought to Justice

PS I miss you and try to get a book from the library called Apache Vengeance, it's good reading.

'Warm Love'. Van Morrison. The fella I used to see at parties in Belfast is now coming through the radio into my cell. *'The sky is crying and it's time to go home …'*

Just when I feel like I know how this place works, like I'm getting a handle on things after the committal hearing, the cell door is banged open.

Get your stuff, Armstrong. You're moving.

What? Where?

Wherever we take you. Now fucking move!

But my solicitor is coming today.

Not my fucking problem.

Me, Gerry and Paul are handcuffed to screws in the police van. We take off like we're being chased. Motorbikes roaring, sirens screaming, people in ordinary cars stopped at the side of the road wondering who is being transported. Monkeys again, and yet it's all become sickeningly normal. Screeching round the corners of Winchester until we hit the motorway. Feel sick. Wish I knew where they're taking us. Trying to think of prisons. I've only been in two: Winchester for the last three months for the murders I didn't commit; and the two months I spent in Brixton for the telly I didn't steal.

Somewhere along the motorway we roar past Alastair. I don't see him, but he can't miss us. Lights, sirens, police escort. He's wondering, correctly, if I'm inside the van. Wondering whether he should turn around and follow us. It is the first of many ghostings we will all experience – no notice, no warning, and you're suddenly moved. And just like that, you disappear – like a ghost. And if your mammy is coming from Ireland or your solicitor is on the motorway, that's just tough – murdering bastards have no rights.

I'm not thinking about Alastair now. I'm too busy looking at the road signs, trembling when we hit the same motorway we took for Guildford, but now we're going into new territory. We're going in a different direction. I can see signs flashing past as we speed along the M3. It seems that we're heading for London. That makes sense. If Carole is right and we're going to trial some time in June, they must want to keep us close to the Old Bailey.

We talk quietly. Between us we know of only three prisons in London: Brixton, Wormwood Scrubs and, the most notorious, Wandsworth. We all go silent when we realise this. I try to reason with myself.

Oh Jesus, Wandsworth … I'm going to get sick.

You don't know that it's Wandsworth. It could be Brixton or the Scrubs.

I can't deal with it. I won't survive.

You will. Not long until the trial. Remember, Carole said second of June – that's only six weeks away. Now breathe in, slowly – that'll stop it.

Breathe. Okay.

Good. You better say a few prayers now, just in case …

In case what?

In case it's Wandsworth.

Wandsworth? Oh, Jesus Christ …

The van heads into southwest London and I can hear Benny or Gerry talking. They're saying that it must be either Brixton or Wandsworth, as the Scrubs is in north London. I'm too busy trying to breathe and pray to talk. *Our Father who art in Heaven …*

~

Late morning, 22 October 1975

I've been sitting in the cell under the courtrooms of the Old Bailey all morning. Sitting. Standing. Pacing. Waiting. Listening. For footsteps, for a shout, for anything that will tell me the jury is back. To say that the verdict is in. It has to be soon. How long can it take? I'm swinging between abject despair and glimmers of hope. Weighing it all up. Carole refuses to believe we'll get done. Every time we've talked about it, I realise she has no idea how close this could be. Me, Gerry and Paul are less hopeful, but we don't say this to her.

Then the judge tells the jury that he will accept a majority. After five-and-a-half weeks he wants this over with.

2.07pm

Must have dozed off, because I definitely didn't hear anyone come down the corridor.

Jury's back.

It's been 27 hours and they have a verdict. Not sure what this means. I'm shaking so much I'm not sure I can make it upstairs to the dock.

~

24/3/1975

Dearest Paddy

This place is driving me mad, we can't even play football on exercise now. I'm so fed-up I still haven't got Gerry's letters, if he sent them that is, but I could do with something stupid to read. I still haven't heard from Lisa but I'm gonna write later on if I get a chance. I don't know what's wrong with my hands and wrists, they keep swelling up and one finger is twice the size of the others and I've taken the skin off it.

They just played Donovan's 'Sunshine Superman' – it's really brilliant. Mag used to play it every night nearly cos Richard had the album and he used to leave it at Caroline's with all the other albums of his and everyone else's. Oh I keep thinking of all the evenings we used to spend there when her mum and stepdad went on holiday. That was about the best 3 weeks I've ever spent …

It's nearly 2.00 and I'm still locked up – it's driving me blooming mad. The two colours I never want to see again are yellow and white, unless its dex or sulphate of course. I wish I could paint this cell black, with stars and a moon on the ceiling in fluorescent paint. It would be quite effective. You never saw Caroline's room, did you? It's got a great scorpion covering one wall and footprints on another really freaky wall.

How are you anyway? As fed-up as me, I expect. I'd be away working somewhere around now, out in Newmarket or Devon. I've just found out you're in Brixton. I wondered what Anne was on about. It took about 5 minutes to work it all out. I might get to see you now. I hope so. God, has that cheered me up. I only wrote to you in Winchester on Wednesday. I wonder what will happen to it. I'm so happy now. I'll be able to sleep knowing you're under the same roof, oh it's unbelievable. I'm wondering if you'll get this letter now, if not it's another wasted one. I only wrote to Gerry yesterday but I didn't post it.

I'll close now. Hope to see you before June, much before June.

God Bless.

Chin up

All my love

Carole

xxx

God Bless The Innocent
And May The Guilty
Be Brought To Justice

Now that we've been committed to trial they've moved us from Winchester to Brixton, and for the first few minutes I'm delighted. I can do this. I know this place and how it works. Someone is looking after me. Thank you, Dad. Thank you, Granny. Thank you, Gertie. You're all looking after me today. They take Gerry, Benny and me inside and we're back in reception, but I'm not the new boy – I've been in this place before. It wasn't good, but I survived two months. I can take another couple of months until our trial.

What I'm about to find out is that going into Brixton as an IRA prisoner is a very different experience from being there on a charge of stealing a television. It wasn't nice before, but it's an entirely different story now.

Look at these fucking photos.

You filthy animal.

You piece of scum.

Murdering bastard.

I'm half naked and still not used to this drill. The screw who is doing my admission is thumbing through the contents of my file. I can't be bothered even trying to see what's inside it. After the committal hearing and hours in the back of a van from Winchester to London handcuffed to a screw, I'm tired and I don't want a punch in the face for daring to look at information about myself. It'll all be lies anyway.

The screw admitting me is breathing noisily, his face is red, like he's having a heart attack, and his pupils are massive. He's staring at a photo. I can't see it, but it's clearly not just my mug-shot. He points to it now before shoving it in my face, so close I can't make anything out. He calls another screw, who comes over and looks at this and other photos. He's thrusting them in my face, far enough from my eyes so I can focus on them now. I think I'm going to faint. Lone limbs torn from their owners. Bloody faces. Blood-soaked clothes. A pub front that has burst open at the seams onto a quiet street with an empty bus stop. Grey, ashen rubble. Shards of glass strewn, shining and jagged. Blood on the pavement and a curtain ripped from its rail, hanging drunkenly out a window, exposed to the elements.

You fucking piece of shit. You murdering paddy bastard. Get him the fuck out of here before I tear him apart.

Every single person who processes me will see these photos. They'll
follow me to every prison and they'll be one of the first things that any
screw will see when they open my file. And during the Hull Riots, less than
a year after our conviction, other prisoners will come across my file. They'll
read the comments that screws have written about me and it will devastate
me. Now, though, in October 1975, as we await the verdict of our trial and
we are still technically innocent until proved guilty, nobody believes this.
And even when they do believe me, what use is it?

When they finally throw me into my cell in Brixton, I lie on the bed and
scrunch up into a ball, hands on my head. I done nothing but they've still
managed to make me feel ashamed. Worthless. Starting to wonder if maybe
I did something and I didn't even realise it.

Was I so out of it that I've blacked it out?

Well, in that case, Paddy, that means that Gerry and Paul and Carole and
you all blacked out at the same time and blew up two pubs. How the fuck
could that work?

I know it doesn't make sense, but how can so many of them believe it?

Because those bastards in Guildford made it all up – and now everyone
believes it. You have to keep a clear head about you or you'll go mad. You'll
go round the bend and you'll be no use to anyone. You need to keep sane for
this trial or they'll do you, just like they said.

Right. Keep sane. I didn't do it.

You didn't. You never did nothing like that. It's not in you. It's not in
Carole. It's not in any of you.

No, it's not. Those FUCKING BASTARDS! I HATE THEM I HATE
THEM I HATE THEM …

I'm terrified here. In some ways it's better than Winchester – we get a
couple of hours for association out on the wing each day. So instead of having
to walk in a circle and have a conversation, we can actually sit down, or go
into someone else's cell. This is closer to a regular Category A prison, where
all the A prisoners are together. All the murderers and nonces and terrorists
in one wing. I'm here with Gerry and Benny (I'll only get used to calling him
Paul during the trial); Giuseppe and the others are in another wing.

I'm coping okay. I won't be close to anyone for a long, long time – how can I trust them? But we're all looking out for each other. I feel safer here for some reason. One day someone comes running in. *Did you see it?* See what? *One of the IRA prisoners has been burnt. Another inmate poured boiling water from a tea urn over his head. He's in a very bad way.*

Over the next couple of days everyone's talking about it, and we realise that the urn had been transported from downstairs. To get it to the second floor would have meant help from screws – there's no way anyone could do that alone without being seen. We quickly realise that means this was a case of screws helping inmates to attack another inmate. A Cat A IRA prisoner. I can't relax from that day on. Constantly looking over my shoulder, watching my back. Petrified. Back to no sleep and sitting against the back wall, watching the door.

The tiredness is making me feel crazy. Feel like I'm losing it. Losing myself. Some days I come to and find myself pounding the bed, the wall, the door. Blood on my knuckles. *FUCK FUCK FUCK FUCK FUCK FUCK FUCK SHIT SHIT SHIT SHIT SHIT SHIT SHIT.*

It's only when I hear other prisoners or screws screaming at me, telling me to *shut the fuck up or I'll kill you*, that I really come to and wonder how long I've been shouting for. How did I get to this point?

The letters from Carole, the thing I rely on for a wee dose of sanity, are coming less frequently now. She is slipping into a depression, so far away. Growing ever more angry and bitter as months pass while we wait for our trial. For now, though, I'm just happy to get a letter from her, as there has been none for several weeks. Anything to take me out of the darkness.

Number 290719
Name Richardson CM
Risley Remand Centre
Warrington Road
Risley, Warrington
Cheshire

8/5/75

Dearest Paddy,

I really feel sick. For a while I thought everything would be alright, even if I did only see you once a week, but now I won't see you for months before we go to court. Why did they have to move me? It's worse here than Brixton, and from what I've heard I'll be locked in all day except exercise. I'm 200 miles from London, so I very much doubt if I'll get many visits, and the rules are so different. It was bad enough when you were in Winchester but it's even worse now and I don't know what I'm going to do. Why the hell did they move me? It was enough to be in prison in London, but now I'll go completely mad. I'll get none of the privileges I had in Brixton or anything.

How are you anyway? Keeping well I hope, not getting too depressed. I don't know whether I'll get my Valium night medicine. It'll drive me up the wall because even the stuff at Brixton wasn't that bad.

I really cried coming up here when we came the same way near enough as when we were hitch-hiking around past Birmingham, St John's Wood, even within half a mile of the old squat, past the Red House, the Swiss and everywhere it was awful. I haven't even a photo of my little sister or any of my papers. My solicitor is going to go mad because he wants me to read them until I know them off by heart. I don't think he will like having to come all the way up here twice a week either, he hasn't even got a car. Now I'm starting to wish Anne didn't get bail. At least I'd still be in Brixton. They don't seem to take into account the cost of going backwards and forwards for everyone concerned. I'm down to my last packet of fags. I can't do any knitting so bang goes your jumper and the baby clothes for Patsy. I think I'm going mad already. I'm sure I heard a cow just now.

I really miss you. I don't know, you seem so far away again. At least in Brixton you were only over the road ... But I think my solicitor will raise hell over this so I may be moved again. It's so stupid, an 8 hour journey for 15 minutes, so that means my mum won't be able to get up. Nan and Grandad won't, Lisa won't. It's really sickening, but Guildford CID will pay for it in the end. They know now it wasn't me but they are too pig-headed to admit it. But the truth always comes out in the end so they'll pay and pay damn well.

Anyway, as long as you are ok it's alright. You'll have to write to me now so there, you can't get out of it. Tell Lisa where I am and tell your solicitor so he can tell mine. Anyhow I still have you, you little pig, so you should be grateful. I can't even say see you soon on this one, but I'll write on the condition I get a reply. I'm going to write to your mother tomorrow and tell her what a good little boy you are (I'm a great liar) but I'm going to, so for now chin up...

Love and peace always

Love Carole

Bless The Innocent

May the Guilty

Be Brought to Justice

Peace

Love

Hope

to all mankind

~

Early afternoon, 22 October 1975

The stairs to the court feel like a mountain, my legs are lead blocks. There's a mark on the wall. A chip in the concrete. I'm cold. I'm warm. Dizzy. Have to get to the top. The screw beside me isn't saying a word. In a few minutes it'll all be over. This agony will be over.

They're opening the doors and I want to bolt now. The screw must feel me straining against it. He's nudging me forwards and somehow my feet are moving. In a matter of minutes we'll be leaving this court as guilty or innocent. And somewhere inside me I know what will happen and resolve that, no matter what the outcome, I will never let myself lose sight of the fact that I'm innocent. And nothing they say can ever change that.

~

Winter and spring passed somehow and now it's the summer. It's 2 June 1975 and unseasonably cool. Apparently it's been snowing in the Midlands and even in southern England. We're still here, awaiting trial. Thought the trial would be starting any day now, but it's not; that was just a rumour apparently. The trial will take place in September, they tell us. Another three months away. Just before my 25th birthday. With any luck I'll be down the Memphis Belle getting drunk by then, assuming I'm not still barred.

Finally, my mammy and our Josephine have the money to come to visit me. I don't know it, but they've had to apply to a local fund. *Go down to the pub to see a man. Ask for some money – to see our Paddy in jail in England. He's on remand. He'll be out in a few months, but we need to go and see him. Haven't seen him in 18 months.*

Mammy can take holidays from her job in Queen's University in June because the cleaners get the same holidays as the students. So she and Josephine take the boat and then make their way to our Eileen's place in Welwyn Garden City. They stay with Eileen for a couple of weeks. Josephine should still be in school, but she hasn't gone back since the day they heard I'd be charged for the bombings. In a few weeks she'll refuse to go back to Belfast with Mammy. *What's the point?* she says. *Nothing to go back for. May as well get a job here and send money home to Mammy.* Nobody can dissuade her. She's grown up overnight, my baby sister.

For now, though, it's June 1975 and she's about to come into a Cat A men's prison to visit her big brother. This will be the first and only time I'll see my wee sister in prison, so traumatic is the experience for such a young woman.

It's all cloak and daggers. They all want to see me – Mammy, Josephine, our Eileen and her husband, Jim – only I can't have that many visitors. So Eileen and Jim let on to be visiting Gerry. We both come down to the visiting room and there they are. I see Mammy and Josephine for the first time since I left Belfast, more than 18 months ago. Mammy looks as shocked at my appearance as I am at hers. She looks years beyond her 49 years. She takes in my scruffy hair, the trousers hanging off me, and sighs. We hug.

Josephine is unusually silent. Shell-shocked. They searched her coming in. She looks around wide-eyed and I remember her tender age. Eileen and Jim have to sit with Gerry at the wee table near ours and we whisper across to each other. Mum and I have the talk. I tell her I didn't do it and she believes me.

Well, how are they treating you here?

Ach, it's not too bad.

You've lost weight, son.

The food's not great, but it's okay. How are you, Mammy?

We're fine, aren't we, Josephine? Aye, just fine – don't you be worrying about us, son …

Everything is fine. Everybody is good. The way we speak most of the time, I could be in a local hospital getting my appendix out. Hoping for a bottle of Lucozade with the gold paper on it and a wee bar of chocolate. But this is the way I want it. What's the point in getting everyone upset? And, I tell myself, at least I know they won't go back to Belfast worrying about me.

Mammy asks when the trial will be. She tells me apologetically that she won't be able to come back in September – she'll have to go back to work. I know this. *It's okay, don't worry. I'll be out soon enough afterwards and then I'll probably come home. Bring Carole to see everyone. Just got to get this trial out of the way first. Sort all this business out and then I can settle down. Be over soon. Don't be worrying, Mammy. Don't be getting upset, Josephine.* But she is – Josephine is crying. The only one who does. The tears that we all have inside but can't cry. Won't. Mammy hushes her. I worry that Mammy will cry now, but she doesn't. She never does. She'll play her part and I'll play mine. It's tiring, but I promise myself that, no matter how bad it gets, I won't worry them. I won't ever add to their burden.

I watch them leave. Mammy's head is down. Josephine looks back. I wave at her, trying not to register the pain in her eyes. My sister can't believe that she has to leave me here. She'll never forget that moment, she'll tell me more than 40 years later. It will never leave her. The fear, the anger, the loss. Not even 16 and visiting me in a Category A men's prison. Goodbye, baby sister.

~

It's autumn and, while the leaves are getting ready to fall, we're going to trial. It's been nine months and 12 days since the night when I was arrested. Almost a year of my short life. In reception earlier, Gerry and I saw screws reading the newspapers. They don't try to hide the headlines. *Snipers Guard the Old Bailey as Bombers Go on Trial.* We haven't been convicted but we're already *the bombers.*

Seeing our faces on the front of these papers makes me realise just how big this thing is. A shiver runs down my spine. Our transport arrives, an armoured prison van. Paul Hill is already there when we get in, inside his own individual cubicle. He smiles, but he looks shaken. It's the first time I've seen him in months. He was taken to Belfast to face charges. They've done him for the murder of a British soldier in Belfast. I still want to shake him, but when I hear that he's been in Wandsworth, I feel bad. They say that's one of the worst prisons in London, if not all England.

After crossing London, we approach the gates of the Old Bailey. Electronic detectors scan every single vehicle coming into the court car park; the jury are escorted in under armed guard. A helicopter whirrs overhead. This is costing the state a lot of money. They'll want their money's worth from us. They'll want blood.

They let us out, one by one. I stumble behind Gerry and Paul, praying I won't fall. We're linked with a chain. Like dogs. Up a bridge and into a cell to wait. Just before it starts, we're brought up from the cells and into a corridor to wait until we're called. And suddenly she's in front of me, handcuffed to two female screws. Carole.

It's the first time I've seen her in six months, and how she's changed. Pale, drawn, lost-looking. She's written to me occasionally, but her letters are different now. She's still in Risley. Away from people like Annie Maguire and far away from London where she could have received visits from Lisa, Maura and her mother. She's been isolated, and that's made her angry and confused. We all sit together on the bench and wait. There's a few words of comfort between us, but there's no doubt about it – we're all terrified and, deep down, we know that they'll do their utmost to make us look guilty.

Court Number 2 of the Old Bailey – our home for the next five weeks. My eyes are drawn upwards to the ornate high ceiling of this courtroom with the chandelier hanging down. The room is far bigger than I'd imagined. It's very intimidating. The gallery is full of people, all staring at us. Paul's mother is here, but we don't have much support in the room. Nobody is up there for me. My mother is at home in Belfast, scrubbing the

floors of Queen's University. I'm torn. I'd hate Mammy to be here, to see me
like this, to hear the lies they'll spew about me. But at the same time I wish
I could jump into her arms or hide behind her back, like the child I used to
be. Have her make it all okay.

And then I see it – the sword of justice. It hangs above the judge's
platform and suddenly I'm heartened. Justice is what we are here for. I look
at Carole and take her hand, squeeze it. Surely it has to be okay.

A man in a wig and red robes walks in. This is a man who has never been
scared of no-one. Mr Justice Donaldson, later Lord, is the judge. There's an
all-male jury and, while I don't notice it now, Gerry later tells me two of the
jurors are black. We hope this means they might help us, as they're usually
nicer to us in prison. We're grasping at straws. Anything.

We listen to the charges. On and on for three pages. My head is spinning.
It's like watching a film except it's me they're talking about. Me, two lads I
grew up near and a girl I met in a pub just over a year ago.

We're all charged with murder at Guildford; Paul Hill and I are charged
with murder at Woolwich; and then I am charged with reconnaissance of
the King's Arms in Woolwich. Apparently I took photos of the place as part
of the planning. I don't think I've ever even owned a camera in my life,
never mind used one.

We're asked to plead.

Not guilty, I stammer

Not guilty, says Gerry.

Not guilty, says Carole.

Paul looks defiant. After his time in Wandsworth and the murder charge
in Belfast, he's angry. His mouth is set in a line and I realise he's going to do
something. He refuses to plead. *I refuse to take part in this. I refuse to defend
myself. Your justice stinks.* Oh, Jesus! This is going to look very bad for us.
They'll hate us before we've even started. Why can't he just shut up?

It takes the prosecution two days to set out their case against us. I try
to forget they're talking about all of us and imagine I'm watching a film.
This isn't real. In those first few days we all hang onto every word and
return to our cells exhausted in the evening. A crime of *military precision,*

photographic reconnaissance, targets planned, the courting couple. At night I
fall asleep with unfamiliar terms ringing in my ears.

They show photos of some of the victims before playing their trump
card. One by one, they bring the victims into the courtroom and into the
witness box. The effect is immediate; there's a ripple of shock around the
courtroom. These aren't just people in photos, they're real people with
missing limbs, angry scars, ugly burn marks. They're in pain, bitter and
traumatised. Some of them refuse to look in our direction. Others stare at
us defiantly, and I want to get sick. I feel so sorry for them. I want to run
over to them and say, *I'd never do this. I'd never hurt anyone. I swear. I'm
sorry, but I didn't do it.* Instead, I will them to see the innocence in my eyes,
the softness in me, the boy who would hide behind his mammy, who played
with his sisters and their friends, the teenager who'd stay with the women
rather than fight with the men. Can't you see that I could never do such a
thing?

Our spirits lift and fade again but we're trying to be optimistic. You have
to hang on to something. Sometimes I wish I could stand up and shout and
scream. But I never would. On the occasions when Gerry and Paul do it, we
have to calm them down.

During the first two weeks of the trial there are explosions in London. A
time bomb explodes outside a hotel coffee shop and a few days later another
soldiers' pub is hit, near an army barracks. Nobody is killed. Nobody thinks
to ask who is doing it if we are all here and the 'Maguire Seven' are in prison
awaiting trial for their part.

At the start we're all hopeful. Who would believe this? They have
confessions, but they don't make any sense. It's obvious that we're a pack
of immature hooligans whose past-times include drink, drugs, petty crime
and gambling. We know enough about the IRA from home to know they'd
never have us in a month of Sundays. Plus Alastair and the other solicitors
have found more than a hundred discrepancies when they compare all our
statements. It doesn't add up at all. Anyone can see that.

And then there's Carole – the strongest case of all. Carole couldn't
have done it, because she couldn't physically have had time to travel from

Guildford to Elephant and Castle in the time they said. There is a list of witnesses, from bouncers on the door to Frank and all his bandmates and friends, who can testify to it. There's nothing ambiguous about that at all. And if she wasn't in Guildford, then I couldn't have been either, since the whole case against the two of us rests on this 'courting couple' hypothesis.

I listen closely to the cops who interviewed me in Guildford and I can't believe that these well-dressed men and women can tell lie after lie after barefaced lie. And if it's not lies, it's omission. As they describe the courting couple they fail to mention that when eight different witnesses who saw this couple were shown a line-up of women that included Carole, not one of them picked her out. Not one single person. And that included a private who had given a detailed description of this couple. In fact, he described the woman as having 'natural blonde' hair; Carole is clearly a brunette in her photo that same evening at the concert. And he described the man as having 'wavy' dark hair, whereas mine at the time of the bombing was straight, long and fair.

The prosecution also fail to mention that I was never given the opportunity to be in an identity parade. Nobody ever picked me and nobody ever exonerated me, because I didn't get that chance. Presumably, after nobody picked out Carole, they decided to abandon that approach.

They produce a Smith's pocket watch they say was found at a flat I lived in for two weeks. They make a big deal of it – apparently it's the same brand as one found in the debris and used to make the bomb. In fact, it is a very common type of watch, so common that about a million of these watches were in circulation in England in 1974. They've torn apart all the squats and this is all they've found. No explosives. No bomb-making materials. No evidence whatsoever. If an IRA bomber was going to live in a squat – something everyone knows they would never do – wouldn't it make sense that he would keep his equipment near him? Even I can reason this out.

By the end of the first week we're all exhausted from sitting up straight, trying to look like responsible, caring people who wouldn't be capable of murder. Focusing. Listening. Watching the jury's reactions. Carole and I somehow manage to never react.

Two weeks into it, when I say that we're not going to get anywhere with these liars, that they're determined to do us, Paul and Gerry don't disagree. Only Carole refuses to believe it. *They have nothing,* she insists. *Everything will be fine, Paddy.* She's already ordered a pint down the Old Bell in her head, but I can see the way it's going. They're pummelling and twisting the truth into so many knots, twisting it inside-out, creating doubt where there should be none, until it's impossible to see what's what. I know that if it wasn't me sitting here pleading for my life, if I were a juror listening to those earnest, upstanding members of the police force and then looking over at us, a bunch of dishevelled, drug-taking layabouts, I'd be ready to convict.

And so I start my twenty-fifth year in the dock at the Old Bailey. Happy birthday, you murdering Irish bastard.

Carole tries to keep my spirits up. She draws me silly pictures using the paper they gave us at the beginning – in case we need to write anything down. We play hangman sometimes. The irony of this isn't lost on us. They debated the hanging issue in Parliament just recently, before this trial started, and we're trying to be flippant about it. Pretend it's not real.

Sometimes we get so bored, so tired, so giddy that we start giggling. We don't mean to, but it's just such a mind-blowingly different world from the one we all inhabited just a year ago. Paul and Gerry do the same. Gerry tries to distract us when we're in the box. He even makes Lisa giggle during her testimony. At times we attract the attention of the court, and they must see us for the immature, uneducated and bored young people that we are. In many ways none of us really believes all this yet; it's just too far-fetched to be taken seriously.

Days turn into weeks and already it's October, but it's still warm. It's the beginning of the drought in England that will come to a head next summer. I can't sleep at night. Having to sit calmly, impassively, and listen to the police talking, lying over and over again, is physically draining. You can't even look too upset or, worse still, angry, in case the jury is looking. Can't do anything that might make me look like a man who could be capable of killing and maiming innocent people. It's draining.

The police tell the court that they didn't beat us, didn't threaten our families, didn't threaten to hang me out a window. They gave us plenty of breaks and lots of sleep, they assure the court, looking innocent and upstanding in their expensive suits. And no, they weren't armed when they arrested me.

One of them tells the court that we confessed willingly – something that is not unusual, according to Walter Simmons, head of Surrey CID. *Most defendants readily admit their guilt,* he explains calmly. No mention is made of the hours we spent denying it. Crying. Swearing. Pleading.

Paddy Armstrong was pleased to confess, he tells the court. He reads out part of my statement and makes much of the words I apparently said. *I'm pleased I've been caught. It's nice to tell someone all about it.* This is what my first statement says. The officers took down our words exactly as they fell from our lips. Apparently. What hardened IRA murderer would actually say those words?

A few minor victories keep our spirits buoyed. They all say that none of the arresting officers was armed. And then one admits that he was. I want to jump up and shout, *See! See, I told you.* And later Gerry's QC describes a tattoo that Gerry saw on the arm of a policeman who rolled up his sleeves before beating him. The policeman is asked to show the court his upper arm and there it is. Exactly as Gerry described it. Doesn't look good for the police.

Me, Gerry and Paul are going to enter the witness box. Carole's QC doesn't want her to do it. She says she's willing to, but he insists. She looks so fragile. Some days she's her old optimistic, carefree self. Other days she's brimming with anger. Eyes red. Raw. I never know what to say then, in case I say the wrong thing. I just pat her arm and hate myself a little more, if that's even possible.

Paul is the first to be called to the witness box, and what an introduction to the Guildford Four. He's sarcastic. Irreverent. Cocky. Refuses to answer questions or else counters them with his own. And yet he's also funny, articulate and entertaining. Given how bored we are by this endless talking that makes no sense for hours at a time, this is a welcome diversion. We all get a thrill from watching him go into verbal battle with some of Britain's greatest legal minds – it's our equivalent to giving these people the two fingers. But that's the short term, and we all know that it can't look good.

And now it's me.

Alastair has been preparing me for going into the witness box. I'll be up against Sir Michael Havers. It won't be an easy ride. But if I do what Alastair tells me, I'll get through it fine.

Never answer a question you don't understand, Paddy. Some of these guys wrap the question up like a Christmas parcel. If you don't understand what he's asking you, don't answer. Even if he makes out that you're as thick as shit, keep going until you know what he's asking. If you don't know the answer to a question, do not give one, because if you do, you'll lie. Keep your answers short. Rambling on will do you no use.

I nod. That last one suits me fine because rambling isn't something I do. If anything, I say too little.

And now they're calling me. I don't know where I'm getting the strength to stand up and walk, but somehow I'm suddenly there, in the witness box. Don't shake too much. Don't ramble. Don't make up an answer. Make sure you understand the question.

It starts well when I'm questioned by my QC. I explain that I confessed out of pure terror, that the questions had been put to me in such a way that all I had to do was agree. I know that most of the jury won't understand this, they look like the kind of people who work and have families, but I'm trying to explain how I was off my head on drugs when I was arrested. *Barbiturates. Tuinal. Speed*, I tell the court.

As I describe it, I can hear the glass in the front door of the squat cracking, the wood splintering, the moment just before they storm through it. My voice keeps going, speaking the truth. *The first I knew was a crowbar coming through a window … Two of the officers carried guns. One was Detective-Constable Attwell. He put it to my head and said, 'Don't move or I will empty this chamber into you'. The other had a gun at the other side of my head.*

I describe the kicking, the punches to the head, the threats. I want to vomit when I remember nine policemen crowding around me until I drown them out with my tears. I tell the court everything, hoping they'll see the truth in my eyes, hear the fear in my voice.

I know the question is coming, but even when it does I have to work hard to explain myself. *Why did you confess?* Have to stay calm so I can make them understand. When I look up I don't see the jury or the gallery; instead I can see Attwell, Simmons and the rest of them towering over me. I'm back there and almost drown in my memory of that moment when I decide it's safer to give them what they want, before they kill me. Attwell is looming over me, saying that if I don't confess soon, they'll come and throw me out of the window and put it down as suicide. There I am again, falling apart in that little room in Guildford, with the photos and the diagrams of the pub screaming at me from the wall opposite. When I try to describe it, I know there's no way that any judge or jury can ever imagine the scene, because it sounds made-up. Still, I try.

I was crying and shaking … I started to make the statement. Being hit and thrown against the wall had affected my mind.

For an entire morning I'm cross-examined by Havers. *He's an uncommonly rude man*, Alastair says later. I agree. What I notice most is that he blinks a lot. Like an animal. Maybe a deer or a strange bird, I'm thinking. That makes me feel better. Makes him seem less threatening. This is a serious underestimation of a very clever man. I'll soon realise that he's far more aggressive than this, like a cheetah, lurking, waiting to pounce, tear you apart. For now, though, this thought is keeping me from throwing up all over this witness box.

It's getting harder to remain calm as he pummels me with questions, his voice dripping with disdain and incredulity. I'm finding it harder and harder to remain composed. My voice is shaking and I'm trembling furiously, like I'm cold, but I have to keep going because this is my only chance to tell the truth, to tell them that I never done no bombs at all. Havers sees my weakness, hears my terror and redoubles his efforts to make me crack. I try my best to answer him.

I confessed because I was afraid – afraid they'd kill me.

I said it because they wouldn't listen to me when I told the truth.

I did it because I was exhausted from sleep deprivation, still on Tuinal, a highly suggestible drug. And because I couldn't take any more. Because I figured everybody would know I never would.

I told them I was in the IRA because I knew Guildford was one of their jobs.

I involved Paul Colman because I needed something to say.

I made up details because when I told the truth, they just kept asking me until I said what they wanted to hear.

And I implicated Carole, my girlfriend, because they said she'd already admitted it.

I confessed because they gave me no other option.

I say that I could describe where the bombers had sat because it was on a map on the wall in front of me, in the police station, but no matter what I say, no matter how much truth I tell, Havers tears me to shreds. I'm so relieved when I realise that we're finished, because I'm close to tears. I only just about manage to answer the last few questions.

You have committed murder – multiple murder – because you were frightened into it. You say you were frightened of the Surrey Police when they interviewed you? So why did you not tell the Metropolitan Police when they interviewed you about this?

I was scared they would go and tell the Surrey Police, I say.

Would you also have lied to Sir Robert Mark, the Police Commissioner?

Yes.

And I mean it. I would have lied to anyone. Because who really believes that one member of the force is going to defend a squatter with a Belfast accent over one of his esteemed colleagues – what would be the point? This makes perfect sense to me, but Havers manages to make me look like a lying murderer, which is exactly what those policemen want.

Alastair will tell me later that I've done a good job. That I did exactly what he told me. Years later, though, Gerry will say that I looked like I was almost in a coma, *mumbling and bumbling along in the thickest Lower Falls accent you can imagine.* It hurts to hear that, but I did have a thick accent, of course, and I've never been as petrified in my life as the time I sat in that chair, facing that courtroom.

Gerry is up after me and he too talks about the violence, the intimidation, the threats. I hear accounts of his time in custody that I haven't heard before, and at that moment I realise that he had it even harder than me. His was definitely more brutal. This softens me towards him. I hold onto my anger towards Paul for a long time, but I can almost feel my anger towards Gerry dissolve there and then, as he describes his experiences.

When we three have all entered the box, it's announced that they will read aloud a statement from Carole. Now I can see that they did exactly the same thing to us all. I can imagine her voice as it's read aloud to the court. *The statements I wrote were virtually dictated to me and I wrote down what they said and suggested to me ... I was forced to go along with what was happening because I was terrified of them and of what further treatment I would get if I continued to deny my involvement.* Exactly what they did to all of us. Bastards. Fucking lying bastards.

One of the biggest obstacles for my defence is my alibi, or lack of one. Fortunately, Alastair has managed to track down Thomas and Jacqueline Walker, two of the people I lived with, who remember seeing me on the night of the Guildford bombing, when I was dog-sitting. Both tell the court about seeing me that evening, but when questioned their versions differ slightly. In fact, the details they disagree on are irrelevant, because while Thomas remembers me walking out of an argument just before 7.00pm, Jacqueline says I lent her my radio between 6.00pm and 7.00pm and was in most of the evening. Between both of these testimonies it would have been impossible for me to have been in Guildford planting that bomb, given that the 'courting couple' were seen leaving the pub at around 6.52pm. And yet because they're a couple who have lived in a squat and because they disagree slightly on minor events, Havers completely undermines their testimonies.

I watch as my former flatmates enter the box and are demolished by Havers. Even though they can all put me in that house in Linstead Street on the night of the bombing, either because they remember the dog-sitting event or some other detail, Havers focuses on the tiny and irrelevant inconsistencies, and in the end they, like me, are made to look like degenerate, unreliable liars who are wasting court time.

Gerry doesn't have much of an alibi either. Patrick Carey, whom he saw that night in a hostel he was staying in, has gone home to Northern Ireland and flat-out refuses to come back to testify. Or at least that's what we think for a long time. In fact, he will later tell Gerry that he did come over, that legal aid paid for it and he was there, sitting in the waiting area of the Old Bailey, waiting to testify. When the case got delayed he was told that he wouldn't be called that day. *Come back tomorrow.* When he asked where he should stay that night, he was told he'd have to make his own arrangements. He had no money, so he went back to Heathrow and used his return ticket to go home. As we all wait for Gerry's alibi, we know none of this. All we hear is that Mr Carey has not turned up. Leaving Gerry with nobody.

Meanwhile Paul's alibis for the Guildford bombing are his girlfriend, Gina, and her aunt, who he'd stayed with in Southampton, as he did every weekend. Again, Havers manages to drill holes into every detail, creating doubt at every turn. In the end his alibi is also in tatters.

In spite of the demolition job Havers has done on our alibis, we're all hopeful that Carole's unshakeable alibi will free us all. As our legal teams tell us, if she's one half of the courting couple, then the Crown will have to prove she was there in that pub in Guildford with me. There at 6.52pm on Saturday 5 October 1974. Their failure to do so will put the entire case in jeopardy because we all implicated each other. If her case falls, then so too will ours.

Carole is in the unique position of being able to account for almost every minute of that day and having several alibis to prove it. She has Lisa, who can explain that they spent the whole day together. She has Maura, who can tell them that both Carole and Lisa visited her in work when we were allegedly sitting in a Wimpy Bar in Guildford, waiting for the pubs to open. Finally, and critically, when Carole and me were apparently planting the bomb under a pub seat, Frank Johnson can testify that she was in a bar in London with him and Lisa, and from there they went on to the gig, the same gig where she was photographed with members of the band.

Lisa is called first. She's nervous, you can see it. She looks young and immature. She speaks very quietly. But given that she's only just turned 17 a few weeks ago, that's all understandable. She's also terrified of the law now because the police have been trying to intimidate her since last December. They've been going around to her house constantly, going through her room, taking things like photos, letters, notes, anything they think might be incriminating. Yet in spite of all this, she stands there and holds her ground. She answers the questions they ask as best she can.

In the middle of it all, Gerry makes a face at her and she giggles. This doesn't help. She also falters on a few points, including if she remembers Carole asking me to mind Leb and whether I was in the squat when they got home that night. The police have shaken her, made her doubt herself. In the end they make her look like a wild-child who was high on the night of the bombings and has concocted the whole story. The prosecution will use her life-style to conclude their comments by telling the jury that she regularly took LSD, barbiturates and amphetamines. Which is true. And there are a couple of small details that she isn't 100 per cent sure about. Except none of this changes the fact that she was with Carole all day, from when they woke in the morning until the moment they fell down asleep in the room we all shared. And ultimately that she can attest to Carole being in London, not Guildford. Everything else is irrelevant.

Maura is called. She is due to be Carole's witness. We're hoping that she'll be a credible witness because, although she's only 15, she lives at home and has a part-time job. She should seem more together. She can tell the jury that Carole and Lisa were with her on the day of the Guildford bombings. That they were in the shop where she worked until late in the afternoon. Maura's testimony means that Carole couldn't have been in the Guildford Wimpy that afternoon, making final arrangements to blow up the two pubs.

The problem is that none of us has heard from Maura in ages. She was in touch with Lisa in the early days after the arrests, but since then she's disappeared. She was sent a summons, compelling her to appear today, but she doesn't show. Another alibi ruined. We're all upset, but Carole is devastated. Her friend has let her down. She was already told they hadn't

heard back from Maura and that she may be in Ireland, but I think she'd
been hoping for a last-minute miracle. As hurt as Carole is, in her true kind-
hearted, optimistic style, she writes to Maura that day:

> Your name was called out in court today, but you never appeared. Never
> mind, it will all be over soon and I can come and see you in Ireland as
> not going to stay around Kilburn. The only good thing happening now
> is that I get to see Piggy every day. May God bless the innocent and may
> the guilty be brought to justice.

Piggy, of course, was her affectionate name for me.

In 10 years' time Maura, then in her late twenties and safe in the
knowledge that the police won't come after her, will come forward and make
a fresh statement. She will reiterate what she told police in February 1975:
that she saw Carole and Lisa that day. She won't be able to verify where Carole
was that night, but she will be able to put a massive hole in the story that at
5.00pm Carole was in a Wimpy Bar in Guildford. She will describe, in detail,
that day in February 1975 when two policemen from Guildford CID came
looking for her, to talk about the statement she gave to Carole's solicitor. She
will describe being brought to the police station and how, when she eventually
got sick of the accusations and was cheeky to the police, they slapped her
across the face. Eventually, her mammy marched her out of the police station
and soon after she was on a boat to Ireland, to live with relatives. Away from
the trial. So when the summons arrived for her to appear as a witness at the
Old Bailey, Maura ignored it and stayed in Ireland.

For now, though, it's still 1975 and we're on trial, waiting for Maura to
appear. And Maura is still a 15-year-old girl whose mother is determined
to protect her from Guildford CID. She is living in rural Ireland, hiding the
whole story from the relatives she is living with. She feels that what she's
doing is right. She doesn't believe that Carole will go to prison or that she
could possibly play a part in preventing it. So she is over there and we are
here, waiting expectantly until we're told that she's not coming. It's not good
news for Carole's case. It's bad for us all.

Frank Johnson is Carole's last witness. This is the big one. The one who can get us all off by proving that he was with Carole and Lisa from the time they met in the pub right to the end of the concert, all through the time the 'courting couple' were seen in the pub.

To convince the jury we are guilty, the prosecution must prove that Carole had been in Guildford at 6.52pm, which is when the 'courting couple' were seen leaving the Horse and Groom pub. She had to then make it to the gig in Elephant and Castle by 7.45pm, when she was seen by the bouncers. That means she had to get from Guildford to Elephant and Castle in 53 minutes. Carole, and her solicitors, are confident that Frank's testimony will be watertight.

Within a short time of his being in the box, the prosecution manages to make Frank look like a liar. He colluded with Lisa, they say; he's an IRA sympathiser and he lied about the times. They produce his second statement, the one he will try to explain was made under extreme duress. In his coerced statement, Frank changes the time they arrived at the gig to about 8–10pm, making it possible for Carole to have got from Guildford to the gig. This is the statement he made under the threat of arrest and murder charges. Threats made while he was detained in Guildford police station for two days. Many years later he will explain how terrified he was:

> I was willing to sign anything. They said, 'We'd like you to make a statement', and I said, 'Just rewrite whatever you want. I'll admit to doing the whole thing on my own if you want' … Because I thought … I'm going to be safer in prison than I am in this place. (McKee and Franey, *Time Bomb*)

The prosecution insists the second statement is the true one; Frank insists his original statement was the real version.

Frank is standing in the box now and they're tearing him to pieces. He has two convictions for possession of LSD. He looks like a bad liar who has changed his story to protect his friends – an IRA sympathiser, an unreliable witness. Years later Frank's statements will be analysed by Barrie

Irving, a prominent psychologist at the Police Foundation. He will find that
Frank could have had no motivation for concocting the alibi. And after
interviewing him, Irving will conclude that Frank is an honest person. A
totally reliable witness.

But none of that can help us now because the Crown manage to portray
him as a dangerous fantasist. Like Lisa, he is rubbished and belittled by the
prosecution in order to discredit us. And it's working. Even we can see this,
as exhausted as we are by weeks of legal arguments. Ultimately, this will
stick with the jury.

Carole won't blame Frank, none of us does. He did his best, but we
know only too well how the Crown can twist things to suit its argument.
Frank, however, will never forgive himself. Just eight days before he dies
of cancer, in November 2013, he will ring Alastair and ask him to come
and see him. To say goodbye. They had kept in touch over the years. Frank
will tell Alastair how he blames himself for giving in to police pressure.
For making that second statement. That, because he allowed the police
to bully him into changing his original statement, Carole lost her only
objective witness. The one who could have freed her. Freed all of us. Frank
will describe his years of living with post-traumatic stress disorder – how
he lost his belief in any kind of justice, his self-worth destroyed, and was
never able to settle anywhere because he could never feel secure. He was a
victim of corruption, just like us. Different kind of sentence. I don't know
if telling all this to Alastair on his deathbed gave him a sense of peace at
the end. I hope so.

So, now that the prosecution has completely destroyed Frank as a
credible alibi, they still have to prove that Carole could have planted the
bomb in Guildford and then made it to the concert in 53 minutes. They
won't be able to do it, we reason. In October 1974 this trip would have been
done on the old A3, which was nothing like today's road – back then it was a
mixture of dual-carriageways and two-lane roads through a series of villages
and traffic lights and roundabouts. It just wouldn't have been possible.

As the timing is critical, the defence asks a law clerk to drive it. He does
so in a hired car on a Saturday evening, observing the speed limits. It takes

64 minutes. This would have had Carole arriving there at 7.58pm, much later than the 7.30–7.45pm time that witnesses gave.

The prosecution also employs someone to do the trip: PC Heritage, a traffic-control driver. He does the trip in 45 minutes, which would have allowed Carole to leave the pub at 6.52 and arrive at the gig with a couple of minutes to spare. What they fail to mention to the jury is that the PC does it in a six-cylinder Triumph 2.5 – a nippy little car by any standards. Nor do they mention that he had the 'twos and blues' roaring, or that he ignored the speed limits. There is also no evidence that he did the journey on a Saturday night, in similar conditions to those the bombers would have encountered on the night of the bombing.

When Alastair repeats the journey a number of times in his E-Type Jaguar on a Saturday night, the best time he manages is 52 minutes, without observing the 1974 speed limits. That was just one minute less than Carole would have needed to be at Elephant and Castle by 7.45pm.

The 45 minutes that the prosecution says it took Carole to get from the Horse and Groom is literally the time it takes to drive from door to door, not making any allowance for enough time to get out of the pub and into the car and from the car into the venue. In order to do this she would have to have been driven at high speed down crowded roads in rush-hour traffic on a Saturday night, have pulled up directly outside the door of the gig, jumped straight out and sprinted into the concert. All without being noticed.

None of it makes sense. Tiny details like the bus stop and double yellow lines outside the Horse and Groom are ignored. Nobody can establish where the getaway vehicle would have been parked, but at a minimum it would have taken her five minutes at either end to get to the car in Guildford and then another five minutes to run to the concert venue from where she would have been dropped off in London. Another fifteen minutes nobody can account for.

We will only later think to ask why, if the concert and Frank were an alibi concocted by the IRA to get Carole off, she didn't remember this when she was arrested. If you have an alibi rehearsed and ready, you wouldn't wait

weeks for that person to walk into a police station to confirm it. No, she'd
have gone straight to her solicitor and never been arrested.

And if the IRA had given her an alibi, wouldn't they have given us
all alibis? Why give me a dog and a bunch of other squatters who spent
evenings robbing chemists' and getting stoned, and whose stories are slightly
different? Why give Gerry an alibi who won't appear? Why just give an alibi
to a 17-year-old English wild-child with no real knowledge of or interest in
the Irish republican movement and hang the rest of us out to dry?

Unfortunately, these questions will only be asked later, as the
inconsistencies begin to stack up. The trial is massive and our teams are
experienced, some in criminal law, but they don't have hundreds of hours
of police time and endless other resources to throw at the case. Our team
certainly doesn't have access to half the information the police has. And they
definitely don't have any knowledge of the files that are marked *Never to be
shown to the defence.*

~

Afternoon, 22 October 1975

The foreman is looking at us standing in the dock. He's opening his mouth
to speak. I'm standing, or I think I am. I need to shift my feet a little, check
that this is real. That I'm not in my cell thrashing about, going to wake up at
any moment. That I'm not in Linstead Street, stoned on a mattress.

I need to concentrate on the heat I can still feel from Carole's hand on
mine just moments ago. This could be our last day in prison after almost a
year, she's thinking. Or our first day for 10 or 20 years, I'm thinking. She's
thinking that within hours, or at worst a day or two, we'll be down the pub,
getting stoned, cuddling on a mattress somewhere and waiting for those
bastards to get what's coming to them. I'm thinking, They're going to do us.
She believes in us. In the jury. In justice. I don't. I know it when I see their
faces. They can't look at us.

And now the foreman is talking. His lips are moving.
Unanimous verdict.

GUILTY.

GUILTY.

GUILTY.

GUILTY.

They've found us guilty of everything. I've been done for Guildford and Woolwich.

Carole almost collapses and has to be held up by a female screw. I watch her and know that I can't let on how scared I am. Have to keep it together for her.

Donaldson is going to retire to his chambers to consider the sentences and closing remarks, he tells us. And although it should be the longest 20 minutes of my life, later I will barely be able to recall it. I can barely remember the cell they take me to. What do I think about? I have no idea. Probably nothing. Gerry tells me later that for the entire time I'm a deathly shade of white, shaking convulsively.

They've brought us back to the court for sentencing. My legs must have moved, but I can't remember. Donaldson returns. He informs us that had we been convicted 10 years earlier we most certainly would have been sentenced to death. He laments the fact that we haven't been charged with treason, a crime that carries the death penalty.

When Donaldson speaks to us it's like I'm under water and his voice is miles away.

Patrick Armstrong. Life. His eyes are fixed on me the way a cat looks at a mouse trapped under its paw. This is where most judges stop, but he doesn't stop. He goes on. *Life, with a formal recommendation of not less than 35 years.* I don't yet understand the nuances or how unusual this is, but I get what he's saying. I will not be leaving prison for at least 35 years. In case I'm in any doubt, he elaborates. *I do not mean by this recommendation to give you ... any reason for hoping that after 35 years you will necessarily be released.*

For a short time I hold the dubious honour of having received the longest minimum recommended sentence under the Murder Act 1965. I'm shaking uncontrollably, but somehow I've managed to stay standing. If

Carole weren't so close by, I'd be going insane. Have to keep it together for her. Keep it together, Paddy.

Carole is sentenced *at Her Majesty's pleasure* because, although she's 18 now, she was 17 when the bombings took place. *It will be for Her Majesty's Secretary of State to decide how the order in respect of the murder convictions is implemented … You may go.*

I don't really understand this, but all it means is that the State can decide when Carole's released. It doesn't mean it's any less a sentence than anyone else's. Carole clearly understands and for the first time since the trial began she loses it and explodes. *You bastard!* she shouts at Donaldson. *Take her down,* he says, and she disappears and she's gone. It will be years before I see her again. The woman I asked to marry me. The woman I hoped would be the mother of my children. My love.

Donaldson fixes his stare on Paul.

Paul Hill, your case is the worst … In my view your crime is such that life must mean life. If as an act of mercy you are ever to be released, it could only be on account of great age or infirmity.

Paul has been given a sentence that's worse than all of ours. He's never getting out.

Gerry is also given a life sentence, and the judge qualifies that he'll do no less than 30 years. He controls himself and later the papers will describe him as *impassive*. We'll realise soon enough that we have been tried and convicted a hundred times over by the press before, during and after the trial.

Take them down.

CHAPTER SIX

We're just two lost souls swimming in a fishbowl …
(Pink Floyd)

C an't move. Arms pinned to my sides. Won't move. Too heavy. Fingers stuck to the side of the bed – my legs are stuck too. What is this? Don't know what's happening. It's like there's something on top of me. A pressure. Forcing everything down. I feel like I'm tripping – on something strong. But I'm not. Stone-cold sober. Far too sober.

The cell is cold. Even more so than normal. I feel like I'd see my breath if I could just open my eyes – like there's a window open. Just. Want. To. Move. But my head's stuck – can't lift it off the pillow. It's like I'm asleep but aware of everything around me: the stink of the slop bucket that reaches every corner of the room; the damp breeze under the thin blankets; the incessant chirping of the birds outside the window who think it's daytime because of the unnatural lighting in the prison grounds.

There's something different. Something new here. Can't put my finger on it. A new smell, an aura of something. If I didn't know better, I'd think there was something or someone nearby – something right here in the cell with me …

~

Thirty-five years. Can't get it out of my head. I'm standing here in the cell complex of the Old Bailey, looking at Alastair and my barristers, and just trying to keep it together. Thirty-five years. They're talking to me and I can hear them; I can hear my own voice. I'm trying to say the right things, whatever it is that you say when you've just been handed down one of the longest prison sentences in history. Don't want to blame – can't blame anyone, or at least not anyone in this room. They did their best. But I knew this was coming. They were always going to find us guilty.

But 35 years. Alastair will describe it as *a mind-bender*. That's exactly what it is. Bending my mind more than any substance I ever took. Whatever I had expected the judge to say, that wasn't it. None of us was prepared for that. Not us, not our solicitors. Even the jury looked shocked.

It's not the 35 years part that we're surprised about, Paddy, Alastair explains. *It's the 'not less than' part that's unexpected. Harsh, we feel.*

Yes, it is harsh. I nod. *So who will decide if it's 35 years?*

That will depend on the Home Secretary. And the parole board. Your behaviour.

I see. Even though I really don't. *And so what now, Alastair?*

Well, there's no grounds for appeal, Paddy. No new evidence, you see.

No, no.

So we've no grounds for a mistrial.

Nod, Paddy. Just nod. Apparently we can't even appeal the sentence, because there's only one sentence for this crime. Life. The only sentence that could have been handed down.

We didn't see this coming – nobody did.

No, no, we didn't.

But we won't give up, Paddy.

No, please, don't. So what happens now?

New prison.

I see. Not Brixton, then?

No, it will be a proper Category A prison. Could be anywhere, to be honest, Paddy.

I'll be fine … Yes, yes. I'll get in touch. When I'm settled. Don't worry … Thanks … for everything. Thank you.

Thirty-five years. Minimum. Life. My life. End of story.

The reality of this situation is stomach-turning, terrifying. I've been arrested before. Remanded. In a prison. In a court. Solicitors, judges, witnesses. I've been through all that before with the arrest over the television last year. And then acquitted. Happy ending. Kind of.

This … this is completely new territory for me. Guilty? Convicted? In a van going to prison? To a real prison? For 35 years. *Thirty-five years?* Ten years more than I've actually been on this planet.

Somehow I've never imagined this moment. Never allowed myself to. I knew they'd do us for it – it was obvious from as early as the second week of the trial. They were going to say whatever it took to make us look guilty. And yet, even though I said those words to myself and thought those thoughts, I realise now that I never really believed it. Never went further than the *Guilty* moment. Never considered what would happen next.

Moving away from the Old Bailey. Away from the flashes, the shouts. *You should have been hanged. Bring back the death penalty. Irish bastards.* Roar of motorbikes, the sirens, the other traffic outside and the world. In the middle of London, a city filled with beautiful old buildings that I wanted to visit one day. Right beside the sights that everyone talks about, that they come to see. When I'd got a few quid together, I'd have come here. Brought Carole, too, bit of sightseeing, nice meal, a gig somewhere. Not now. Maybe in 35 years, when I'm nearly 60 and Carole is in her fifties. We can shuffle around on our weary bones and see it through old eyes.

Silence in the van. There's nothing to say. Even the screws attached to us are quiet. Paul's biting his cheek, Gerry's staring into space, pale and shocked. If anyone speaks, I don't hear them. A thick fog has swallowed me whole. The world's passing us by here. It's as if we're driving away from it – almost like we're leaving it. Which we are, really.

London Bridge. And now the suburbs. No motorways yet. We can't be going back to Brixton, I know that. So it has to be somewhere else. As long as it's not Wandsworth. Something about that place that scares me and I've never even been there. That's the one place where I know I would never cope. I wouldn't last a week.

We're still going the right way. Kennington Park Road. Oval cricket ground and … wait … we're going towards Clapham. Looking at Gerry and

Paul. They know it too. Paul's mouthing it. *Wandsworth.* Oh, Jesus Christ, please, no. I knew that would happen. Knew I'd end up there. They'll kill me. They'll fucking kill me. Oh, Jesus. I'll kill myself first.

The gates of HMP Wandsworth have opened for us. I knew it. It was always going to be Wandsworth. Later I'll realise that I've had my eyes shut for most of the journey, rocking back and forth like these men in a film I'll see a couple of years later. *One Flew over the Cuckoo's Nest.* Completely insane. Me and that film. But when I prise my eyes open they're taking Gerry and Paul out. They're going into Wandsworth, but I'm left here, chained to the screw. They're closing the door again. Barely get to say goodbye, I'm so shocked.

North this time. Still in London. It's Wormwood Scrubs. A huge old prison with every group you can imagine locked up together. This is a proper Category A prison, with massive wings full of scary people. The cockney gangsters, the Irish, the blacks. Everyone sticks to their own.

Into reception, and I have absolutely no expectations whatsoever and at this stage ritual humiliation feels like the least of my problems, so it's something of a blur.

Irish bastard.

Look down. Just get through it. Answer the questions.

You'll rot in a fucking prison before we let you out.

Say nothing.

You won't know what's hit you, paddy bastard!

Don't react.

Special dietary needs?

Shake the head.

Should have hanged the lot of you.

Try not to take it in. Stand there, take the abuse. Freezing-cold water. Can't feel my feet. Don't react.

Lice powder. Stripes. Cat A. Just put it on, Paddy. Don't look at them.

Just wait till everyone hears one of the bombers is here. You better run and hide, bomber!

Hold back the tears.

Not such a hard man now.

Look down, Paddy. Keep looking down.

Look at this fucking IRA bastard.

Just leave the spit. Wipe it later. Do nothing.

You make me fucking sick.

It's nearly over.

How'd you like to lose an arm or a leg? We can arrange that, can't we?

Blink, Paddy, blink. Don't give them the satisfaction.

Take him away.

That's it. Just move. Keep walking until you get to the cell.

And this is it. My cell, for however long they decide. I could be in this one room for 35 years. It's sparse and chilly even when it's sunny outside. Uncomfortable. Impersonal. Perfect, as far as they're concerned. Perfect for waking in, for eating and drinking in, for writing letters and reading in. For pissing and shitting and bleeding and coughing and fantasising. For listening to music, falling sleep, waking, screaming, crying. For growing old. For dying in. This could well be the place where I die – only the time is uncertain.

It's only early evening. The food smells of vomit. It's cold and congealed. Just like Brixton. Did I really wake up there less than 12 hours ago? That doesn't feel possible. It feels like days ago that I woke up and waited for them to take me back to the Old Bailey, to wait on the verdict and then the sentencing. Is it less than a few hours since I saw Carole … Carole … Carole?

The bright orange light on the ceiling means that the screws don't have to turn on the light when they glance in through the flap during the night. It's like sleeping in a lighthouse. I'll get used to it. I'll have to. For now, all I can hear is the sound of my own breathing and some sounds far away. Occasionally there are footsteps. An aggressive bang at my door, just to remind me they're there, that they can see me, makes me jump. Apart from that, silence.

It's dark now and an unusually warm night – around 22 degrees, which is hot by anyone's standards. It's still 22 October 1975, longest day of my life.

But it's not over. I will remember this even more so as one of the longest, most terrifying nights of my entire life. Not knowing what's ahead and wondering how, and if, I'll manage to handle it at all.

Staring at the orange light. Minutes have passed, or maybe hours. There are holes in the fabric on either side of my mattress. Every time someone peers through the flap or walks past my door, I grip the mattress even tighter. I don't remember when my skin broke through the coarse fabric but it must have done because I can feel the horse-hair scratching and tearing open the tips of my fingers and my hot blood seeping out, soaking the flimsy fabric covering the mattress. I barely register it. Can barely feel it now.

No less than 35 years. It's not a real number to me. My entire lifetime and another 10 years. Two of Carole's lifetimes. By then my mammy will be dead, surely.

Hour after hour the orange light haunts and taunts me. It's moving. It's a face. It's the Devil. It's Gerry. Paul. Carole. Dirty Harry. Donaldson. Mammy. Josephine. The longest night.

Finally, there's a shrill noise and sounds of furniture moving, feet pounding the floor. I don't know if I slept, but I must have. And my first night is over. At last.

Fortunately for me there's a big Irish cohort here. Lot of IRA men. They sit together at two tables in the canteen. They've heard I'm here. Wave me over. I grew up with fellas who were in the IRA. I know plenty of them, but I've never spent much time with them. Here, they're the only people I have. Nobody else wants to even speak to me. I'm the fella who murdered all those innocent people in Guildford. Just another IRA bastard. So even though I've always stayed clear of the IRA in the past, I realise quickly that I'll need them in here if I want to survive – or at least until people realise that I'm innocent.

IRA prisoners are hated in English prisons. *Murdering scumbags. Evil bastards.* As Category A, we are the lowest of the low. Prison is exactly like society and communities – a proper hierarchy where everyone has their place. The nonces have always been at the bottom. Despised. Above them are the murderers, and so on. IRA prisoners have managed to buck the trend: hated by prisoners and guards alike, they are down there at the very bottom – lower even than the nonces.

Imagine being the most hated person in your work, in your community – more so than people who rape children. There are no words to describe what that does to you. Now imagine that you aren't a strong person, a fighter. You avoid conflict and confrontation at all costs. This is me. I'm someone who is comfortable with my family, with my girlfriend, when I have one, and with my small circle of friends. They are who I stick to. They know me, they like me. That is me and that has always been me. Up until a few months ago, I always stuck to my circles. Now they're gone and it's just me, in this prison, after being sentenced. And as angry as I feel, as difficult as I'm finding it to forgive them for dragging me into this, for giving my name, at a time like this I could do with someone like Gerry, or even Paul.

Even more than the dangerous criminals, the people I need to watch are the screws. They have access to your food, your clothes and, most frightening of all, your cell – any time. And if they want to mess with you, they can do it in a heartbeat. They play mind games, some of them. Wait for me to relax and then one of them, a huge bastard with a strong northern England accent, bursts in. *Cell search.* As if I have a bomb or a few sticks of dynamite tucked away under the excuse for a pillow.

Search, I discover, is a misleading term. It suggests a polite and orderly cell check, but they turn the place upside-down – throw everything around the cell, break things, tear them up, send them flying from one side to the other, often with a mock-apologetic smile pasted on their face. *Oops, did that break? Sorry, Armstrong. Oh, did you want to keep that photo? Well, you can put it back together, I'm sure – you've got enough time to do it!*

The first time it happened, I didn't know what to do.

I don't know what you're looking for. I haven't got nothing here.

That's for us to decide.

I swear. Sure where would I get it?

You fucking IRA bastards could magic a bomb from a bowl of porridge.

I don't know nothing about bombs. I never did those bombings in Guildford.

Yeah, and my mother is the Queen, you lying bastard. Now get the fuck out and let me do my job.

Their hatred and disgust is almost tangible.

The terror will take months, years even, to subside. But it never goes away. Ever. I tell myself: I'll get used to this. I won't be so scared in a few months. Won't be on the edge of tears at every moment. Jumping. Watching the door. Checking my food. Smelling it. Testing it gently with my finger. Waiting for the pinch of the glass tearing into it. Jumping if anyone comes too close. And the showers. Don't know if I'll ever be able to relax in them. That's where they'll jump you, when you're at your most vulnerable. It will be a very long time before I'll relax in a prison shower, if ever.

I'm shivering and pumping sweat, my heart palpitating. The orange light is illuminating the room and I can still see Dirty Harry coming towards me with a gun and me moving back towards the open window. Mammy is below, ready to catch me, her hands worn from scrubbing, reaching out. Carole is beside her, tripping on LSD. Laughing. Holding flowers. And behind them is a girl with no arms. Looking at me. And I'm falling, falling towards her, away from Mammy, away from Carole. Towards that faceless girl with jagged flesh. And I know she won't be able to catch me …

With the images fresh in my head and beads of sweat rolling into my eyes, I look around. I must have fallen asleep. I've no idea what time it is. My headphones are still on my head. Pink Floyd's new song is in my ears. It's only been a few days since I first heard it, but since then it's been haunting me.

I will never forget the first time I heard it. I was lying on my bed, trying to fall asleep. That's my technique. Sleep away this hell. And just as I was dozing off, I heard it, as if it was floating through the walls and straight into my soul, bypassing the brain. It started with the understated sounds of a guitar instrumental. Found myself nodding my head, tapping my foot. And then the gentle plucking eased its way into a more insistent, spine-tingling plucking as the acoustic guitar came in. Finally a voice appeared and it was magical – took me out of my body, far away from this cold, grey cell, in the way that only music can.

So … so you think you can tell
Heaven from Hell

I found myself nodding along to the drums as they come in, tapping my leg, listening to the piano tinkering in the background, when the soulful voice reached out to me again and suddenly I found myself upright, like I'd been shot. *'We're just two lost souls swimming in a fishbowl …'*

I was all goosebumps. It was like an electric shock. I wanted to howl along in pain, like an animal, and weep in ecstasy all at once. This song was written for me at this exact moment, in this very place. Someone has found a way to articulate every emotion I've felt over the last 18 months. This unnatural hell that I'm locked in is exactly like a fishbowl, and me like a demented fish. Round and round a grey, bleak yard on exercise, just a stone's throw from the real world, where people are living their lives. If I strain my ears, I can hear the distant roar of traffic. Round and round a pissy, dark cell where, if I crane my neck from the window, I might glimpse a field or a building outside. Round and round this godforsaken prison. Stuck. Pawing at the unbreakable glass of this fucking fishbowl. Hour after hour. Day after day. Year after year after endless bloody year.

And suddenly I was thinking of Carole and my mammy and my sisters – wishing they were here or, ideally, that I was there. Anything but this.

And Carole, wherever she is, somewhere on the other side of the country or maybe in the same city, for all I know, Carole, God bless her, is going round and round in her own fishbowl. A lost soul, like me. We're just two lost souls and I wish we could at least be together in hell, especially on a day like this. I'd like to share this moment with her, feel her beside me, lose myself in her for a moment. Wish you were here, Carole.

I had to know what it was before it disappeared. I followed the fading notes of the instrumental to the next cell, where another inmate was listening to his radio. A nice English fella I'd spoken to a few times.

What's that song there?

That one – do you like it?

Aye, it's brilliant

Yeah, it's a new one.

Who is it?

It's Pink Floyd. It's called 'Wish You Were Here'. Not long out, I think.

It's ... dead good. They're class.

Yeah, they are, man. You should hear the album, Paddy – it's fucking
amazing. *Blow your mind*

Aye, it would surely.

And now, just days later, I'm lying here, my hair and my eyes soaking
wet. And the images from my nightmare won't leave me. There's me falling
from a window of Guildford police station, falling, falling towards the
faceless girl looking at me, away from Mammy's outstretched arms, away
from the beautiful walk with Carole. Wish you were here.

~

Somehow it's December again. The end of 1975. 'Bohemian Rhapsody' is
playing on every radio station. Freddie Mercury asking the questions: *'Is this
the real life? Is this just fantasy?'*

I know what he means. *'No escape from reality.'* None at all. Only 'I didn't
kill nobody, mamma.' Didn't plant no bombs, didn't make them. Wouldn't
have the faintest idea how to, even if I'd wanted to. But I never did want to.
And yet here I am, the second Christmas away from my mammy and my
wee sister Josephine, in a cell just big enough that if I stretch out I can touch
both walls. The second Christmas of 35, by the looks of it.

One day in the first few weeks, after I've slopped out and I'm filling up
my water jug at the tap, there's a wee fella standing crying. He's only young.
Skinny lad, with a shaved head. I keep filling up my jug until I can't ignore
him any longer.

Are you all right there? What's wrong?

I just got nine months.

Nine months? Are you serious?

Yeah! I can't believe it.

Nine months. For fuck's sake – is that all?

He sniffs. *Well, what did you get?*

I got 35.

He looks appalled. *35 months – Jesus!*

No, not 35 months – 35 years. Now go and do your time.

He recoils a little, shocked. I know he wants to ask me what I'm in for, but he thinks better of it. I'm obviously a very dangerous character and he's scared now. He's slinking off, away back to his cell, and for the first time in months I'm smiling. Nine months! Jesus Christ.

To keep myself sane I do things like adding up other people's terms. There are eight cells in my part of the wing here. Most cells have three people in them. As a Cat A prisoner I get my own. When I get to know the prisoners in the other seven cells I add up all their sentences; even combined, theirs is still less than mine. Most of them are legitimate criminals, but I'm going to be here longer than all of them put together. I have to laugh, because if I don't I might kill one of them – or myself.

In the lead up to Christmas the news is filled with more IRA attacks. I hear some men talking about something they have just heard on the radio about a suspected IRA siege, so I turn on my radio and it's the first story I hear. As I listen, I have no idea how much this will impact on my life.

Three armed IRA men on the run from police have burst into a flat in central London and taken at least two people hostage.

Officers have now sealed off the corner of Dorset Square and Balcombe Street, in Marylebone, after a car chase through the West End during which shots were fired.

The gunmen are believed to be members of an IRA hit squad which has been behind a number of attacks in the capital and Home Counties over the past few months.

They are accused of shooting dead TV presenter Ross McWhirter at his

Enfield home a week ago, and also of carrying out attacks on London restaurants, the Hilton hotel and the Army public house at Caterham in Surrey...

The couple being held hostage are John Matthews and his wife, Sheila. There are reports they have a young child as well, although these have not been confirmed.

Police appear prepared for a long siege. A large mobile headquarters has been brought in and there is an army personnel carrier in a nearby street where several diplomats are believed to live.

Donna Martin, who lives in Dorset Square overlooking the siege address, was watching from her window:

'About 50 cars arrived at my doorstep. We all rushed to the window and I have never seen so many guns in my life. We saw the policemen with a car which was riddled with bullets.

'Then the police came into our flat. They all had guns and were wearing flak jackets.'

The gunmen were cornered after they attacked Scotts restaurant, in Mayfair. It was the second time the building had been targeted. On 12 November a bomb containing ball-bearings was thrown into the restaurant, killing one and injuring 15 others.

This time, police were lying in wait and when the gunmen opened fire from their car, a Cortina, they were ready to give chase.

The Cortina was pursued through the busy West End traffic to Gloucester Place in Marylebone. A number of shots were fired and the windscreen of the getaway car was shattered.

The driver could no longer see where he was going and stopped the car. Police later found a holdall in the car containing two sub-machine guns, a Sten gun barrel and a clip of ammunition.

The four gunmen ran down Balcombe Street and finally burst into a five-storey block of flats owned by Westminster City Council.

Mrs Matthews is reported to have opened the door of flat number 22B to see what all the noise was about and the men smashed their way past her and barred the door.

[Source: http://news.bbc.co.uk/onthisday/hi/dates/stories/december/6/newsid_4261000/4261478.stm]

The siege takes over the English and international news for the six days the men remain in the flat with the Matthews. A large mobile headquarters has been brought in and the army are stationed in nearby streets. The media have camped out nearby and are capturing every moment possible. It's all anyone is talking about.

Terrified of expressing too much interest in anything that looks like IRA activity, I nonetheless can't help being as fascinated as everyone else. It's impossible to look away anyway because it's reported on the hour, every hour, for six days and even in the weeks afterwards. And initially I'm as thrilled as the other inmates to have a temporary distraction from the monotony of prison life. But this is quickly replaced by a deep horror, knowing that two people around my mammy's age are being held, probably at gunpoint, by Irishmen. I'm mortified and petrified. Once again my fellow-countrymen are causing havoc just miles away from me. I can only imagine how furious the English public must be to see this play out. They'll be baying for the blood of these men. And I am stuck in here, at the mercy of the people who are being terrorised on a daily basis.

I start praying for them to let the couple go and come out with their hands up, but the days are mounting and the situation hasn't changed. Inevitably, the comments begin – full of horror and glee, prisoners and screws alike. I've protested my innocence so many times that, at this stage, the people here either believe it or they don't. But that doesn't seem to matter now because, guilty or not, I'm Irish and 'an IRA prisoner', so that makes me a legitimate target now. I'm also an easy target – they see my softness, my regular shaking; for some it's too good an opportunity to pass up.

See your scumbag Irish friends are at it again, Armstrong – terrorising innocent people. You should be shaking, you murdering bastard. We're rounding you all up one by one – you'll pay for this.

Just you fucking wait till they get those bastards out of that flat – they'll be sorry they ever fucking set foot in our country. You'll be seeing your Balcombe Street friends in here soon – that'll make you happy, I'm sure.

On the sixth day of the siege, 12 December, the Balcombe Street gang, as they are now known, are forced to release their hostages and surrender to the police. I don't know any of the four, but I will meet them eventually. I wonder if they've any idea what lies in store for them once they're convicted?

~

As the Balcombe Street gang, just freshly arrested, are sitting in a cell like mine in another prison somewhere, I'm here eating a prison Christmas dinner for the second year in a row, trying not to wonder what Mammy and Josephine are doing, who they're eating with. If Mammy is upset. Worrying about whether she's been able to rouse herself from the bed today, go to mass and cook a dinner. Or will Josephine have to shake her from her drowsiness, somewhere in the afternoon, and force her to eat something?

Think about the men in here who have families, Paddy. Focus on something else. People who are worse off. Men who you see coming back after a visit, their eyes ringed with dark shadows, tinged with a faint redness, their mouths tight with grief.

At least I'm not married with children. If we'd been arrested a few months later, I might have been married to Carole. She could even have been pregnant in prison. Doesn't bear thinking about. And look at Paul Hill there. As angry as I am still, I think of the wee girl that his Gina will have to bring up on her own. No daddy. And all the missed firsts – first steps, first words, first day at school. It must be so heartbreaking.

And suddenly it's New Year's Eve. Just a stone's throw from where I am lying in my cell, people are out there celebrating, meeting friends, dancing at parties, getting drunk, stoned, falling in love, having sex, getting married, having children and lives. Celebrating the past year and welcoming in the new one. Living. Meanwhile I'm looking back on the last 12 months: three prisons, a committal hearing, a trial, a verdict and a sentence. All in one year. More pain, more frustration and more injustice than I or most people have experienced in a lifetime, all squashed into one year. And the last few

My dear mammy and daddy, Eileen and John Armstrong, on their wedding day. They had a joint wedding with another couple. This is the only photo of them together and the only one I have of my father. C. 1948.

My darling wee sister, Gertie, RIP. This is the only photo that exists of her. It was taken shortly before we lost her, aged 2. She's wearing a sailor suit here – the same outfit she was wearing the day she died. When my other sister Josephine found this years later, she originally thought it was a photo of herself as they look so similar. 1957.

On a typical day during the Troubles, you could be walking along the Falls Road and meet an armed soldier who would quiz you about your name, address and where you were going. As scary as it was, it quickly became normal. Here I am (*middle*) on one of those days with a friend from my area. August 1969. (*Belfast Telegraph*)

Me (*second from left*) in a dapper suit and tie with my friends after the Corpus Christi Procession. Note the street sign above: Guildford Street. It's like a portent of doom, though I had no idea at the time. 1969.

Me holding my new baby nephew on the balcony outside our new home in Divis Flats, not long before I went to England. *C.* 1971.

A rare photo of two special friends, Lisa Astin and Carole Richardson, just a few months before our arrest. It would be a long time before they would be reunited again. *C.* October 1974.

A typical night in a pub in Kilburn. Notice my white belt and trendy jumper. My fashion sense changed when I left Belfast but I still fancied myself as pretty cool. 1974.

The shocking aftermath of one of the Guildford pub bombings (The Horse and Groom). Photos like this and others were on the wall as I was being questioned in Guildford Police Station. October 1974. (*John Carter/Associated Newspapers/REX/Shutterstock*)

Gerry, myself and Paul are taken away in a police van. One of us is showing the peace sign and you can see we're handcuffed. It's still not real. October 1974. (*Trinity Mirror/Mirrorpix/ Alamy Stock Photo*)

My mug shot in the police station. This was taken after a three-day bender. At that stage I still believed I would be out in a few hours. December 1974.

One of us is taken from a police van into the Guildford Magistrate's Court. They used to throw a scratchy blanket over our heads but it never blocked out the screams and taunts from the angry crowd. December 1974. (*PA Archive/PA Images*)

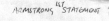

SURREY CONSTABULARY   EXHIBIT No. 10

Station or Section: C.I.D.   Division: Guildford
                               Date: 4th December, 1974

Statement of: Patrick ARMSTRONG

Age of witness: Born 24th September 1950

Occupation of witness: Labourer

Address: 14, Algernon Road, Kilburn, London, N.W.6.

    I, Patrick ARMSTRONG wish to make a statement. I want someone to write down what I have to say. I have been told I need not say anything unless I wish to do so but whatever I say will be written down and may be given in evidence.

                (Signed) P. Armstrong

    I'm pleased I've been caught. It's nice to tell someone all about it. I'm going to tell you everything I've done right from the beginning. I joined the I.R.A. in 1969 and did my training in Dundalk. The training lasted two weeks. That was the official wing. All my family are Catholics. I was born in Belfast. I joined the I.R.A. because the Falls Road area was attacked. It was after that I made up my mind. I left the official when they called their truce in 71 or 72 and joined the Provisional. I was a Volunteer and had

One of the statements I was apparently 'happy' to make at Guildford Police Station. I still find it so strange to read it and accept that a judge and jury could have believed those were my words. December 1974.

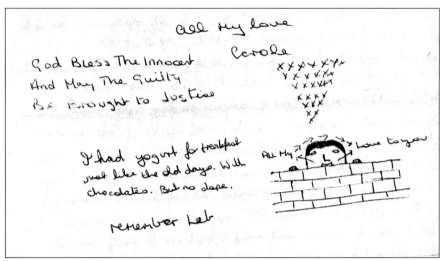

Carole wrote to me a lot while we were awaiting trial. Her letters kept me sane during that time. She used to sometimes include wee pictures in them and always signed off with a handful of kisses and the same message: 'God bless the innocent and may the guilty be brought to justice'. 1975.

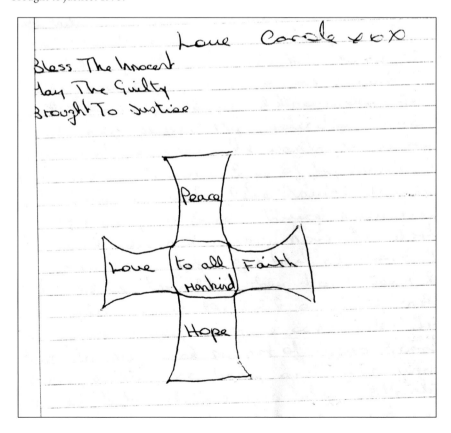

While Carole and I went out the back door of the Old Bailey into waiting cars, Gerry walked out the front door to the waiting crowd. He made his famous speech before waving to well-wishers and was then escorted off in a car. We had no idea how challenging life would be when we got out, but we were soon to find out. October 1989. (*REUTERS/Alamy Stock Photo*)

Carole just after our release, where she is happiest – with a horse. She still looks so young and innocent here in spite of having spent 15 years in some of the toughest women's prisons in England. October 1989. (*PA Archive/PA Images*)

A happy reunion after many years. *(From left)* Frank Johnson, Carole, Ros Franey, Alastair, Grant McKee, Lisa and myself. 1989. (*Frank Pocklington*)

A decent beer in a real glass at one of my first civilised dinners in 15 years. 1989. (*Frank Pocklington*)

Pat Mulryan, Daniel Day-Lewis and I on set at Kilmainham Gaol, Dublin, during the filming of *In the Name of the Father*. Pat and I acted as advisors on the film. Daniel used to follow Gerry and me about listening to our accents and asking us questions. 1993.

Gerry and I in London posing for photographers. After the huge success of *In the Name of the Father*, Gerry in particular was constantly followed by the press. We both look a bit rough here. Life was a little crazy for a few years. February 1996. (*Irish Times*)

The Three Musketeers, Pat Mulryan, myself and Paddy Reilly, just before my wedding. We scrub up okay considering how little sleep we got the night before! 1998.

Caroline and I pose with her family (*above*) and then mine (*right*) at our wedding. This is one of the rare times that I'm not making a funny face in a photograph.

Caroline and I at our wedding. Doesn't she look gorgeous? And then there's me … making a ridiculous face.

My very dear friend and solicitor, Alastair, myself and his beautiful wife, Pat, at our wedding. I'm caught off guard making a smart comment while nursing a pint of Guinness. They were incredibly relieved I had met a good woman. Pat said it was like watching her own child get married.

Me and my babies, John and Sophie, on our first family holiday. Who would have thought this could ever happen? Certainly not me! *C.* 2004

Tony Blair's letter of apology. While long overdue and greatly appreciated, it failed to mention many of us by name and ultimately was quite hurtful. At least it sent an unequivocal message to the world, especially those who thought we got out on a technicality – we were innocent. 2005.

10 DOWNING STREET
LONDON SW1A 2AA

THE PRIME MINISTER   9 February 2005

The Guildford and Woolwich bombings killed 7 people and injured over 100. The loss suffered by their families will never go away. But it serves no-one for the wrong people to be convicted for this awful crime.

It is matter of great regret when anyone suffers a miscarriage of justice. There was a miscarriage of justice in the case of Gerard Conlon and all the Guildford Four, as well as Guiseppe Conlon, and Annie Maguire and all of the Maguire Seven.

And, as with the others, I recognise the trauma that the conviction caused the Conlon and Maguire families and the stigma which wrongly attaches to them to this day. I am very sorry that they were subject to such an ordeal and injustice.

That is why I am making this apology: they deserve to be publicly and completely exonerated.

An extremely sad day. Myself, Paddy Hill of the Birmingham Six, and other friends and relatives of Gerry Conlon carrying our dear friend from St Peter's Cathedral, just off the Falls Road, at Gerry's funeral. June 2014. (*Brian Lawless PA Archive/PA Images*)

I finally get to introduce my old pal Jim Sheridan to my family at an outdoor screening of *In the Name of the Father* in Merrion Square, Dublin. I hadn't seen Jim in a very long time but it felt like it was only yesterday that we were on set in Kilmainham Gaol. August 2016.

Caroline and I are reunited with our dear friends Alastair and Pat to celebrate the 25th anniversary of our release and to commemorate the 40th anniversary of the bombings. Taken at their home in Surrey after we visited the memorial garden for the victims of the bombings. It was a very emotional trip. October 2014.

A very emotional reunion with my dear friends Lisa Astin (little sister) and Maura Kelly when they came to Dublin to see me. Within minutes, the 20 years since we last saw each other had disappeared. They brought Louise, Carole's daughter, with them and I was so overwhelmed to meet the beautiful young woman Carole had raised. We talked and laughed and cried together. *(Left to right)* Caroline, myself, Lisa Astin, Maura Kelly, Louise and Mary-Elaine. 2016.

While writing this book, my dear wee sister Josephine and I take a trip down memory lane and visit all the old haunts around the Falls. I haven't lived there since 1972 and it takes my breath away how much it's changed, and yet, standing outside my old primary school, St Comgall's, it feels like I never left. 2016.

My baby, Sophie, and I getting ready for an Arsenal match. We always wear our Arsenal tops and head down to our local to cheer on The Gunners. 2017.

Mary-Elaine (my dear friend who wrote this book with me) and I. She's posing and I'm messing, as usual – some things will never change. 2017.

months spent sleeping, eating and shitting in one small, dark room with an orange light. I've felt every moment of it. And sooner or later I'm going to have to come to terms with the fact that I am facing 35 years of this. If I can do it.

For me, New Year's Eve and the first day of the year in prison will always be an incredibly painful time – knowing what I've lost and what I still have to lose. That first one, the new year of 1976, is no exception. When the raw anger and pain have subsided, I hope that I can just put my head down and bide my time until we can maybe appeal. I don't know that 1976 will be a year when the bombing and shooting will escalate and anti-Irish sentiment will grow even more. In a single night, before the first month is out, another 12 bombs will explode in London's West End. And I won't come out of my cell unless I have to.

My time in the Scrubs, as it's known, is a blur. I'm a living sleepwalker. I must be eating, sleeping, washing, leaving the cell for exercise. I have a faint recollection of playing football, but it's all a blur. I shut down because it's all too much to take in. Carole barely writes now, and when she does she's depressed. The screws destroy her letters on me. Make them into tiny confetti pieces, along with the letters from Mammy and my sisters. So glad they will never get her earlier letters, which I have given to Alastair to mind.

Our Eileen comes to see me when she can. Brings me whatever I need – clothes, books and records. Finally, my dear mammy arrives over on the boat. She's been alone in Belfast since last summer. Working her fingers to the bone so she can come and see me as soon as possible. She must be heartbroken with all of us over here. Josephine is still living with Eileen and Jim and their kids. Harriet is over here, too. On this Easter visit I've asked Mammy to bring my records over – there's a record player here and I might even be able to buy my own one, if I can get the money together.

And there she is. Almost a year since I saw her last. My poor mammy has lugged over anything she can carry. She arrives in on the first day laden down, but all I'm interested in are the records I asked her to bring from home. I look at them.

Jim Reeves? That's not mine. Why'd you bring him?

Sure isn't he great, Paddy. I love him.

You might listen to him, Mammy, but I don't.

Ach, give him a wee try, Paddy. You'll get to love him.

Aye, Mammy, I'll give him a try.

I don't. I've no intention of ever letting a Jim Reeves record make contact with any record player in my vicinity. And so I do a swap with another prisoner who likes him and get a Pink Floyd record in exchange. Jim Reeves. Jesus!

Mammy can only stay a couple of weeks and then she has to go home. She takes our Josephine back with her. I think that after a year in London, Josephine has realised that no matter how bad Belfast is, the grass isn't very green over here. With me in prison and with us having the same surname, she's living in fear of someone putting two and two together. One person at her work already has – a Protestant man from Belfast. He hasn't said anything, but the next person might not be so nice. I'm relieved she's going back to Mammy – I don't want her to be associated with Public Enemy Number 1.

And so she leaves Eileen's house and she and Mammy sail from Heysham to Belfast on a rickety boat. It's the last sailing ever for that boat, and for our Josephine. The next time she comes back will be in a very long time, and it will be on a plane. Unfortunately for my dear mammy, she has many, many more boat journeys ahead of her.

The music brings great comfort, one of the few you can get in prison. Screws can't take it from you. They can break our records or even our record player. They can take radios. They can try to take my mind even, but they can never remove the music from my head. The chords, the lyrics I listen to closely and analyse like I never did before. The rhythms, the refrains, the soulful voices – they are mine and nobody can take them from me. Even in the darkest times, when it feels like nothing could rouse me from the depths of this despair, a melody will come from nowhere to comfort me. I'll find myself humming it and lose myself in it. David Bowie's 'Life on Mars', one of my favourites from my first year in London. I can find happy or sad lyrics in almost any song, anything to fit my mood.

Sometimes I hear music floating up through the thin walls. Rock and roll, classical. Not my usual type of music, but it's nice, I realise. Some of the older prisoners listen to the classical stuff. I wouldn't play it myself, but sometimes it's just what I need. Soothing. Takes me away from all this. And other times I'll hear Buddy Holly's voice crooning and suddenly I'm transported back to Milton Street and my dad is there, reading the paper, humming along as Mammy and Granny chat away while dusting every tiny corner. And there's me and Eileen and Harriet, running in and out of the house. The sounds and smells of the Falls Road will suddenly fill my ears, my nostrils, unbidden.

When the cell doors slam shut at 8.00pm I lose myself in lyrics and sounds on the record player, on Capitol Radio or Radio Caroline. Wonder if Carole is lying there, listening in another tiny cell, to the same songs. Thinking of me.

I'm lying on my side one night, facing the wall, with my eyes firmly shut. There is no orange light in my room, no cell door. It's just me and the radio. And then Louis Armstrong's velvet voice creeps into my cell. '*I see trees of green, red roses too … And I think to myself, what a wonderful world.*' Suddenly I'm 18 or 19 again, getting ready to go out with Margaret Hutchinson. It's a soft evening and I'm just home from work. A wee bit of money in the pocket of my dapper suit. I've a clean shirt that my mammy ironed and a cool black tie. I wonder if I can get past my sisters before they notice I haven't washed my neck? Standing in the kitchen, wondering if tonight will be the night, and Louis Armstrong is in our kitchen, too, singing to me. '*What a wonderful world.*' You couldn't say it any better than that – it's a bloody brilliant world. I've got a girl, my Margaret, and I'm meeting her tonight. And who knows what will happen? Ronnie McCartney and half the other boys on the Falls want her, but she's mine. And I can't believe my luck.

~

Still can't move. Feels like the breath has been sucked out of me and now I'm weak and floppy on the bed. Couldn't move if I wanted to. And I realise that it's time. So I open my eyes.

As my eyes flicker open, I don't need to move my head at all, because he's there at the end of my bed. My dad. Looking at me.

I'm petrified. Why is he here? Trying to move again, but I can't. Stuck to the bed. My fingers are resting in the hole I've scratched out on the mattress, my eyes darting around the cell. The orange light is still glaring at me, but it's not bothering me for once. I feel like I should be asleep, but I'm not. Wiggle my fingers again slightly. Definitely real. He's still there. This is really my daddy. Thank you, God.

~

There's a bookie in the prison. There's one in every prison, I'll soon realise. Bloody fantastic! Now I can have a wee flutter using my tiny prison wage. Food has no joy for me and I don't smoke that much, so this is how I'll spend the minuscule amount that I have. And when I don't have enough, I get a wee tab. It's in control, though. For the moment. A very welcome distraction. I have a good eye for a horse, people tell me. I'm lucky, but not a big enough punter to ever be a worry for a bookie. I enjoy having something new to focus on. The odd adrenaline rush in an otherwise drab and joyless world.

But then, just when I'm settling down, not jumping at every shadow and every unexpected noise, I get ghosted. Moved to another prison with no notice. One minute you're here, the next you're frantically grabbing your bits and pieces and they're shoving you into the back of a prison van.

We're leaving London, but beyond that I know nothing. The only thing I can see is that we're heading north. Tougher there, I've heard. Shudder. I catch brief glimpses of the countryside and even though my view is distorted by the iron grilles on the window, breaking the fields and sky into tiny squares, I can see the burnt grass. It looks thirsty from the drought that continues to blight England. I know the feeling of being in desperate need of sustenance, of dying for the want of the most basic things. Love. Fresh air. Friendship. Trust. And even more love. I wish I could lie on the thirsty looking grass of these wide open fields, stoned, with my arms around Carole. Listening to the birds and looking at the sky.

The van is slowing in front of a security gate and only now do I know where we are. HMP Hull is my new home.

~

Shortly after they're sentenced, in one case receiving three life sentences and 192 years, my solicitor, Alastair, receives a call to say that someone from an IRA Active Service Unit (ASU) has admitted to the Woolwich bombing – the bombing me and Paul were done for.

It all happens around the same time as I find myself in the back of that van, tearing its way out of Hull and into the English countryside. While I'm trying to snatch a look out of a tiny barred window, just 100 miles away, in Manchester Crown Court, the trial of five Irishmen involved with one of the ASUs is beginning. In the dock are Brendan Dowd and four other men, charged with the bombing campaign in London and Liverpool. Charges against them include conspiracy to cause explosions and murder, imprisonment of hostages and possession of arms, explosives and ammunition. Unlike us, they don't deny the charges because, also unlike us, they're fighting for a cause. The five men spend most of their 10-day trial in the cells, unrepentant and unwilling to recognise the court – another stark contrast to our compliant and terrified defence.

This is all relayed to me by Alastair. He's still my solicitor even though, now that we've been tried and convicted, we're no longer entitled to free legal aid. But as he will tell me many times and many years later, he can't get us out of his head. So he'll work for free. This isn't an area that he normally works in, but after our trial he has a lot more experience and he's not willing to give up. Of the various human rights cases he's involved in, ours is the one that's keeping him awake at night. He decides he will keep working on it in his own free time and for nothing. Gerry isn't that fortunate, nor is

Carole. But eventually Alastair is allowed to represent the three of us. Paul's solicitor will help out for a while, but in the end Alastair will take over his case too. All without charging a fee. I will soon realise how lucky I am to have this extraordinary man in my corner. In our corner.

It's June 1976 and as I'm settling in to HMP Hull, Alastair is having his first meeting with an ASU member – Joe O'Connell. He's trying to find out what really happened that night in Guildford. In the short time they spend together, O'Connell tells him that none of us was involved with either Guildford or Woolwich. And Joe's in a position to say this because he was, by his own admission, involved. He is one of the men responsible for those bombings. For doing what we were meant to have done. He will later be able to tell Alastair about another member who was central in both bombings – Brendan Dowd.

Dowd agrees to talk to Alastair. Sensing the importance of this interview and not wishing to jeopardise it in any way, Alastair has the foresight to bring a court stenographer to record it and a retired Metropolitan Police superintendent, James Still, to conduct it. In addition, prison guards will be present. By doing the interview this way, Alastair can never be accused of manipulating Dowd's testimony.

Over almost five hours, Dowd describes the Woolwich and Guildford bombings with a level of precise detail that nobody else has been able to give thus far, including information about where the getaway car was parked, the exact location of the pubs involved, details about the weight and construction of the bombs, plus a drawing of the inside of the Horse and Groom pub that had only ever been published in one local newspaper. All the information we couldn't provide, because we didn't have it, didn't know it.

Everything Dowd says corresponds to the forensic evidence, but even still there's nothing to prove that he hadn't made the bomb and I hadn't planted it. Certainly he will implicate himself, but in order to clear me Alastair will need to prove that Dowd was actually in Guildford, because throughout their investigations the police were only ever looking for one man for this bombing. The only man who was unaccounted for after their exhaustive interviews, and this same man and his companion made up the 'courting couple' the police were searching for. If Alastair can prove that man was Dowd, then the police will have to admit it couldn't have been me.

Finally, Dowd offers a detail that makes Alastair's head spin and confirms that his belief in me has been justified, his instincts right. This is something which, until now, Alastair has never heard of. *Two old guys with shopping bags*, Dowd says. He describes two older men he noticed sitting in the pub. They had big white shopping bags with them. The pair were sat on a bench next to Dowd and they had two rounds of drinks before leaving. *Just beside me*, he says again. *Carrier bags. Must have been waiting for a bus.* He draws two circles on the map to show where the two old guys had been sitting. *Had some large bags of groceries with them. I think they must have been waiting for a bus*, he repeats.

Alastair doesn't know it yet but the two old guys, Leslie Hutton and Arthur Jones, had indeed been in the Horse and Groom while they waited on their bus home to a nearby town. They had been interviewed by the police and made statements in the days following the explosions. Both remembered a couple being there who, they told police, were neither military nor market people. No significance had been attached to the pair, because they left before the explosion, which is why they were never referred to in court or called as witnesses. And because my legal team didn't see all the statements that the police took, they never saw two statements from Hutton and Jones. Naturally, therefore, Alastair has never heard of these witnesses.

By the time Alastair leaves Dowd and the Category A high-security wing of Albany Prison, he feels very strongly that he has discovered something of huge importance. With all this new information, his real work now begins – to find out more about the two old fellas with the shopping bags and, if it amounts to anything significant, to make a case for an appeal.

~

While Alastair is slogging away in his own time and also trying to do his day job to pay the bills, I'm sweating in HMP Hull. The ongoing drought means that showers are few and far between. The air is full of the sharp smell of sweat. But I'm in with a decent Irish population, including Paul Hill. Once I get used to the place, meet a few people, I realise that one prison is just like the next. Some different rules, a different bunch of dickheads running the place and its own unique number of crazy people per head of capita, but at the end of the day a prison is a prison. Except Hull is like a Victorian prison – one toilet and three baths or showers to every 50 men. Stretched to its absolute limits. It's inhumane and the prisoners are unhappy with the conditions and getting very restless. I just don't realise yet how much.

The only area they seem to have invested money in is the security. Encircled by sensitised steel fences with barbed wire on top, it would be a hard place to escape from. The CCTV on the roof means they can watch you from anywhere. And they never let us forget it. The floodlights are like nothing I've ever seen before – it's so bright that even on the darkest night it's like a dull day inside. Even the birds are confused by it and some of them twitter all night long in the unending daylight. I sometimes wonder if there are a whole load of these tiny birds passed out in their nests during the daytime because they've been up all night, chirping away outside my window.

Bizarrely, birds are very popular in some prisons, and Hull is no exception. Lots of the men have them in cages in the corner of their cell and they're treated like a precious child. I'm torn about this. There's something bizarre about a bird in a cage inside an even bigger cage, and I can't work out if it's cruel of the inmates to keep them or if it's fair enough – we all need company after all. In any case, I don't get one myself. Soon enough I'll be very glad of that decision.

I'm set to work quickly here. I work in the textile workshops and the wages are pitiful. You basically work for free. There's also a woodmill here, called the Mill, and it causes a lot of problems. It's a serious operation, not unlike big factories in Belfast, with an actual woodmill on-site alongside an assembly shop and a spray shop. This is a proper job for the men who work there and inhale the dust, paint, lacquer and other chemicals. Only prisoners who insist on it get masks and ear plugs, even though an inspector who visited once noted two words – dust and noise! I will learn later that the woodmill in Hull makes prison-cell furniture that's destined for prisons in Iran.

With our paltry wages we pay for tea, milk, tobacco. You can also throw in money if you want to be in the film club, make a donation for prisoners in the Segregation Unit (solitary confinement) or buy more stationery and stamps. I like the film club, but writing one letter a week is more than enough for me. I'm finding it harder and harder to write anything because there's just nothing to say. *Same shit, different day*, as I'll hear Americans say many years later. When I do, I'll want to laugh and think how they have no idea what it's like to do the same shit each and every day for year upon year, but I certainly do.

Just as I'm settling in to the rhythms and ways of this place, an Irish lad comes up and asks if I want to play football. It's a hot summer's day, too sticky to lie in an airless, stinking cell. In this heat, no matter how many times you slop out, the smell of urine permeates everything – my clothes, my mattress, under my skin. And now, with so few showers allowed, I can almost taste it.

I decide I can't get any sweatier, so football outside sounds like a nice option. And so begins a summer of banter and craic. One I'll remember for a long time. What starts out as a little league somehow becomes the Irish All-Stars versus the English. We decide to have a best-out-of-three competition.

The first match is on a stinking, record-breaking hot day. I'm in goal and extremely grateful because, even though I've lost weight, I'm not sure I could run around for too long in this heat. Everybody has their T-shirts off and spirits are high. The game is a cracker and in spite of the heat and the sweat and the exhaustion, we win. The Irish All-Stars gallop around the field, like we've actually won something. Like we're no longer the underdogs. The murdering Irish bastards.

The craic begins afterwards when a couple of fellas ask me to let in a goal in the next match. I look over at one of the fellas on my team. *Are you joking? See him there? He's a big man in the IRA. He'd fucking kill me if I did.* It's funny. We all have a laugh. And I realise that it's not the big things in prison, it's the little moments like that – it's the laughs and the stupid things that will get me through this living nightmare.

A few weeks later, towards the middle of that long, drought-filled summer, we're ready for round two. Our English inmates are under pressure. If the Irish All-Stars win this one, we'll be two up and we'll have won, because it's the best of three. I'm in goal again and I see a ball coming towards me. I dive and somehow, in spite of the relentless heat, I manage to grab and hold it. *Save!* I run out of the goal, somersault and somehow land on my feet. I'll pay for it later when my back and neck ache, but today I feel alive and important and not like a piece of shit at the bottom of a screw's boot.

Later in the same game I let in a goal and curse myself. The English win 1-0 and now we've both won a match. We'll play the decider in a few weeks. Or so we think.

The atmosphere in Hull among prisoners is very amicable. Our relationship with the screws is a different matter, though. They're evil bastards. They would destroy your personal belongings if you looked at them crooked. These are the type of fellas who get a custom-made peaked cap, designed specifically so it comes down over their eyes. They think they're in some film or something. And because they're dying to nick you, they'll fuck with you for no reason at all. Interfere with your visits for stupid, nonsensical reasons. Throw you in solitary at the drop of a hat. I try not to let it get to me by keeping my head down, a tactic I've discovered gives me the least amount of hassle. Sometimes, though, just existing is enough for them. It's very unsettling when you know one of those screws is around.

The night it all starts it's coming towards the end of association, just before lock-up at 8.00pm. Association is the only time of the day when we can move freely about the wing, go into each other's cells. It's only a couple of hours before lock-up, but it keeps everyone sane. I'm in my cell, talking to another prisoner, waiting for the screws to come around to tell us the doors will be shut soon. This fella's a real laugh – he has the funniest stories. I'm sure half of them are made up, but he makes me laugh so much I don't care.

So this night, just before shut down, he's telling me a story that I'm really having a hard time believing, but he's insisting it's true.

I swear to your Catholic fucking God, Paddy.

Ah, now, less of the blasphemy.

Oh, fuck, yeah, sorry.

Ah, I'm only joking. I curse all the time in here. I never did before – my mammy would kill me if she heard me.

So anyway, I put that fucking ad in the paper and my missus saw it there a couple of days later. I swear to you.

So what did it say?

'*Holiday homes to let. Lovely spot. Sunshine all the time. Nice time. Hull prison.*'

So he's telling me this story and I'm saying what a gas man he is, not knowing if he's pulling my leg, and suddenly there's banging and crashing and shouting and the sound of feet thundering along the wings.

This isn't the norm. My heart is racing. I'm tempted to barricade myself inside. I don't want the wrath of the screws on me. But the sound isn't from the screws, it's the prisoners. They're smashing and shouting and screaming. The fella with me looks at me, lets an almighty roar out of him and rushes out. He can't know anything more than I do, but he doesn't care, doesn't hesitate.

Listening to the wood splitting and a roaring that's so primal it's terrifying, I can't help looking outside after him. What I'm about to witness will stay with me for ever. On our landing and on the one above, prisoners are throwing furniture around, smashing it, dumping it over the landings. I have no idea what it's about, although things have been getting tense the last few weeks – so much so, even I've noticed. Conditions are getting worse in here. Between the terrible facilities and the increasing brutality, people aren't happy. I've put my head down and the screws have left me alone, but not everyone has been so lucky. I'll find out soon that the riot I'm now looking at started after a prisoner was brutally beaten for no reason; and then prison management wouldn't listen to the men who were trying to get some sort of justice for him.

I pause momentarily. There's no sign of any screws around. The prison belongs to us. I blink again, and then something in me snaps. I run back into my cell and grab the thin wooden table in the corner and fling it against a wall. My mouth is open, my jaw slack, awestruck as I watch it sail through the air before it hits the wall and *crash!* It splits into fat, jagged pieces, clattering to the ground. I've never done anything exactly like this before, but I do remember the feeling of adrenaline. I've been here before. Briefly.

I'm 19 and the adrenaline is pumping through my veins as I tear down the Falls Road, flinging bottles at the RUC and army trucks. This is one of the rare moments when I've ventured out of home and joined in on the chaos. There are cries as all the young lads shout above the noise.

Fucking bastards is all youse are.

Smash!

Get youse all out of our fucking country.

Bang!

Get that one there, Malachy.

Aye, I will surely, Marty.

Fuck the Brits!

Crash!

And as quickly as that memory comes, another comes crashing in on top of it. Waves on a beach threatening to drown me. I can hear their voices in my ear. *Murdering Irish bastard. Fucking IRA killer. I can throw you out that window. Just fucking sign it, you lying bastard.*

Need to get rid of these voices in my head. Shut them up, even just for one night.

Smash! The bed is upside-down. I'm tearing furiously at the sheets and blankets and feeling them straining against my hands and finally yielding – *rip!* Fling them in the air and they fall down around my feet.

I can see Dirty Harry's face in the chair as I fling it furiously against the wall. *Crack!* The wood splinters my finger but I don't care. I'm in charge and I have the power here. No-one here to crowd around me, to make me cower on the ground. To spit at me, threaten my mammy. Nothing they can do to me here. I take one of the legs of the chair and ram it through the window and the smashing sound is like a fine melody to my ears. When I've run out of things to break in my cell I charge out to the landing, to look for more. Anything that makes me feel alive, in control.

There are people running everywhere, throwing things over the balconies, shouting like maniacs. I can't believe my eyes when I see men levering off the thick wooden cell doors, reinforced with metal, by destroying their hinges, and then using these doors to crash through locked doors. They'll be used as barricades. The only people still hiding away are the sex offenders, and so they should.

Some of the men who started the protest, including Paul Hill, have got into the Segregation Unit so they can free the men in there. To do this they have to climb outside and break through the roof into the Seg., fighting off screws along the way. Finally, the screws have all fled and it's just the prisoners inside.

I feel like I'm back in one of the squats, having a wild party. Someone has turned on the music and within hours it's mayhem. Wild dancing, singing and drinking prison hooch. There's thick smoke in the air – the sweet smell of ganja.

On and on it goes all night long. I've barely eaten anything except some crisps, a tin of coke and a bar of chocolate that someone got out of the canteen when they broke in, but I don't care. The hash is flowing freely, we don't have to hide it and this is the best party I've been to in a very long time. I think about how much Carole and Lisa would enjoy it and for once I don't wish I was anywhere else. This is too crazy to miss.

All night long people are smoking, drinking, dancing while others are roaming free around the prison, looking at the places they've never been allowed into. Some people are searching for their files, but they can't get them. They're locked inside the administration block, a separate part of the prison that we can't access, and the screws have made it clear they won't be letting us anywhere near it. There's obviously a lot at stake. Some of the men want to see what's written about them; Paul Hill is determined to see his. But I don't know if I want to see all the lies they've made up about me.

What's the point? It will only make me angry and bitter when I don't feel like that for the first time in months.

As we all clamber out onto the roof for some fresh autumn air after a night of wild abandon, we're blinded by the flash of cameras and shouts from down below. The press are waiting. Some of the prisoners start shouting demands, while others are making banners. A few of them work out the wording and we end up with *Four screws beat one prisoner* and a few other messages.

We can see that the people below want to listen, so a man is pushed to the front to speak. We all stand there behind him, our arms around each other, while he talks about the degrading and inhumane prison conditions, the workshops where we're treated like slaves, the brutality that's commonplace. There are chants to support him – *Yeah, that's it, go on* – while others whisper things for him to say. He talks about our hopes, our demands, our anger and our contempt for this brutal system that isn't reforming anyone.

Later someone starts a chant and everyone joins in: *Fuck the Shah of Iran.* Most people don't know what this is about, but it's a reference to the furniture that's being made here in brutal conditions, using cheap labour, and then shipped out to Iranian prisons. It'll be interpreted as a political message, though, its meaning lost on many, but we know what it means.

Children arrive a while later and gather below, delighted, as some of the lads throw sweets down. The solidarity among the prisoners is incredible. It's difficult to describe and, despite what happens afterwards, it sustains me through the many dark nights. It's a sense of unity that I never again will experience in prison.

We go back inside and the party continues. I find I'm losing my sense of time because the routine is gone. It's a bit overwhelming. I've been in prison for less than two years and already I'm institutionalised. I'm not complaining, though, when I can binge on a dinner or breakfast of tobacco, hash, sweets, crisps, chocolate and tins of fizzy drinks, all raided from the canteen.

Some fellas look like they haven't slept at all and are off their heads on hooch and whatever else they've managed to get their hands on. Eventually people start slinking off to have a rest before reappearing for the next session. Somehow I manage to curl up and fall asleep on a mattress I find flung in a corner of the wing.

When I wake up, I barely know where I am. I finally work out that it's Thursday morning, so it's been two full nights of mutiny now. I look at the men around me and everyone looks pretty shattered. Filthy clothes, dishevelled hair and big grins on their faces. I partied hard in London, spent entire weekends off my head, but even by my standards this is a pretty good party. We all know it will have to end, but not yet.

We go back out onto the roof and the cameras and the children look like they never left.

Some men have finally got their hands on their files. When they come out with them, they're very upset. I know it's coming, but I don't ask for a while. Finally someone comes up to me and tells me.

We've got your file, Paddy.

Well. Is it a bunch of lies?

It's not, actually. Here, have a look for yourself.

He hands it to me. It's just a short file – like an introduction to me. I start to read and there it is in front of me. *This man is believed to be innocent.* Just like that. I haven't even been in prison for two years and it's written down there in black and white. *Believed to be innocent.* It explains that I'm not accepted by the IRA leaders here, that I don't behave like an IRA man and that I wouldn't be the calibre for one. It's an insult, I know that, but it's one I'm more than happy to accept. I'm not, I never have been and I never will be IRA material. I don't want to be. There are men who will fight our cause and I understand that. We need people to fight. But I could never do it. Never will.

Paul shows me his file. I don't understand it all, but it's pretty damning. It says that he is a potential hostage-taker, a non-conformist, rebellious, subversive and that he would escape given the chance. It talks about his relationship with Gina, his girlfriend and the mother of his wee girl, and says that the relationship must be ended. And it says, *Never to be released.* He's shaking with rage. I nod. I don't know what to say to any of this.

Finally, amidst rumours that the army or the SAS will be brought in and that snipers are waiting to pick us off on the roof, we realise that this could turn nasty very quickly. It's decided that we'll take a vote. Most people agree that we should end it, rather than surrender. A man is sent out to negotiate the terms and conditions. We are also acutely aware that we will be punished, so we need to protect ourselves and try to limit the damage. We will obviously be leaving here, so we ask for the Hull screws to be the ones to take us out – not because we like them but because, if they beat us, we'll know their names. If they bring in strangers, it will be impossible to know who did it. We also demand a GP to check us.

Sixty-seven hours after it started, the riot is over. Screws come back on the wing, but they don't touch us. Later on they'll go into cells and destroy whatever is left. They'll get the budgies and let them out of their cages. The budgies will fly out the windows, destined for certain death, and I'll see grown men cry when they find the cages empty. I walk down to my landing and I'm shaking. I know what we've negotiated, but I don't trust them. The doctor checks us on the way out. And that is the end of Hull. We will never get to play the final match in our Ireland versus England competition. It will forever remain 1-1.

On the bus to Strangeways Prison in Manchester, there's 12 of us on board. All cuffed to at least one screw. The mood is quiet. We're all very tired and I'm wondering what kind of a place this will be. It turns out the name says it all. It's a strange and horrible place that used to have an execution shed in the B wing. It turns out that, of the last two people to be executed in Britain, one was hanged here, just 12 years ago. Would have been us if the judge had his way.

I just want to get to my cell and lie down, but as they take us out of the bus, in handcuffs, it dawns on us: this isn't over. The screws won't be letting us off that easily. While some prisoners, like Paul Hill, have been kept in Hull for another night, getting kicked and battered up and down the length of the wings, we are about to have our own private welcoming party. There's a line of screws waiting for us, with batons. As we run past them they rain down blows and kicks and punches and spit on us. I'm trying to go faster, but the man in front of me is stumbling, so the screws to my right and left can pummel me. The words of other prisoners come into my head. *Put your hands over your head, Paddy – always protect your head.* I try to wrap my arms around my skull, but they're relentless. We're outnumbered and we have nothing to fight back with.

The beatings stop for a while when the screws are worn out from kicking and punching. They start to process us, but they get their second wind as we walk onto the wing, where there's a line of them waiting to pummel us again. Some are new – they missed out on the first round, so they have more energy and fury to unleash. I don't know how I take it but I do, because there's no choice. I learn to almost disassociate myself from it all. Pretend I'm looking down on a complete stranger being beaten. That the blood pouring from the head or the gash in the leg belongs to someone else. I'm an observer, and I feel sorry for that person. And somehow that makes it a little easier to bear.

We all go in front of the governor and we're nicked for the riot. I get almost three months in the Seg. Unit. I'm not surprised – we all knew this was coming. And yet no matter how much I've heard about it, nothing can prepare me for being locked in a square box for 23 hours a day with just one hour of solitary exercise. For having no other humans to talk to, no music, almost no sounds at all.

My thoughts are deafening. They won't stop. Every time I close my eyes I'm back in Guildford or looking at that judge in the Old Bailey, staring at me with his beady eyes, a smile of satisfaction as he bellowed to the guards, *Take them down!* Looking up at Dirty Harry, his fury and his stale breath bearing down on me. Hearing the snarl of the dog outside the interrogation room.

Here there are no distractions from me. No way of escaping. Nothing but me and my thoughts. And it's exhausting. Try to sleep it away, but you can only sleep so much. The first month is the worst. It's unending. Every minute is like an hour, hours are like days and days are like months.

The only thing more disturbing in the Seg. Unit than the silence is the smell. Slop out happens rarely there – maybe once a day, maybe less. As a result, the smell of piss is amplified. I never thought it could get any worse than on the wing, but after several hours in Seg. it gets under your skin, into your hair, your sheets, your food (if they haven't already put some of their own piss into whatever muck they've served you). Eventually I will stop smelling it, but for the first week or two it's nauseating.

On my second week in there, a trolley rolls around with a few books on it. I look for the thickest one I can find. *War and Peace.* I've heard of it, but haven't a clue what it's about. I pick it up and read it. I read it again and again. Half the time I don't remember what I've read, but somehow it calms me down.

There are days when I can't feel calm. No matter what. When all I can do is cry and grind my teeth. And somehow when I come around, become fully conscious again, I'm on my knees, my head against the door and my fists pounding the metal frame. I realise I've been doing this for a while, because my knuckles are bleeding. I don't feel better after it, though, just sapped of all energy. Usually I end up lying down on the bed and passing out.

Occasionally a cockroach appears, or a mouse. I don't mind the mice but the cockroaches make me almost vomit. I manage to kill a couple. The crack of their shell under my boot is the nearest I've come to feeling any kind of satisfaction in weeks. Now a couple of them lie in the corner, on their cracked backs, facing the filthy ceiling.

One day, after I've finished crying, a tiny little parcel suddenly appears at the bars to my cell. I've no idea who it's from, but it's a bit of cannabis. I burn it down, roll a joint and light it up. When I wake up, drool down my chin, after a dreamless sleep, it is dark. Half of the joint is still in my hand. I smoke the rest and sleep again.

And so it goes. Utter torment followed by exhaustion. I don't know how long I've been in here for now, but when I hear footsteps coming I feel crazed. I haven't eaten anything off the plate in days. The less I eat, the less I need. They worry when you do that. They don't want you satisfied, but they also don't want to have to explain anything; they give you just enough that

you don't die. One of the screws comes in, tells me I have to eat. I'm looking
at him and I'm just about hearing him. I'm liable to do anything now. Bite
him, kill him, anything. If he'd come another day, I might have. But there
happens to be a couple of dead cockroaches on the ground. Squashed by my
laceless boots.

Have to eat, do I? Fine, I'll eat this here.

I'll never be able to explain how or why exactly I do this. Almost
against my own will, my hand has reached out, scooped up the two dead
cockroaches and stuffed them into my mouth. I barely taste them. *Crunch.* I
bite down. Don't chew, just one big hard gulp and swallow. And eyeball him
while I do it. I could do it again 10 times over, the way I feel today. It's a low
point, but in my two years of incarceration there have already been so many
low points that I barely recognise just how low it is. Almost insane.

When my time in solitary is over and they open the door to let me out
and back to my cell, it takes hours before I can speak in full sentences.
Nodding and monosyllabic sentences are all I'm fit for. I probably look like
I'm being sullen, but Seg. has left me almost mute.

My head's been pounding for weeks now and I'm finally allowed to see
a doctor. When I tell him about my headache, he tells me to stop wanking
so much. That might be funny if a mate says it when you've a hangover,
but when it comes from a prison doctor after you've had a headache for
two weeks, when you can barely see straight for the noise in your head, it's
infuriating. I surprise even myself when I growl at him. He jumps. I'd like
to smash his head in, if only I could see properly. He scampers out of the
room, looking back at me like I'm a feral animal. And in this place, some
days that's exactly how I feel.

~

Daddy's looking at me. And although I can't move my head I can see him
perfect, and I can't believe that he hasn't changed. And how clear he is,
just sitting there. I've been trying to conjure up his face in my memory
for months, years actually, without success. I don't have a picture of him

and it's been tormenting me. Even if I could get one I wouldn't because they'd tear it up. I don't keep pictures of anyone any more. Won't give them the satisfaction. But now I don't need one because there he is – his round face, dark eyes and thick, dark hair. His warm smile. He's looking at me so serenely. I just wish I could touch him, but I still can't move. It's like my muscles have been programmed for this moment. They won't even allow me to struggle. *Relax*, they're saying. *Enjoy this moment. Lie back and take him in, every tiny part of him. It's been a long time since you've seen him. You need this.* And I do – desperately. I've never needed to see my dad as much as I do at this very moment. Breathe, Paddy. Breathe and take it all in.

~

They've ghosted me. Again. This time I'm not sorry – Strangeways was awful. On first sight HMP Wakefield seems more modern. I'm heartened by the big electronic doors, the bright lights in the entrance and a half-civilised reception. I'll soon learn that it's as archaic as any other Victorian-style prison and that the bright lights that greet you on arrival are frighteningly deceptive. This is a dark place, filled with evil; a prison full of nonces. Most of them look completely harmless, but they're deviant bastards who have raped children and women. The Cambridge rapist is in the cell next to me. Some of the fellas tell me stories about the women he attacked and I wish I didn't know because the idea of what he's done to women makes me feel sick. I think of someone touching our Eileen or Harriet or Josephine or Carole or Lisa and I feel my fists clenching. I never utter a single word to him or even look in his direction.

One prisoner points out a man who looks like he wouldn't harm a fly. He nailed a woman to the floor after raping her, he tells me. That image keeps me awake for nights. There's another man who killed his gay lover and then apparently kept him in the bath so he could keep having sex with him for days on end. For some reason we find this one funny, maybe because it sounds so implausible. Some of the stories that go around are so crazy, I never know quite how much to believe. I'm reminded of David Bowie crooning in 'Life on Mars' – '*It's the freakiest show*'. This brings freaky to a whole new level.

Half the time a story goes around the entire prison and nobody even knows who started it. In some ways it's more a form of (admittedly very dark) entertainment, to get through the monotony of it all. And yet I've been put in the same prison as these people. It's so insulting. Degrading.

Giuseppe Conlon is here, too. He's so frail-looking. He always was, but now he looks like he'd break in two if a screw or inmate gave him the slightest push. He was given medication in his last prison and says he was much stronger then, but he can't get it here. He's a brave man. Tells anyone who'll listen that he's innocent. *My name is Joe Conlon. I'm an innocent man.* He loves his horses too and we talk about the old days, working on the boards in the bookies. As awful as it is that I'm here, I can see that his situation is so much worse than mine. He's an old, sick man who just wants to be with his son Gerry, but they keep moving him around. He'll die in here if they don't do something soon. There's nothing I can do for him except have a chat with him now and then when I see him out of his cell, which isn't often these days. Everyone is good to him. You can't but be outraged for him.

Around the same time as I'm moved to Wakefield, more ASU men are being tried. This time it's the four Balcombe Street boys. Their trial will be an open-and-shut case. There's no lack of evidence: flats found full of guns and explosives, forensics, eye-witnesses, not to mention the fact that they held a couple hostage for five days.

In the long-standing IRA tradition they all refuse to recognise the British court, so they refuse to plead as the charges are put. Unusually, though, they add an additional reason.

I refuse to plead, says Joe O'Connell, *because the indictment does not include two charges concerning the Guildford and Woolwich pub bombings. I took part in both, for which innocent people have been convicted.*

And even though this is the very first time that there has been a suggestion, in public, of a miscarriage of justice, this reason is never mentioned in the national press, except in *The Guardian* and the *Surrey Advertiser*, Alastair tells me furiously. O'Connell and the others give specific instructions to their legal teams to show evidence that will tie them to the Guildford and Woolwich bombings. It's a decent thing to do.

It comes out during their trial that Douglas Higgs, the principal scientific officer for the Crown, had linked the Guildford and Woolwich bombings with numerous other bombings, a link that he later removed from his statement. Under questioning, it's revealed that Higgs was told to leave out this part by a Sergeant Doyle of the bomb squad, who in turn was told to do this by the commander of the Anti-Terrorist Squad, Jim Nevill. When questioned, Nevill tells the court that he was ordered to do it by the Director of Public Prosecutions. It also becomes public knowledge that when the Balcombe Street men were arrested, they admitted to Guildford and Woolwich and denied knowing myself and Paul. And yet when Eddie Butler, one of the Balcombe Street gang, mentioned this to Peter Imbert and Jim Nevill, the very same officers who had questioned us in Guildford, they brushed him off. *We'll see you about that later.* But they never did come back to talk to him about it. And why would they? It didn't suit them to hear the truth. And also, my senior interviewing officer, DCI Style, interviewed the Balcombe Street men and failed to ask them a single question about the Guildford bombings, despite knowing that they had admitted carrying them out.

Towards the end of their trial, Joe O'Connell stands in the dock and speaks. Later, I read a transcript of what he said. The judge tried to interrupt him many times, but at one point he managed to speak uninterrupted for several minutes. When I read the transcript I want to cry with joy and stick it in the faces of those Guildford CID bastards. We'll have our day. This is exactly what we need. We'll have to get an appeal based on this.

We are all four Irish Republicans … We have recognised this court to the extent that we have instructed our lawyers to draw the attention of the court to the fact that four totally innocent people – Carole Richardson, Gerard Conlon, Paul Hill and Patrick Armstrong – are serving massive sentences for three bombings, two in Guildford and one in Woolwich. We and another man [Brendan Dowd] *now sentenced have admitted our part in the Woolwich bombing. The Director of Public Prosecutions was made aware of these admissions* [in December 1975] *and has chosen to do nothing.*

I wonder if he would still do nothing when he is made aware of the new and important evidence which has come to light through the cross-examination by our counsel during this trial ... Taking Mr Higgs [the principal scientific officer for the Crown in the Guildford trial] *first, he admitted in this trial that the Woolwich bomb formed part of the series of those bombings with which we are charged; yet when he gave evidence in the earlier Guildford and Woolwich trial he deliberately concealed that the Woolwich bomb was definitely part of a series carried out between October and December 1974 and that people on trial were in custody at the time of some of those bombings. Mr* [Donald] *Lidstone* [the forensic expert for the Guildford trial] *in his evidence for this trial tried to make little of the suggestion that the Guildford bombing had been part of the Phase One offences with the excuse – and this appeared to be his only reason – that the Guildford bombing had occurred a long time before the rest. When it was pointed out to him that the time between the Guildford bomb and the Brooks club bomb which followed Guildford was 17 days, and the Woolwich bomb which followed that was 16 days, and that many of the other incidents with which we are charged had equal time gaps, Lidstone back-tracked and admitted there was a likely connection. Those two men, Mr Higgs and Mr Lidstone, gave evidence which had no place in their true conclusions as scientists; they gave evidence which they must have known was untrue. The evidence which they gave was completely following in line with police lies so as to make the charges stick against those four people. Why? Because Nevill knows that the truth means the end of the road for him and many other senior police officers and because his superiors know it would be a dangerous insight into how corrupt the British establishment really is. This shifty manoeuvring is what we, as Irish Republicans, have come to understand by the words 'British justice'. Time and again in Irish political trials in this country innocent people have been convicted on the flimsiest of evidence, often no more than statements and even 'verbals' from the police. Despite the oft-reported claim that there is no such thing as a political prisoner in England ... As volunteers in the Irish Republican Army we have fought to free our country from its bondage of imperialism, of which this court is an integral part. I have made this statement on behalf of the four of us in the dock.*

The Balcombe Street gang are convicted in February 1977 and given lengthy sentences. Thanks to their confessions, we're going to get another day in court. Two years, to the month, after our original sentencing, we're going back to the Old Bailey. Alastair is indefatigable. When he's not in prison visiting me, he's visiting the others – Gerry, Carole, the Balcombe Street fellas. He talks to anybody who can help our case.

I don't know it now – and I won't know it for a long time – but cracks are starting to show in Alastair's marriage. Working non-stop, for free, to try to liberate a group of people (Public Enemies No. 1, 2, 3 and 4) who were convicted of bombing two pubs in his own hometown does not make for a happy marriage. His wife isn't coping with it all. Her husband, as far as she's concerned, is an IRA sympathiser, which translates as a traitor to his own people, to the people whose relatives were killed, to those who were maimed. He's also putting their own lives at risk, she tells him. Which he is, I suppose, because although he doesn't tell me then, he receives regular threatening letters and phone calls at his office, calls that his staff take. His office is broken into and he lives with the feeling that he's being watched. And one day he'll receive a letter to say that he's been sentenced to death by the National Front – a three-page letter describing exactly how they plan to do it. And yet in spite of all this, or perhaps because of it, he continues to work for us because he feels it's his duty. He is literally the only chance we have, and he knows it only too well.

Of course he won't tell me *any* of this at the time because he's too busy working on our case and doesn't want to worry me or make me feel any worse than I do. The ultimate professional. I'll only find out years later, and no matter what I do for the rest of my life I'll never be able to pay him back. How can you put a price on a life, put a value on a stranger believing you, having faith in your innocence enough to help you for free, losing a marriage as a result, enduring threats on his life? I literally owe this man my life because he is the only one who was prepared to take on the 'bombers' when no-one else would.

On the way to the Old Bailey, for our appeal, it's like I imagined the last two years. Was I really in Brixton? In Winchester? In the Scrubs? In Hull? In

Strangeways? And now we're back where we started, walking into the Old Bailey, hoping the truth will be heard. Better late than never.

And there she is. It's the first time I've seen Carole since we were sentenced, two full years ago. Paler now. Thinner. The light in her eyes has dimmed. It's actually more painful to see her than not. Confirms my fears that prison is crushing the life out of her. She squeezes my hand under the table, and for the millionth time I am in awe of this beautiful woman who holds no grudges or bitterness.

She's the strong one – the one who holds us together, who give us hope when they're tearing strips off us, rubbishing our claims of innocence. She's like the man I wish I could be: strong, reassuring, hopeful. Me, I'm still a quaking wreck who can never trust in the fairness of their process. Maybe it's because I grew up in Belfast on a diet of discrimination, automatically presumed guilty. Or maybe it's just me.

The appeal will last three weeks and I'll soon realise that I'm right. They've no intention of letting us go. There's far too much at stake here. Far too much to lose. As the MP Chris Mullin will tell me many years later, they would be willing to sacrifice small lives for great reputations. *Our* small lives and *their* great reputations.

We're tried all over again: by the court; by the three judges, who peer at us like we're vermin; by the media. Everyone. It doesn't matter that the Balcombe Four testify for us. That they get up in the box and say that they did it and we didn't. The minute details they provide about the planning and execution of the bombing, including the weight and make-up of the bombs, are all ignored. The hire car, the car park in which they left it and the two old men they describe, the ones Brendan Dowd had told the police about – all either ignored or undermined. And even though they hold up under cross-examination, just because they are hazy about irrelevant details (understandably so, given that it's now three years later and they did around 50 attacks over their 18-month campaign with the London ASU before they were caught) none of it is given any weight.

In the end the prosecution will argue that, yes, the four Balcombe Street men were obviously involved in Guildford – they've shown that they know details only the bombers could know. And, yes, there may well indeed be direct links between Guildford, Woolwich and other bombings – others that none of us four could have been involved in because we were in custody. But, they will insist, that doesn't mean we weren't all in it together. The Balcombe Street men, they'll suggest, are just trying to get their mates out of prison, even though we were all involved together. By their very unrealistic and flawed rationale it seems that about eight or ten people all went to Guildford to bomb two pubs. As little as I know about this kind of thing, I know that would never happen.

And while I'm certainly no legal expert it seems ludicrous to me that, given their access to such sophisticated intelligence about paramilitary organisations, none of the judges asks why these very articulate, disciplined men who kept to themselves would associate with the likes of us young hooligans. Nor do they stop to ask why, when we were confessing, we didn't mention any of these boys who are now admitting to the bombings. If we had pointed the finger at one another, if I had implicated my girlfriend, and Gerry his own auntie, why in God's name wouldn't we have mentioned men who were actually responsible? Nobody ever wonders aloud why they've never found any of our fingerprints on any of the explosives or guns or other bomb paraphernalia in the flats they raided. The same flats where they found those of O'Connell, Dowd and the other ASU members. If we were all in this together, then surely our fingerprints should be somewhere. But they're not. And yet this is never mentioned in court because they know that to vocalise it would undermine their case.

Instead, in his closing statement Lord Roskill clouds the whole case in fake confidence and certainty, justifying the unjust and the unjustifiable. He tells the jury that *we are all of the clear opinion that there are no possible grounds for doubting the justice of any of these four convictions, or for ordering retrials … We therefore propose to dispose of all these applications for leave to appeal by refusing them.*

In disposing of our applications, he is proposing to dispose of another 30 years of our lives.

~

Maybe it's because we don't see it coming this time. Or maybe because we've built our hopes up. Whatever it is, we're devastated. As cynical as I was at the beginning of the appeal, I believed we would get justice. Even me.

Alastair is devastated too, which makes me feel bad. *It's okay*, I say. *You did your best.* Because he did. I nearly want this as much for him as I do for me. *We won't give up*, I say. *Where to now, Alastair?* Once again these bastards have made me feel guilty. Somehow I always manage to gravitate back to a position of guilt and shame. Even when I've done nothing. Especially when I've done nothing.

I stew on all this in the van to my next home – HMP Long Lartin. I'm angry now. How could they do this to us? We're innocent people. We know it and they know it. The real perpetrators have confessed. Why couldn't they just fucking admit it? That's what we're all thinking as they send us down again, to serve out the rest of our sentences – until old age or, in the case of Paul Hill, infirmity. How can they let innocent people rot?

It's a naïve perspective, of course. As Chris Mullin said, our small lives were easily sacrificed for the sake of their great reputations. Two years later, when the Birmingham Six's appeal is also denied, Lord Denning will encapsulate the feelings of the establishment perfectly.

If the six men win, it will mean that the police are guilty of perjury, that they are guilty of violence and threats, that the confessions were invented and improperly admitted in evidence and the convictions were erroneous ... This is such an appalling vista that every sensible person in the land would say that it cannot be right that these actions should go any further.

~

In the two years since the appeal I've become comfortably numb. Which is infinitely better than the roaring, screaming agony of the first few years or the black dog that kept me in bed for days on end, unable to rise or dress or eat or speak for months. Nicely numb now. My hands like two balloons. My feet in bandages. My mouth dry, my tastebuds useless and defunct. It's not pleasant, but at least it doesn't hurt as much.

There's nothing you can do about it, I've decided. There's two choices –
get angry or get over it. Just do the fucking time. Get rid of all that fury. And
maybe I'm not happy. How can I be? Maybe numb is as good as it's going
to get in here. It's a sorry excuse for a life, but maybe it'll keep me alive and
sane for a while longer.

I arrive at this conclusion after those painful periods of anger and
depression. It happens when I see this fella who came in a few months
earlier. I saw him when he'd just arrived. About 30 he was. Good-looking
man. Healthy. Tall. Dark hair. Next time I see him it's a few months later
and I can't believe it. I'd never have thought it possible to see someone so
transformed in such a short space of time. He looks about 60 now. His hair's
almost entirely white. A roadmap on his face. Aged overnight. It's the anger
– you can see it in him. It's destroying him. Eaten up by the unending *Why
me?* and the *What if?* Dying slowly, one pointless, unanswerable question at
a time.

The little things get me through. Mammy's visits. She comes to see me
once a year now. She was coming over every few months on her holidays,
but she couldn't afford it. And now that I know I'm in for the long haul,
what's the point? The visits are still torturous. I'm lying, she's lying, and
we both know it. Everything's rosy in the garden of prison, everything's
fine back in Belfast. We're all great. And so the charade continues. There's
moments when I give her tiny insights into prison life, like when she says
that she heard some prisoners take drugs. I start laughing and she's shocked.

You don't do that, Paddy, do you?

Course I do, Mammy. What do you think I'm getting the money off you for?

Whack! I'd forgotten how quick she can be.

Jesus, Mammy – I'm a grown man. You can't do that.

Yes, I can, and there's one for your cheek.

Whack!

The three screws pretend not to be listening, but their eyes are nearly out
of their heads looking at this wee woman who's normally so restrained. I'm
laughing, even with the ringing in my head.

Sometimes I get stuck into something. A distraction, albeit temporary. For a while it was the gym. Circuits. Everyone was doing them. Jumping up and down on a step for 30 seconds, lifting weights, star jumps. Round and round and round. It felt good. I was getting stronger and leaner and sleeping better. I got six months out of that before there was a rumour that a breakout was planned, so I was sent on a lie-down in a local prison. Solitary in some small prison for a few weeks. When I got back it had all changed. Nobody was doing circuits anymore, so I didn't bother. I did miss it for a while. It made me feel better.

Another time I decide to study. A few of the IRA lads are doing it. They're very educated and I'm not. I'd like to know more about history, so that's what I choose. An Open University course. They tell me to write an essay about the Troubles, my version and then from the perspective of an English person. There's an old dear here – a bearded lady – who teaches English to a few of the others. She says she'll look at it. I give it to her. *Biased*, she tells me. I say nothing and send it off. It comes back from the Open University person a few weeks later with a B+. It was good enough for them. When they ghost me to another prison in the middle of my studies, I lose heart and that's the end of that. But it gives me heart that I can learn, even at this age.

The few precious and consistent distractions in my life – music and sport – are what stop the fire from going out altogether. They help the few embers in me to keep going. Like the Cup Final in 1979. Arsenal versus Man United. I've followed Arsenal since I moved to London. We're all in the television room, packed in. There's me and one black fella who are passionate supporters. Me for Arsenal, him for Man United. He's a big fella. Massive. I'm tiny by comparison.

It's a fast game. Frank Stapleton has already been down on the ground, but he's back up again. And then Brian Talbot is passed the ball and, boom, it's in the back of the net!

I'm up and running around the room, my jersey over my head. My friend is shaking his head. *Just you wait, Armstrong. We'll nail you bastards.*

And they nearly do a few minutes later, but somehow our goalie pushes
the ball over the top of the net. They keep trying to push forward, but they
can't. And then they get one in.

That's a fucking foul. A handball. Ref!

No it's fucking not. It's a goal.

I'm screaming at the TV, but the ref's on our side and it's disallowed.
Still 1-0. And while we're still arguing Liam Brady is dribbling the ball up
the side of the pitch, passing it to Stapleton, and he's heading it and …
GOALLLLLLLLL! It's 2-0 and we're at the end of the first half. I'm dancing
around the room, much to the amusement of the others. The big fella is
standing against the wall, fuming.

The minutes are ticking on and we've annihilated them. Clock's at 60
minutes and it's still 2-0. *You couldn't score in a brothel,* I laugh. Clock's at 70
minutes – still 2-0. I'm nearly sick with the excitement and even he's starting
to laugh now. They've no hope. It's 80 minutes down. Nothing from Man
United. *Hope is fast fading for Man United,* the commentator has just said
and I'm laughing my head off. *Just switch sides,* I tell him. *I'll get you a jersey!
Forget them there losers.*

He's given up. Just four minutes left now. It's all over bar the shouting.
My friend is screaming, but it's useless. They'll never score. *Pass it,* he's
screaming. *That's it. Go on, McQueen, get it in! Come on, come on …*
GOALLLLLLLLL!

It's 2-1 to them. They've finally scored, after 87 minutes. Big deal. I'm not
worried. There's three minutes left and they'd have to score again to equalise.

But less than a minute later my friend is up on his feet again as the ball's
passed to Sammy McIlroy, who's just sent it sailing towards our goalie. No,
no, it can't … *Yessssssss,* he's screaming. *Fucking yesssssss! Two goals in one
minute. Go on, the Red Devils.*

Arsenal were preparing their victory speeches and now they're dumbstruck,
the commentator is saying. I'm almost crying. It's 2-2 at the 88th minute.
Fuck it – it's going to be a draw. Watching the clock go down. Two minutes
left. One minute, and now they're talking about what an amazing turnabout
this is. I can barely watch it.

Everyone has written us off. The final we nearly won. But wait. Brady's got the ball, taking it up the front, passing it over, and Alan Sunderland has caught it on his foot and is sending it away again, towards the goal, sliding as he does, watching the ball sailing, sailing and … it's in, it's fucking in. *GOALLLLLL!*

The crowd are going insane. The players, the managers, they're all up off the bench. The commentators can't believe it. I can't believe it. Within seconds the whistle goes and I'm crying. We've done it. I look down at my friend; the thick rolls on the back of his neck are bulging out. His head in his hands. He can't believe it. I pat him and laugh. He turns around. *Just wait, Armstrong. You just wait.* I laugh even more.

I see him the next day in the weights room. He's there lifting what must be a couple of hundred pounds. I laugh at him. For a man who's lifting an enormous weight, he's incredibly quickly up on his feet and bounding purposefully towards me. Everyone around us moves back. I lock eyes with one man and his eyes have doubled; his pupils are tiny dots in the middle of a massive shock of white. I've no time to even move. I'm too busy noticing everyone else's reactions and marvelling about how nimble he is for such a bloody massive man. Before I know it he's got me on the ground, pinned me down with one hand and with the other lifted my massive bar bells over my chest, and I'm there, stuck like an insect that's rolled over on its back and can't get up. Nobody has moved, and for a moment there's a complete silence. Then I start laughing and he starts laughing. He's hysterical and everyone is just looking at the pair of us – this 22-stone English fella looking down at me, a 13-stone Belfast fella, pinned to the ground, and both of us crying we're laughing so much

Yes, I'm comfortably numb most of the time, except for the brief minutes like this when I can laugh. This memory and winning that FA Cup Final will get me through another few months.

And suddenly we're speeding like a freight train towards the end of this decade, of which I've spent almost exactly half in prison. I'll be 30 next year, and my wee sister is in her twenties. I have four nephews I've never met

– some born while I've been in here. They've grown up while I've been in prison. Only ever visited me in a prison – never seen me outside one. Never known any different. Somehow it's become normal.

While I can account for every painful moment of the first couple of years, time is speeding up now and it feels like the outside doesn't really exist any more, even though I can see it if I squint from an upstairs window. I'm no longer interested in it. When I happen to glimpse it, the news is like a film. Like something people make up, so I don't bother with it. It's the only way I can make this bearable. Pretend time has frozen out there while I'm here. The only contemporary aspects of my existence are the films I see every week in film club (and they're not exactly news) and the music I listen to. But even that's rubbish. I'm growing old in front of my eyes. Young fellas are coming and playing this rubbish on their record players. I listen to the radio less and my own records more. It works for me.

At Christmas 1979 we're looking down the barrel of the new decade, and me and my mates plan an almighty party, prison-style. Me and John, Liam, Gerry and Paul have gravitated towards each other. Not Gerry and Paul from Belfast – these are English fellas. Some people find it strange that I wouldn't just stick to the Irish prisoners, but I've nothing against the English. They didn't put me here. Guildford CID did. I can't take that out on every English person I meet. Some of my best friends are English. The girl I wanted to marry is English. My solicitor is English. In fact, the Irish Government have done very little for us. So I've no problem with most English people. Just the system that put us in here. And I'm bloody glad to have those friends at a time like Christmas and New Year. They stop me getting low. Distract me.

We can get away with certain things, I discover. The screws turn a blind eye to our activities if we keep quiet. We manage to get in some acid on paper. We cut it up and put it into coffee. I lie on my bed and there's Donald Duck and Mickey Mouse walking across the cell. Fuck it – I've seen stranger stuff in here, so it isn't really that weird to see two cartoon characters appearing.

And when the hash and acid run low, we brew our own hooch using apples, potatoes, yeast and hot water. I ask one screw for the apples and spuds. He laughs and tells me to piss off, but the next day a big bag of them comes up to my cell. When it's ready we seal it up in plastic bags and then wait. For the week or so it takes to ferment we store it in containers, hidden in behind the pipes, encased in wood, in the showers.

We have a special screwdriver that one of the lads made in the workshop so we can open up the pipes and remove the hooch. There's no smell from it because of the steam from the shower, but even still the screws must know it's there. They ignore it. Sometimes it's very weak and other times it's like rocket fuel. It doesn't take much to get me drunk any more so I don't really care.

There's a Christmas tree downstairs. Some decorations. Everyone is in a better mood. Staff are a bit more relaxed. So we plan our party, get the hooch ready. Put our money together and get enough for a decent bit of food. It's not family, but it's as close as I'll get in here. Someone is playing the radio in the background, Christmas music, while we drag a big table out onto the wing. Get some knives and forks. Plates ready. Some of the men are cooking up a big chicken with spuds and vegetables for everyone. If I let myself imagine, I might be able to pretend I'm not here. Just ignore the cells a few feet away, the screw pretending not to watch us. We're just a few mates enjoying ourselves, eating a meal together. Later, laughing in a cell, having a drink and a smoke. Everything is fuzzy around the edges and then it's nearly 8.00pm. Time to shut the cells. Lie in my bed. Christmas Day, Paddy. You're still in prison, but it's okay. You can do this. New decade coming. Turning 30 soon, but don't think about that now. Float away now on this buzz. Float into the eighties ...

~

A few IRA lads are going to escape. They've told me. I'd like to go with them, but they don't offer. Most people think I'm nice but they know full well I'm not what an escapee is made off. Too soft. I agree to help them anyway. Might as well. They can't possibly extend my sentence, so I've nothing to lose. The lads have bailed me out a few times now with my gambling debts. Given me tobacco and other bits and pieces. Made sure nobody gives me hassle. Everyone now knows I'm not one of them, but there's an unspoken agreement that they have my back. It's the least they can fucking do, I think sometimes.

We're making ropes in my cell. They show me how. *So we take three long pieces like this. Tie them at the top. See? Then you plait them like this, Paddy. All the way down. That's it.* Make it nice and strong. My arms are getting tired, but we're nearly there. We've been doing it for a week now and it'll be finished by tomorrow. They'll go tomorrow night. We're just finishing off for the night when the cell door opens and this English fella comes in. Looks about for a minute. Nobody's saying anything – just looking at him looking at us. He leaves and we continue. He might say something, but hopefully by the time he does it'll be too late.

I'm on the wing when I hear them coming. A group of screws and the governor.

Cell search!

Fuck. No time to do anything. They're in my cell now and I'm made stand at the door and watch them. Try to keep my face impassive as they lift the bed, and there it is. It's obvious what it's for but I'll deny it when I'm called down and nicked for attempted breakout.

Before I know it I'm back in the Seg. Unit, and soon after that I'm sent on a lie-down to Durham Prison. There, it's weeks in a cell that's so small you can't stretch out properly, and where cockroaches, mice and rats run wild.

When I get out, the IRA lads are gone – all moved to different prisons. I'll meet one of them a few years later and he'll thank me. *No problem – sure I'd nothing to lose.* Neither had they. It's the one thing me and the IRA prisoners have in common – all in here for a very long time and with absolutely nothing to lose now.

CHAPTER SEVEN

Precious time is slipping away ...
(Van Morrison)

It's 3.15pm on a cold Thursday in December 1987 and we're in the shed – me, the PO supervising us and a few of the other men who work on the garden party. We've been working for hours and are enjoying a break. The steam from the mug of tea warming my hands is wafting out into the freezing air.

From this vantage point we can look down on the rest of the prison grounds and out onto the fields. The other prisoners are out on association, and up until a few minutes ago they were all just walking around, talking, stretching their legs. Now everybody has stopped.

I can't quite believe what it is that I'm seeing. In the last 13 years I've been in more prisons than I have fingers, but I've never witnessed anything like this. There's a helicopter just yards away. *Probably Paddy Hill and Gerry Hunter coming back from the Court of Appeal in London,* one of the boys says when we first hear the roar of the engine and the whirr of the blades and all look out into the distance. It's the day of the Birmingham Six's appeal and sometimes they bring them back in a helicopter instead of in the van. *Yeah, that's most likely it.*

But it's not.

There's something not quite right about this. It's been whirring around for a while, advancing and receding through the clear winter sky. It looks like it's going to land on the other side of the wall. Lowers down and disappears for a moment, but then suddenly lifts up gently, the blades appearing first, and hops over the wall. It's quite impressive for such a big machine.

We're watching, our mouths open, as this whirring monster drops lower and lower onto the football field, just opposite where we are. This is not where a helicopter would normally land.

And now, as if in slow motion, there are two figures, in stripes, running towards it. Prisoners. Making for the open door of the still-whirring machine. We don't know it yet, but it's John Kendall and Sydney Draper. From what I know about them, Kendall is a gangland boss and Draper was done for murder. I've barely ever spoken to either of them, but they both seem like pretty hard men and I tend to avoid that type if possible.

Right now, though, it's just two figures running and it reminds me of one of those films – the ones where everything is in slow motion. Their arms stretching outwards, as if to propel their bodies forward, their legs driving them closer and closer to the open door. They couldn't be. It's too simple. Too obvious. Someone must be coming behind them to nab them. But there's nobody. Everyone has just stopped. Staring. Spellbound by these two cartoon-like figures. I can't believe it – they're leaning in towards the door and it looks like they're going to jump in …

~

It's the summer of 1982 and after my lie-down in Durham I'm being transferred to HMP Gartree, another maximum-security prison in the heart of rural England, somewhere between London and Manchester.
From my limited view through the van window I can see that this is a beautiful part of the country and for a few minutes my spirit soars and I forget the kind of place I'm going to. Meadows and birds and endless blue skies. I can imagine lying in one of those fields with Carole, staring at the clouds and laughing at something. Maybe this place could be better than the others. Maybe, just maybe, this won't be so bad.

But once again they've succeeded in building a place that's intent on sucking the marrow from everyone's bones. Not unlike the other prisons I've been in, it's the kind of place where they've invested more money in the security than in the basic facilities, like showers and toilets. Grey building after barbed-wire fence. From a cell window or the exercise yard there's little evidence of the magnificent scenery just yards away.

Maybe they put people like me here because, if you escape, there's nowhere to run. It's just fields for miles, a few roads. If there's civilisation close by, I'll certainly never see it. It would explain why they send the likes of the criminal who called himself Charles Bronson here, a man who will arrive a few years after me, dubbed the most dangerous man in the country by the English press. And not long after I leave, Fred West, a serial murderer and rapist, the most utterly vile example of humankind, will be sent here. I've never come to terms with the fact that I am deemed to be just like such men. That it is seen as an appropriate place to put someone like me – innocent and soft.

In spite of its drabness, there's a substantial Irish population here, some of whom I've met before. That makes it easier to settle in. I don't have to proclaim my innocence any more. Seven years in, prisoners know we didn't do it, screws know we didn't do it. The dogs on the street know it, for God's sake.

When I arrive I'm put onto C Wing and a few weeks later I meet a man I've heard a lot about. Paddy Hill. Also in prison for bombings he knows nothing about – the Birmingham pub bombings in his case, which happened just a month after Guildford – this is a man who knows exactly how I feel. We have a lot in common. We're both Paddys from Belfast, except he's Patrick Joseph – Paddy Joe for short. A small, solid and lively man from the Ardoyne area, he's an instant friend. You can't help but like the man. The first time we meet he slaps me on the shoulder and tells me that he's heard all about me, that we're going to prove our innocence and that whoever gets out first, the Guildford Four or the Birmingham Six, will get the others out. I agree immediately, and just like that we're fast friends.

This little Belfast man, who's six years my senior, is impossible to dislike. He's as subtle as a brick through a glass window, can talk for Ireland and reminds me of a yapping terrier – small, fierce and loyal. He's also great fun. We'll spend many a night having the craic, a smoke in my cell, telling stories, chatting or even singing on occasion. He'll get himself into trouble in prison and spend more time in solitary than most men, but he comes up fighting every time. Most of all, this is a man who will always make me feel like he's got my back. I'll never be in any doubt of his loyalty.

A few years later, another important man arrives in Gartree. My childhood friend and rival in love, Ronnie McCartney. He'll later tell me how shocked he was when he first saw me. Where was the trendy teenager who walked around in a suit and tie? The cool fella who Ronnie looked up to? How had I become so beaten down and neglected-looking. The boy I'd stolen Margaret Hutchinson's affection from saw a very different person looking back at him.

All these years later Ronnie's still talking about this teenage rejection, and I get great mileage out of it. Unlike us, Ronnie is actually an IRA man. In the time since I last saw him, he took up the cause and was in an ASU until his time ran out and the police caught up with him. He will become my biggest ally in prison, a man who'll rescue me from the depths of despair, the brink of insanity. And even though he's a true IRA man, he's loyal beyond belief. Between him and Paddy Hill I have true friends.

Gartree will also be the place where I will meet the one person who knows for a fact that I didn't do it. The one person who can vouch for my innocence with 100 per cent certainty. Joe O'Connell. Of the London ASU and the Balcombe Street gang. One of the men who actually did do Guildford. He's on a different wing in Gartree, but when we eventually meet he looks me in the eye and shakes my hand. *Sorry, we did all we could. Tried to tell them, but they didn't want to know.* I don't blame him. He didn't get us locked up. In fact, he and the other fellas tried their best to convince the courts that we didn't do it and that they did. He nods seriously at me. Listening. He'll do anything he can to help, if ever the time comes. And he will. I thank him. And that's it.

People often ask me about this conversation and are surprised when they realise how short it was. And it's not that it was unimportant, quite the opposite. But what do you say? He doesn't want me to be here, I don't want to be here and we've both done our best to reverse an appalling injustice, but here I am anyway. What's there to say beyond that? It certainly isn't

worth getting upset about, fighting about. So we don't – neither of us is that
kind of person. And so if you were walking past us at that moment, here's
what you'd see: two men talking quietly, nodding, listening, agreeing. And
if you didn't know what we were discussing, you'd never in a million years
imagine that he was apologising. Saying sorry that I'm doing 35 years for a
bomb that he and other members of his ASU planted.

He's a nice man, I decide. In spite of everything. He never meant to
hurt me. I know immediately that we'll never become friends. We're very
different animals. He keeps to himself, serious and disciplined. Typical
IRA man. And I am not. And even if none of this shit had happened, we
still never would have been friends. But there's no animosity and he'll bail
me out more than once during our time in prison together. He owes me, I
suppose.

~

The two figures have reached the door and they're diving inside
the helicopter. The door is closing now and I'm rooted to the spot,
unconsciously clutching my mug even tighter between my hands. Riveted.
These two fellas are actually going to take off and disappear into the sky.

As the door closes and the blades are whirring faster, readying for take-
off, one of the officers near me comes to life. *You forgot their black books,* he
shouts. The black book we all get signed whenever we leave prison. We all
laugh. He'll probably get in trouble for it later – this inappropriate joke –
but for us it's the perfect line at the most surprising of moments.

Somewhere in the distance prisoners on exercise have come back to life
too. Shouting and cheering. We join in from our shed. It doesn't matter who
escapes from prison, you're always behind them. It's an unwritten code.

I've seen many escape attempts – some better than others. Most are
foiled because they're badly planned or someone gets wind of it. The
occasional attempt succeeds, but, Jesus, this one is unbelievable. So simple.
Ingenious.

I can hear an alarm sound somewhere in the near distance. Somebody's finally worked out what's going on. Inside, screws are frantically phoning the local airport in Leicester – following the alarm procedure that was set up in the 1970s. The arrangement is that once Leicester Airport gets the call, they press a button that activates an alarm and an aeroplane is immediately sent up to sort out the problem. Except somebody has forgotten to send the memo to whoever answers the phone in Leicester Airport. Instead the fella in the airport asks the screw why the fuck they're ringing him, they should be ringing the police.

And while all this is taking place, the helicopter has just hit the sky again, disappearing into the distance, destined for who knows where, and those two men are free. Lucky bastards!

~

It's a freezing night in February 1984. One of the coldest I can remember in prison. I'm sitting on the bed in my cell, a blanket wrapped around me, listening to something on the radio, half reading a book. The music on the radio is shit these days. Better off listening to records if I want some decent music, but I'm sick of mine. Need some new ones.

A while back I ordered some LPs from a mail-delivery company and they actually delivered them. To a prisoner. In prison. And sent a bill. When I didn't pay them, they tried to bring me to court. Even sent an order telling me to appear. The prison decided it wasn't worth spending the money on transporting me there. It costs thousands to take a Cat A prisoner up to court. The bloody things they sent me are only worth about 50 quid, if even that.

Sitting here, thinking about other ways to get some new records, I'm out of ideas. Mammy is broke. Eileen has done so much for me, between driving back and forth to see me, bringing me clothes and whatever else I need, that I can't ask her for anything else for a while. I really need some money.

I've another, bigger problem that I've been avoiding thinking about – the reason I'm sitting in here in the first place and not on the wing for association. There's a cockney gangster who'll be looking for me and I need to avoid him because I can't pay him. Bought a couple of ounces of hash and tobacco off him on the tick. Promised him my canteen (credit) in return, but I'd already promised it to several other people for other stuff and now they're all looking for the canteen I promised. But I only get one every week. I can hold the others off for a couple of weeks, but this fella in particular is the angry type. He's going to be looking for his money and I've no way of paying him, as I've already given my canteen to the bookie. So I'm avoiding him – hiding away in my cell.

I don't know how long they've been standing there, but when I look up there's three of them there in front of me. IRA fellas. I get on well with most IRA fellas usually. Don't have a lot to do with them, except Ronnie, but when I do it's fine. These ones, though, they're hard men. They tell me that the cockney gangster's been to see them. Told them to sort me out since I'm one of them. Before I get to say that I'm not, they interrupt me. I'm bringing their names and the IRA into disrepute. I need to wise the fuck up. My little drug and gambling habits have been getting out of control lately, they say. They're going to have to sort me out if I don't sort myself out.

They mean business, these fellas. They're moving closer and I'm shaking. *Just a mistake. Promised two fellas my canteen. I'll pay the cockney fella next week. Won't happen again, I swear.* One of them puts his face up to mine. His eyes are cold. He wouldn't have a problem kneecapping me, that much is crystal clear. He'd probably enjoy it. *We know it won't fucking happen again, Armstrong, because if it does, you'll be in the prison hospital. And you can't be putting on any wee bets from there with broken arms and legs.*

He pulls back and one of them, who's been quiet the whole time, starts to speak. *You'll need to get yourself down the Block. Out of our way. Now. Go see the Chief and tell him you need a wee break. Tell him whatever the fuck you want, but you get yourself down there. A week or two should do it. And when you come back, you pay him back or you'll have us to deal with.*

I'm nodding. *I'll do whatever you want. I'm real sorry, won't happen again, boys.* They shake their heads and walk off. I'll have to do what they say. Get put into the Segregation Block. Suits me fine. Bit of peace and quiet to sort my head out and I'll be away from that cockney lunatic. Take my tobacco and off I go. Head down to find a Principal Officer or the governor.

Paddy Hill's in the Block when I get there. He's been there a couple of days. It started when one of the Hickey brothers, of the Bridgewater Four, was up on the roof running amok. I find out that he was one of four men done for the murder of a 13-year-old paperboy, Carl Bridgewater, back in 1978 but is believed to be innocent. Yet another victim of British justice.

Being the kind of prison where prisoners look after each other, when Hickey got up on the roof to protest, some of the others were passing food out to him, to help sustain him. In the meantime some other prisoners started rioting too, including Paddy Hill. They would have been out on the roof along with him except the screws got to them first, but not before they'd destroyed their cells – broken everything, including the windows, using the metal legs off the beds to smash them in. And so Paddy Hill has ended up on the Block as punishment for his part in the riot.

When he sees me coming down, Paddy's surprised. I'm not normally in trouble. *Have you been rioting too, Armstrong?* I shake my head. Hoping he'll leave me alone. I can't deal with it tonight. Just want to go into my cell and sleep and forget about it. I tell Paddy I'll see him in the morning. I'll deal with it then. He looks at me and I know he's not going to drop it tomorrow.

In the morning I try to avoid him but he's in a cell close to mine so he's at me again, asking what I'm doing here and who sent me down. He's very protective of me, but it makes me feel like an even bigger idiot. Like I'm someone who has to be minded. Which is true, but that doesn't make it any easier to deal with.

I finally tell him the score because I know he won't give up until I do. He's furious. *Who the fuck do those IRA boys think they are, protecting that fucking cockney bollix? I'll sort them out. We'll see whose legs they're gonna break when I go up on the wing. Don't you worry, Paddy, no-one's sending you down here for no cockney fucking gangster.*

He gets the Officer Commanding (OC) of the IRA – a fella from Cavan – and tells him that he wants to see those fellas. Out on the field.

What's the fucking score, boys? Putting Paddy on the Block this afternoon for some cockney fucking wanker? What the fuck are you playing at?

He came up to us, they tell him. *Told us to sort it. So we did.*

Well, listen to me here. You don't work for no cockneys and you don't do his dirty work. You leave him to me and don't fucking touch Paddy Armstrong.

And then Paddy marches straight up to the cockney fella. *I told you before not to give Paddy any fucking gear. Couple of ounces of tobacco or a lump of dope. And you're going to the IRA? Anything happens to him, I'll stab the fuck out of you in front of everybody. I'll send you out in a box.*

And that's that. The terrier has yapped and snarled a bit and I'm off the hook.

Go back to your cell, Paddy. Nobody will trouble you again. And pull your head in for fuck's sake, would you?

I go back up on the wing and I'm left alone.

He goes to see Ronnie McCartney after this and soon after the governor transfers me to B Block. Over to where Ronnie can keep an eye on me. Ronnie asked the screws to do this, he tells me many years later. I'm safer away from those boys.

Ronnie corners me in a cell and tells me to pull my head in. *Don't fucking buy anything you haven't the money for. I'll do my best for you, but one of those wankers could kill you one day.* He tells everyone else they're not allowed to give me anything on tick. If they do, it's their fucking problem because they know what I'm like. I laugh when he tells me this, but I'm mortified. Now I just smoke other people's hash when I can't afford it. I get stoned just as much as before, but I'm not getting threatened.

The real problem is the horses. When I first came into prison I discovered that wherever there are criminals, there's a bookie. The kind of bookie who would take a bet on anything.

And that's my problem – I often can't pay. Especially when I lose. I have a good reputation for picking winners, so they give me credit. And again I rack up a few debts. This time it's Joe O'Connell who bails me out. He doesn't make a big deal of it. Barely says a word. Just tells me to cop on. Watch my back. And even though I know he owes me, I know this isn't right. But if I can't have a wee gamble, I'll go insane – it's the only thing that gives me a lift in this place.

When I go back to the wing after a brief spell down in solitary, I find out that Paul Hill's here in Gartree. It's been years since I've seen him and he looks shocked to see me. He doesn't look fantastic himself, but I know I probably look worse. Later he'll write that I look much older now, my hair going and my eyes dull and tired. I don't look in the mirror very often, but I know he's right.

We get on fine, but our interaction is limited as he's a lot more serious than me. He's not really into getting stoned and acting like an eejit like me and my friends.

When we talk, he mentions the campaign to get us out. It's been gaining strength and more people are getting involved. *It's good, isn't it? We'll get there – they can't keep ignoring us for ever, especially if we get more people to write letters and pester politicians.*

I've zoned out. I used to be able to read books. Remember the days I spent reading *War and Peace*. I read it twice in solitary after the riot in Hull. Found a few good novels along the way. When I had the concentration. And there was a time I could even study. Write long essays. Feels like a long time ago now. Couldn't write a coherent sentence these days if I tried. Find myself dropping a book a few pages into it and often never coming back to it.

Paul's looking at me. I nod. I pretend I know what he means, but the truth is I don't, because I haven't been following the campaign to get us out. Some days I can barely get myself out of bed, never mind write letters like he's saying. *Aye, I'll do that.* Yeah, right, I think. I can't write letters like him and Gerry and Paddy Hill can. I barely write to my mammy or to Carole or my sisters – I'm not going to write to strangers who don't want to know. Don't have the energy. And even if I did, what good would it do anyway? Take on the entire British judicial system? They've taken 10 years of our lives – they're not going to back down now because I write a few letters. It'll take a miracle at this stage. Anyway, I reason, I've seen what happens to the men who fight the system and I know I'm probably not in a much better state than them, but at least I'm not tormenting myself night and day. I don't say any of this to Paul, but he must get the message because he stops talking to me about it.

Some days you wake up and realise another year has passed. Like the sugar I heap into my tea to keep my energy up, time just dissolves and disappears in a split second. And after all this time we've been forgotten by almost everyone except our families, but I'm not going to be worrying them by asking them to write letters.

My poor mammy is almost 60 now and she's still working her fingers to the bone to pay the bills and to come and visit me once a year. One day when I'm waiting for her to arrive, a screw comes into the workroom and tells me to get my things. No explanation. I don't know that she's sitting in the waiting-room, waiting patiently, knowing how slowly the cogs in the wheel of prison work.

I'm signed out and before I know it I'm handcuffed to a screw in the back of a van. We're going to London – I'm needed in court, they say. Not sure when we'll be back – gone all day. They don't care that my mammy is coming – nothing they can do. Shrug.

We get there, and of course I'm not needed in court. A mistake apparently. By the time I'm back, she's gone. It's not unusual, this kind of thing. Happened a lot to us all in the early days. When our solicitors would be coming we'd be ghosted out to another prison.

When I get back I discover that my poor mammy was here, waiting for hours before anyone told her that I was gone and wouldn't be back all day. I can just about see past my tears enough to break up everything I can find in the cell. When I'm dragged down to the governor, he agrees that it was very unfortunate. He gives me a couple of weeks on the Block, but after this he'll let me save up all my visits and use them when Mammy comes over. They'll even agree to take me to a London prison for a couple of weeks at a time so she can stay with my sister and won't have to pay for accommodation. This way I can see her a few times a week.

When I discover it's Wandsworth, I now have to face my biggest fear. But I'll do it for my mammy. Only for her. And this is how I find myself in this hideous place. They've put me working in the mailroom, sewing mail bags.

And there, nailed to the wall, is the chair Ronnie Biggs used to sit on and the mailbag he was sewing before he escaped. Like a trophy. I can't decide if I'm appalled or awed to be looking at it. It keeps me amused at least, which is some help, because the work is mind-numbing. Not that I do the job properly. If they want a stitch every 2mm, I'll do one every 10mm. They might be able to make me work, but I won't do it well. A pitiful rebellion, but it's the only way I can do it.

Mammy's visits are still exhausting. Every time I see her she looks older. Now when she smiles I can't see beyond her sunken cheekbones, eyes dark and hollow. And even though she's the person I love most in the world, it's just too torturous. While it's awful, at least it's easier to pretend everything's okay for a week or two a year rather than a single day every week, so I keep the charade going. And in spite of all the pain it causes us both, I love seeing her. My dear mother.

When I come back from Wandsworth, although I'm happy to be back in a place where the screws are decent to me and the other prisoners let me be, it's hard not to get sucked into a depression again. I've done less than a third of my term and it's only going to get harder as I get older. I'm not fit, I'm not healthy. Gone are the days when I could do squats and jump up and down in a prison gym.

Instead I get off my head every night and drag myself into the prison workshop during the day to do whatever boring task is assigned to me in the metal shop or on a sewing-shop machine. Whenever things get too much, I go and see one of the POs and ask to be taken down to the Block where I can just sleep all day. They even let me take my radio and a book with me, which you don't get if you're there on punishment, but since I'm there voluntarily it's okay. The cells in the Block are tiny, but all I need is a bed. Paddy Hill and some of the other men are down here regularly and you can pass stuff between the cells, so it's nice. And after a couple of weeks, when whoever was looking for me has forgotten or when I feel a bit better, I go back to my cell. Until things go wrong the next time.

I'm lonely too. Despite the numbness that I feel a lot of the time, the one part of me that won't die is the longing for female company. After growing up around women all my life and then being so close to Carole and Lisa, I miss the presence of women.

There's some men in here who write to women they don't know. Get visits sometimes. They pass around the letters they get back. I'm happy for them, but I've never had any interest in that. And given how much I hate writing letters, it would never happen anyway. But there are times when I just long for a human touch. A hug, a kiss. The kind of affection that doesn't happen in a men's prison. The only kind that happens here isn't the kind I want. Not that I don't miss sex. Jesus, I do. Years later I'll be asked what I missed most when I was in prison. *Sex*, I'll say cheekily. But I only like it with women, so I go without.

And just when I think I can't take any more, when I'm spending more time on the Block than in my cell because I have to avoid so many people, salvation comes – in the form of a garden.

It's the governor. *You're going on the garden, Armstrong.* I can't believe it. Normally a Cat A prisoner would never be allowed onto the garden party. It's a really privileged position – the closest thing you can get to a party in prison, all day, every day. It means being in the prison gardens all day long, where you can smoke away, chat, have a laugh, sit down and read a newspaper even. *Really, Gov? Yes, Armstrong. Really? Do you want to now? I do, yes.* He's patting me on the back and for the first time I feel like I've been lucky.

In the beginning I'm working like a dog. Raking, weeding, sweeping, planting, everything. And I feel great. Being outside with my hands in the soil, feeling the soft breath of the country air and even the rain on my face brings me to life again. I feel like I'm waking up from a long sleep, refreshed, energised.

The screw who's over us, Mick Haynes, is one of the nicest screws I've ever met. When I'm tired or not coping, he lets me sit down and read the paper while he does the gardening. Even gives me some tobacco that's been confiscated from other prisoners. More and more these days, I feel like a lot of the screws look out for me, even the Chief. It means a lot to me.

Mick and I joke a lot. I pretend to give him orders and he laughs. We have normal conversations. He asks me about my life in Belfast and I ask him about his. He tells me all about the hawks he has at home and I tell him about growing up on the Falls. I tell him that when I get out of here one day, I'm coming to see his birds. He smiles and says that would be nice. And that's how we get on. Just two men having a conversation. I'll never get the chance to tell him what it means to me, but he makes me feel like a human being again, like a person who deserves a bit of dignity and respect.

I learn about sowing seeds and growing flowers and weeds and so many things I never knew about. Then one day we have an idea – a pitch and putt course for the other prisoners. Wouldn't it be great to have one? We think they'll laugh at us, but the Chief gives us the okay, so we do it. Draw a plan. Measure it. Draw an outline. Walk around it. Inspect it. Talk about it. Argue a bit. It takes days, but we're loving it. And then we're cutting out holes in the grass and at last it's finished. It's a great feeling. We're very proud of ourselves. Me and the Chief test it out. He beats me. It's like I'm not in prison at moments like this. Just two men playing a game of pitch and putt.

The months and even the years fly by now. I've been in for 13 years and for the last three, working on the garden party, things have been bearable. I'm not even sure I want to leave, to be honest. What would I do and where would I go? The telly shows me the changes that are happening outside. The world is a different place. It's moved on and I haven't. I wouldn't be able to cope in it. So this place is just fine now. It's 1987. I'm 37. Never thought I'd spend my fortieth birthday in this place, but it looks like I will. And my fiftieth. I'll be almost sixty when I get out. If I ever get out.

If I do ever get out, the one helpful thing I've learned here is how to cook. My mammy can't believe it when I tell her. The food is so bad here that a lot of people do their own cooking when they can afford the ingredients. The way I dealt with it for years was to pretend to be a vegetarian because I realised that I got better food that way – nothing amazing, but at least I could make a sensible guess as to what it actually was on the plate. Sometimes, when I'm feeling up to it, I chip in with a few other men and we cook together.

An Indian inmate teaches me to make a lamb curry from scratch with some basic spices. I never had a curry until I came to London so it was mind- (and mouth-) blowing to eat it in the beginning. Now I'm used to it, I have a more discerning palate. I show him how to make an Irish stew – my dad's recipe.

As Cat A prisoners we eat on our own most of the time. Breakfast and lunch in the cell. Alone. Some prisoners cook together in the evening time and then eat in one of the cells. I do that sometimes. Depends on my mood. These days I eat alone a lot. A habit that will linger for the rest of my life.

I'm still comfortably numb. Like my space. A bit of solitude. Everything predictable – the same every day. Doors unlocked at eight o'clock every morning, go to work until midday and then back to the cell. Banged up again. Eat. Doors open again at 1.40 and it's back to work. Locked up again at 5.00 – eat. Then association from 5.50 until 8.00, or 8.30 on weekends, and then that's it. Doors locked. Goodnight. No point in fighting it, so you just go with it. In many ways my life is better now. More stable, more routine. Never had this kind of routine, except when I was a child. Something reassuring about the predictability.

It's been so long since I've seen Carole. The letters stopped a few years ago. Every so often one will arrive in the post, but mostly she's quiet. Getting on with doing her time, like the rest of us. I understand. But I miss her. Her voice. Her laugh. Her gentleness. Her quirky way of looking at the world. I wonder if I will ever see her again. If we don't get out for another 20 years, anything could happen to one of us in that time. We may not all make it out of this place alive.

And then suddenly, there she is. After eight years she's sitting in front of me. Carole. Somehow she's managed to get an inter-prison visit after all these years. Now 10 years older than when I first met her. More womanly, more grown up, but still only 27. She's so beautiful.

Sitting beside her in the Cat A visitors' room, with about four screws staring at us, at first I'm tongue-tied. Don't know how to speak to a woman – just her proximity to me is blowing my mind. She's looking at me. Telling me about how the campaign is going. I'm barely listening. I lean over and kiss her. The warmth and softness of her lips, her mouth is unbelievable. I'm laughing and she's laughing and I think I would happily die right now.

We keep talking and acting like teenagers. If the prison guards know what's going on, they don't say a word. They've seen it all before. We keep talking until they make movements. Time's up. I feel like a teenager whose girlfriend has to get the last bus home so she doesn't get into trouble with her parents. We kiss again. And then she's gone again for another few years.

When the band Berlin release a new song in a couple of years' time, I'll hear it for the first time lying in my cell, stoned. Lying on the bed, reading a book, I'll close my eyes and picture Carole in front of me, laughing at me, calling me her *little piggy*. That she needs to fatten me up. The girl I proposed to, sitting at the top of a hill. The girl they took away from me. The girl I should have married when I had the chance. '*Take my breath away …*' And just when I can practically smell her, touch her, a screw will walk by and I'll hear him cackle. *Look at Armstrong. He's stoned – reading a book upside-down!*

Alastair is getting more animated now. The campaign is definitely moving more than he's been telling me. Since *Trial and Error,* a book about us, came out the previous year people have been talking more. Robert Kee, the author of the book, sent me a copy and I tried to wade through it, but it's heavy-going. I kept falling asleep. It was a bit weird reading about myself, but it's nice that we haven't been completely forgotten.

I don't know if the book will have any impact, but something has to happen, Alastair tells me, if we knock on enough doors. *They'll have to reopen the case. Can't ignore us for ever,* he says. Determined. I'm more cynical, although I never admit it to this amazing man who just won't give up. But the fact is that, even though there's been a major book and a couple of documentaries about us in the last few years, and despite the fact that Merlyn Rees, the former Labour Home Secretary, has expressed his doubts about the case, nobody is bloody listening. And to be honest, such is my state of mind that I've barely noticed all this going on around me.

One day I turn on the radio and hear that Douglas Hurd, the Secretary of State for Northern Ireland, has decided to refer the Birmingham Six case back to the Court of Appeal, but not ours. I'm gutted. Of course I'm over the moon for Paddy Hill and the other lads who were done for Birmingham, and I know that Paddy will fight for us if he gets out, but still … what about us?

Gerry's obviously more optimistic than me. He managed to gate-crash his way into an interview with BBC Radio, something I could never do. It really wound up the prison authorities because for the first time since we've been locked up, one of our voices was broadcast to the public. He's found himself a new solicitor too – the one that the Birmingham Six are using. A hot-shot solicitor named Gareth Peirce who fights human rights cases. I'm sticking with Alastair; he's the only one I trust.

~

On that winter's day, just before Christmas 1987, when Paddy Hill, Gerry Hunter and the other Birmingham fellas are up in the Court of Appeal in London wondering if they'll be out in a few weeks, we're back in Gartree watching the blades of the helicopter disappear into the distance, clapping and cheering before the screws come and order us all back into our cells while they deal with the situation. None of us, and certainly not me, have any idea how this escape will end up impacting on everyone.

As one of the few people who witnessed it – my mouth hanging open and a mug of tea in my hand – I'll be somehow implicated by senior prison authorities. Anyone who knows me will never think for a moment that I had anything to do with it, but decisions like this are made on high by people who don't care. I'm a Cat A prisoner, an IRA murderer, so I probably had a part in it. I'm suddenly sent away on a lie-down to a local prison. Taken away from my garden, my sanity, to a tiny cell in a totally strange place. Nobody there who knows me. Nobody there who cares.

After two weeks confined to a cell, minimal fresh air, I'm sitting in the van, dying to get back out on the garden party. I know old Mick Haynes and I will have a laugh about it all. We all will. I'm looking forward to the banter.

Instead I'm greeted by new, higher fencing around the grounds. One of the fellas who escaped has been caught, I hear; the other is still missing. He'll manage to stay on the run for more than a year. They have ramped up the security to prevent this from ever happening again.

So I never get to have that banter I've been missing so much, because I've been taken off the garden party. *You're in the workshop now, Armstrong,* I'm told apologetically. *Security an' all that – you know how it is.* Nod. *Oh, yeah, I do know how it is.* What's the point in saying that what I really know is that I'm innocent; that anybody who has met me knows it and plenty who haven't know it too; that this job in the garden has kept me sane in an otherwise intolerable situation? But I don't, because there's no point. I say nothing. And so, just like that, the only bit of sanity I have is gone. And then everything goes black for a couple of years.

Back in the workshop I'm not coping. Working on this big machine. So loud. Can't think. Can't focus on anything. The darkness in the workshop, the dust, it's all too much. I feel more claustrophobic than I ever have in any cell. Want to just put a rope around my neck and end it all.

How I manage to get out of bed and put one foot in front of the other I don't know. Other prisoners aren't coming as close to me. I haven't washed in days. I caught sight of myself in a mirror a few weeks ago and even I was shocked. My skin is almost grey, my thinning hair thick with grease. I know I should wash, but I just can't make myself. When the bells sound for the end of work, I disappear to my cell and hide away. I stay off the wing during association, and when they come looking I pretend to be asleep until they leave me alone.

And then the day comes when I just can't do it any more. The noise is making me dizzy. I'm going to vomit if I stay in this room for another minute. Rush out, tell the screw I have to leave. He lets me go and I make my way to the Chief's office. He doesn't look surprised when I ask to go on the Block. *Just need a bit of a break, Chief. Away from it all. Not coping at the moment.* He doesn't argue with me. Just takes my laces. I know what he's

doing and normally I'd be annoyed. As if I'd ever contemplate it. But I'm
not sure any more.

A nervous breakdown they're calling it, but I only hear this later. It
sounds so dramatic, but it isn't. Just a very slow, gradual slide into bleakness.
Into a very dark and lonely place.

Solitary is better and worse. The break from the workshop and the wing
and all the people is definitely better. But the silence makes me realise how
noisy my head is. I'm hearing voices and having conversations with people
who aren't here. Mammy. Josephine. Carole. Dad. Granny. Guildford CID.
Dirty Harry. And then he's back: Dirty Harry. Standing over me. Him and
the rest of them looking down at me. Screaming their questions. Fists and
feet and questions and I'm whimpering.

They let Ronnie McCartney down to see me. He's become a good
friend in here. We were never close growing up, competing for Margaret
Hutchinson's attention, but in here he's a lifesaver. And now he's trying
everything he can think of to coax me out of my depression, but I've just
lost the will. Can't take much more. *The campaign is really stepping up*, he
says. *You'll get out.* I've heard this before. Alastair has told me all about it and
some days I'm interested, but not right now. There's a couple of journalists
writing a book about us. Another book. The same people who made a
couple of documentaries about us. Alastair has told me about this too, but
right now I don't care. I just want to be left alone.

Ronnie won't let me be. Keeps talking and talking. Telling me stories.
Trying to make me laugh. Things from our childhood. Other prisoners.
Screws. Women he's been with. Men he's fought. He just talks on and on and
it's impossible not to get drawn out of myself even a little bit. He and some
of the other men do their very best to keep me afloat. They know I'm fading
with every month and year. Trying to lose myself, just get into the banter at
night, forget it with the bit of a smoke, the odd flutter on the horses when
I have money (nobody will give me credit now), but it's not working. And
they can see that.

And so they've pulled me back just enough that I'm not teetering
above the precipice, but there's no joy any more. I'm numb, but no longer

even comfortably so. And other people can see the hopelessness, smell the weakness. It's seeping out of me like a silent gas, lingering in the air. I can almost smell it myself.

Most men would never take advantage of someone in a bad state, the way I am now, but there's always one or two who will. One in every prison. *Murdering paddy bastard – let's give him some shit.* Makes themselves feel better. Shows their mates how hard they are.

In Gartree, in my weakest moment, the person who has the misfortune to pick on me is a black cockney fella. Dying for a fight. He's horrible. A bully. Known for picking on people. Gives the rest of the black prisoners a bad name, as most of them are lovely and we get on great with them. But he likes to go around winding people up. And me in particular. I ignore him for weeks, but only because I've no fight left in me. Nearly 40 years old, for fuck's sake. Can't be dealing with this. But the anger is still there, stacking up nicely like a torrent of water behind a dam. I'm getting closer to losing it and I'm afraid of myself. I might lose it and stab someone, kick their brains in. Walk away, Paddy. You know what can happen. Don't forget …

There's a fella who sits behind me in school. Thick dark hair and a dirty wee face on him. From just a few streets away. Always jabbing me with his pencil, in the back, just where it hurts. And he knows it. Anything to wind me up. Daring me to stand up to him. Knowing I won't. And I don't. Day in, day out, he keeps at it. Pushing further and further, always with that sly grin on his face. For weeks I've been dreaming about him. The same dream: I've got him on the ground and I'm punching him, wiping that cocky grin off his face. Every time I wake up from that dream I feel sick just thinking about it. I'd never hurt anyone like that. It's not me. I hate violence. And so when he continues to torment me, I'll run away and ignore him. Or worse, when he laughs, I'll laugh with him. Like we're both mates and this is a big joke between us. And I'm disgusted with myself for being so weak.

This has been going on in class for weeks or maybe months, and then one day I lose it. He's trying to wind me up – a jibe, or a sly dig. Just enough to set me off. And that's it. I'm on top of him. Trying to hit him. My heart is pounding. And suddenly there's four of my friends pulling me off him.

One fella tried on his own first but he couldn't do it, so there's three others helping him. *Stop, Paddy – get off him – that's enough.* They'll look at me with new eyes now. Half admiring, half bewildered. *You could have really hurt him.* I can't talk about it. Feel sick. Run home. Never tell any of my sisters about it. Thinking of the shock in his eyes as I was looking down at him. Wondering now if he'd really been meaning to annoy me. Maybe he was just joking the whole time. Maybe I'd imagined it all. Misinterpreted it. I want to vomit.

And now, almost 30 years later, I'm on the other side of the Irish Sea, in a British prison, and I can still see that wee lad looking up at me every time one of these boys winds me up in prison and I think I'm going to lose it. I can almost smell his fear as he looks up at me from his dirty wee face, his eyes wide in shock. And I feel their hands pulling me off him. I don't want to feel that again. That's not who I am. More than anything, I'm scared by the adrenaline that surged through me as I was beating him. I didn't know the word then, but that's what it was. Adrenaline release. Power. Taking control. One of the rare times in life I didn't feel weak. And now, looking at this cockney fella all these years later, I know what I'm capable of. I never want to go back there again. That is not the kind of man I am. So I walk away.

But he won't give up, this cockney fella, and he's massive. And he's determined to wind me up. Started with snide comments. Standing in front of me, his elbow sticking out just a bit. Knocking against me. I'm biting my lip and walking away. Pretending it's not happening, that I don't need to nip it in the bud. That's what the other lads are telling me. *Just fucking punch the head off him, Paddy. He's a cheeky bollix.* Can't tell them I'm afraid of my anger. They'll tell me to wise up. They can't see into my head. Can't see the memory I'm playing out from nearly 30 years ago.

I can't avoid him for ever in here. And now the day I've been fearing has come. I'm going from wing to wing, delivering the videos. I bring them around to the lads so they can choose what they want to watch. It's a nice job and means I can't hide away from people. Think that's why they gave me this job.

But today I've the added complication that I've an extra consignment down my pants. A wee parcel that a fella has asked me to mind as he's expecting a cell search. So I agree to mind it for him. *Just hold it for a few hours, Paddy, and I'll make it worth your while.*

I'm distracted by a conversation – something about a film and one of the actors. And then out of nowhere this prick has muscled in on the conversation and starts giving me shit. He thinks I've been slagging him off.

What did you say? Were you calling me names, Armstrong?

No.

Yeah, you fucking was. You was slagging my colour. Fucking racist.

I don't care what fucking colour you are and anyone here'll tell you I'm not a fucking racist. You could be green for all I care.

I know what I heard. I'll fucking kill you, you IRA cunt.

Aye, fuck off, you cheeky bastard.

I have to walk off or I'll hit him. In hindsight I think that maybe I should have just punched him. Had a good clean fight. Others would have jumped in. Backed me up. And that would have been the end of that. Except I'm carrying that packet down my trousers and there's a lot of shit inside it. If it escalates into a fight and screws get involved, I'll be in serious trouble. The media would love it too. If we have any chance of getting an appeal, this could screw it completely.

But I can't dump the bag and then go and hit him, because it's worth a lot of money and then I'd have to pay it back. Which I definitely can't afford to do. Say nothing, Paddy. Walk away.

Oh, look, the hard IRA man is walking away. All fucking mouth. Fucking IRA is just a bunch of fucking pussies. Kill women and children but you can't even fight.

I know where this is heading and it's not good. Why did he have to bring the IRA into it? He knows I don't even hang about with the IRA boys, except Ronnie. After this he goes around the wing talking, saying he got one over on the IRA. Telling people that the IRA is *a bunch of fucking pussies.* And now they're standing around me, these IRA fellas, giving me hassle.

He's making a fucking wanker out of you, Paddy.

Out of all of us.

I nod.

You have to do him, Paddy. Before he does you.

Sometimes I wish he would, I'm thinking.

He's a cheeky bastard. A fucking bully.

What's new? I've had to deal with ones like him all my life. I'm used to it, I want to say. I nod again. *Yes, I know.*

Just do what we tell you and you'll have no more problems.

I know this is true, but I really don't want to do it. What if I lose it? I could fucking kill him and then I'll never get out. But I don't think I can do it. *I'll think about it,* I tell them.

Fuck's sake, Paddy. There's nothing to think about. Just do it.

Aye, right, right. I've finally spoken.

I owe the IRA nothing. I'm doing time because of their bombs and because of Surrey Police. But the IRA are my only allies inside prison a t this stage. Ronnie's keeping me sane in here. If I didn't have Ronnie here, I'd have nobody. And if I'm on my own, I'll do myself in – if one of those cockney bastards doesn't do me first. I'm fearing it more and more every day now, with this fella always sniffing around me. If I don't act soon, I could be in real danger. I just wish I didn't have to. I hate confrontation. Maybe I can avoid it, I'm hoping …

And now, a day later, I'm on the wing and I go into the TV room to deliver a video and there he is in front of me. Watching some documentary. He hasn't seen me. One of the fellas nudges me. A quick nod of the head. *Go on,* it says. *Do it.* And I know it's now or never.

Before I know it, there's a six-gallon bucket in my hands.

Fill it right up, Paddy. Aye, that's it. Now throw all that there sugar in it.

Really?

Oh, aye, it's no good without that. Needs to stick to the bastard. He'll never forget it. Aye, all of it – there's a good ten pounds in there. And don't forget to mix it up. Here, give us one of them there spoons and I'll do it – see? That'll scorch him lovely. He won't know what's hit him, the cheeky ignorant bastard.

The first time I try to lift the bucket, I have to drop it immediately. My hands are shaking too much to do it. Focus, Paddy. Calm. Focus on the weight of the battery in your pocket. I pat the thin pocket of my prison-issue trousers – cheap, stiff and scratchy, the Cat A yellow stripe down the side. The pocket is heavy, and when I glance down I can see the hard edges of the battery.

Gripping the sides of the bucket again, I walk as quickly and casually as I can down the short corridor between the kitchen and the television room. At any moment I'm waiting to be caught. Stall for a moment, almost willing a screw to come around the corner and stop me. Nothing.

Fuck's sake, Paddy, just fucking do it. No-one will ever respect you if you don't stand up for yourself. And he'll kill you one day.

Feel sick to my core. Imagine Carole could see me now. Or Mammy. I'm a peace-loving hippie, for Christ's sake. How have I ended up in this situation?

They're all standing back, to let me go by, and there he is. Still sitting there watching the TV. Completely oblivious. A few men glance over and move back slightly to lean against the wall. Another couple have slipped out the door to keep watch in case a screw comes. One is nodding at me, willing me on, but I can't look him in the eye. I'll do it because I have to, but I can't pretend I'm enjoying this.

As I'm charging towards him, I can feel myself almost step outside my own body. It's like I'm looking down at myself, in slow motion, not actually doing it myself. See the flick of my wrists and slight forward movement of my body. See the water leaving the bucket and it's almost graceful as it sails silently through the air before the splash. It takes a few seconds before I register the high-pitched scream as the boiling, sugar-filled water courses down his head and the back of his neck. He leaps into the air, writhing about and flailing his arms. The syrupy mixture is clinging to him, burning. It must hurt like hell.

As the TV drones on in the background, this big, tough man screams in the most helpless, almost childlike way. I want to grab him. To stop this. But the other men are looking. Men who never believed I had it in me to stand up for myself. I need to see this through.

The door is so close. I could run out now, but they warned me about this. *Make sure he's on the ground, Paddy – if you don't, he'll fucking kill you. Get him down fast.*

They're still looking at me. Steel eyes. *You're not finished yet, Paddy. He's still standing.* I summon up Dirty Harry's face. At will for the first time. It's the only way to feel what I need to feel – otherwise I'd grab this man and hold him and start apologising. So I turn to Dirty Harry. Him and his friends in Surrey Police crowding over me. *Just fucking sign, Paddy. Sign or you'll pay.* Starving me, pissing in my food, saying they'll throw me from the window, lying in the witness box until I don't even recognise myself any more.

He'll fucking kill you, Paddy, if you don't immbolise him. He's a mad bastard. And then the rest of his mates will queue up to take lumps out of you, cos you'll be a weak bastard.

Now I'm tugging the battery-filled sock from my pocket and lifting it. Without being fully conscious of it, I'm striking him anywhere I can reach. The battery is connecting with his arms, legs, and he's flailing. Backing away from me, nowhere to go and then that it's. He's falling. Down. Down. The other men are standing back, watching this large man drop like a sack of potatoes and curl into a ball, wailing and clutching his skin. I'm focusing on the low drone of the TV to block out his screams.

And suddenly it's over. The whole episode has lasted only a couple of minutes and, as quickly as it appeared, my rage has evaporated. It has been replaced with the sharp taste of bile in my mouth.

It's like my conscience has re-entered my body. He's still screaming, tearing at his skin, and I can't bear it. It's the most sickening feeling I have ever experienced. I know I have to move quickly before I show my terror. I'm running out the door and they're slapping me on the back. Others are nodding. *Good man, Paddy – you did what you had to do! Nobody will fuck with you now.* I ignore them, keep going. Straight up to the governor's office, Paddy. Get away from all this. Get to solitary. Just keep moving. Get to the Block. Then you can cry and throw your guts up and beat yourself up with your guilt and fear for hours.

I'm brought in front of the governor. I've known this man for years and I can barely look at him. He doesn't say anything. Sending me to solitary for a month. He could give me a year, for all I care. I don't want the nods of congratulations, the winks, the pretend-shocked looks, the pats on the arm from the other men. I feel like a fucking animal. Worse than I did a week ago, though I wouldn't have believed it possible. A monster.

As luck would have it, after a few weeks of solitary, Mammy decides to come over. If I'd known, I could have tried to stop her. But I didn't and so she's here and there's no time to think of excuses. *Some screw was being a prick. Wouldn't give me my tobacco, Mammy. Fucking bastards.* Anything but what happened. Couldn't deal with the horror in her eyes if she knew the truth.

Suddenly they're at the door. *Visitor, Armstrong.* I'm so out of it I just follow them. Don't ask who. On the way from solitary to the visiting room, where three screws will watch and listen to me and my mammy talking, they take me on a detour. Past the door of the hospital wing. It's open. I glance in, as they know I will, and there he is. I can only see his face, neck and arms, but that's enough. The burns are still raw – like crude patches of pink paint on a glossy, black surface. His skin is destroyed. He sees me looking in and our eyes meet. He looks at me with such hatred. And fear. The hatred doesn't surprise me, but the fear does; that's something new. And although I've been in the horrors the last few weeks, reliving those few minutes again and again, only at that moment when our eyes meet do I realise that I've underestimated the significance of what I've done. I've made a man afraid. I'm appalled by it. Disgusted. Before I can think about it, they're pushing me onwards. *Come on, visiting room.* I'll be able to avoid reflecting on it today, but the image will visit me again and again. Sliding into my mind's eye in the quiet of the night when the only sounds are the creak of the pipes and the occasional whimpers from another cell. Jagged, fleshy stains on the otherwise perfect skin of another human being. Caused by me.

When I walk to the Category A visitor room, guards stand back slightly as Mammy folds me into her arms. I'm trying not to shake. If she notices the shivering or how pale I am or how my unused voice is cracking and breaking, she doesn't say anything. We do our gentle dance, talking about nothing, asking no questions. She tells me about the people who are talking about us. *Heard they're trying to get your Paddy out*, they say to her. People who have avoided her for years. *Heard there's a book out about them? Sure isn't that great, Eileen? We all knew they didn't do it. Sure how could they? Sure Jesus, Eileen, doesn't everyone know that your Paddy wouldn't hurt a fly? Anything we do can do, just let us know.*

Generally, though, Mammy and Eileen ask me very little. They never ask why I need them to buy me a pair of expensive runners that are a couple of sizes too big for me. They're not stupid and they know that if I've been desperate enough to ask there's probably a good reason. It's not really a good reason. It's a valid reason, but not a good one. A gambling debt I have to repay. These days I'm better than I was, keeping the bets small – only what I can afford. But I'm great at picking winners, everyone tells me. So when I tell them that there's a sure thing but that I'll only reveal it if they lend me a bit, I can usually get away with it. Except when I lose.

They take me back to solitary after Mammy's visit, and the grey walls close in on me. I can't take much more of this. I only realise that I'm banging on the doors when I see the blood on my hands. Leave me alone leave me alone leave me fucking alone alone alone alone.

When I'll finally talk about it, many years later, I'll reason that it was simply inevitable. How could someone live through what I had and not be damaged by it? And then I went and damaged someone else. It's the circle of prison life a lot of the time. I hate it, I regret it, I'm ashamed of it. This man didn't deserve this. He was in the wrong place at the wrong time. He wound me up, of course, but if it hadn't been him it would have been somebody else. That's what prison does to you. Changes you, even momentarily. That moment of insanity was part of where I was and what it was doing to me.

~

The nightmares haven't stopped. The scalded face hasn't disappeared, but apparently I've done my time in solitary. *Back to your cell, Armstrong.* I'd be as happy to stay here. Wither away and die. No garden party. Nothing. When I go back on the wing, Gerry Conlon's there. I haven't seen him since our appeal was turned down 11 years ago, and now here is, standing in front of me. He looks all right, but he doesn't recognise me. *Gerry, it's me. Paddy.* He looks at me in shock before hugging me. *Of course, Paddy! How are ya?* Years later he'll write about that day in his book and describe me as 'gaunt and having the sick prison pallor that some men get'. I've only been off the garden party for about six months but already that's how I look. And while we both know that I look like I'm haunted, drowning, neither of us says it. Instead we hug and cling to each other for a moment. Are you drowning too, my friend? I want to say. Do you want to give up and just let them win? Do you? Or is it just me? But out loud, *I'm good, Gerry. I'm great. Happy to see you.*

Within days I'll see how strong Gerry is now. There's something subtly different about him. He's still a hooligan and great craic but he seems stronger, less beaten down. Definitely coping better than me. A bit more grown-up. It's the first time I've seen him since he lost his dad.

It's been eight years since then, but there's tears in his eyes when he describes the day Giuseppe died. *Promised my da I'll clear my name. And then I'll clear his.* I'm nodding, even though I want to tell him to save his energy, because those bastards will never let us go. *You will, Gerry, you'll clear his name.*

He nods. Tells me about his father's treatment in prison. How he was kept on the second floor, even though he was too weak to come down to the ground floor, where the food was served. It was only when Alastair, who also represented him, got an independent doctor to assess him that they moved him to Wormwood Scrubs, adjacent to the hospital. Alastair also got Cardinal Basil Hume to come see him – to try to get him released. The government did finally listen, but it was all too late. The day after Giuseppe died his wife, Sarah, received a letter from the Home Office saying that he had been granted release into her custody. Too little, too late.

And Gerry tells me about British Airways, the only company that flies
to Belfast, refusing to take his innocent father's body home. Fortunately,
Alastair paid for some of the fees for Giuseppe's body to be transported in
England. Then Aer Lingus stepped in and agreed to fly him to Dublin and
then get him to Belfast by road, but the coffin went missing for a few days,
winding up in Hereford, only to finally arrive home with a massive bill of
almost a thousand pounds, which Sarah had to pay before her husband's
body was released for the funeral. *Which I wasn't allowed to attend, Paddy*,
he says. The hurt and resentment in his voice is painful. *My own father's
funeral, Paddy.*

He looks at me. *I'm fighting this. Writing letters. I've even written to
Gorbachev.* I nod. *That's great, Gerry. Letters are good. Yeah, I'll write too.* But
we both know I won't. Having him here is nice, though. He and Paddy Hill
know each other and, even though we all carry our crosses differently, we
each know exactly what the other is going through. A shared pain.

After talking about the campaign in the first few weeks, now we avoid
the subject. It depresses us both and you can't live that way, so we talk
about everything else. Like me, Gerry's mad about his football. Except he's
a United fan and I'm still a committed Arsenal fan, so we give each other a
hard time. Slag each other in the way that only two people who've known
each other since childhood can, in the way that only two people who
understand where the other grew up and what they've been through can. It's
very easy to be around him.

Paddy Hill's in everyone's face, always in trouble, always down in solitary.
Ever since he and the other lads accused of the Birmingham bombings had
their appeal turned down, he's been even angrier. Once again we're all in the
same boat, with no idea where it's going or how to get off the bloody thing
before it sinks and takes us all to the bottom of the sea. Would that be so
bad? I can't help wondering lately.

Despite the anger, the loss and the heartbreak that are never far from
the surface, Gerry, Paddy Hill and I spend many nights in one of our
cells, smoking, laughing, talking about Belfast in the 1950s and 1960s and
comparing stories about the crazy and stupid things we've done in prisons,

and our exploits in London and Paddy Hill's in Birmingham. Paddy Hill tells a great story and always puts me in a good mood.

Just when we're managing not to think about or talk about our case, one day, a warm Saturday in June 1988, the TV tells us about a star-studded concert – the likes of Dire Straits, Phil Collins and Sting will be singing for the release of prisoners. It's about a South African man, Nelson Mandela. I've heard a little bit about him and obviously I wish him well, but what about us?

And now a group of us are sitting watching this concert in the TV room. Bryan Adams and Stevie Wonder have flown in to sing in honour of this man. Even though it feels mean-spirited to begrudge a 70-year-old South African man – someone who is clearly an incredibly important man, who has fought for the rights of his people, who has been in prison for 26 years – even so, I'm really fucking angry. Not with him, but with the people who won't fucking do anything for us. Angry that even though we are just a few short hours away from Wembley, not just on the same continent but in the same country, the four of us, the Maguire Seven and the Birmingham Six have been in prison for 14 years, and who knows how long more? We are innocent, and we have had everything stolen from us. Even Margaret Thatcher comes out and says she won't do business with South Africa until Mandela is released. And yet she's keeping innocent men and women prisoner in her own country. But she's not interested in talking about that.

As these important people demand the release of all South African political prisoners and hear the world roar back its support, Gerry and I look at each other silently.

What about us? I want to scream. We're innocent. Our only crime was being Irish. Being Catholics with Belfast accents. Don't we matter too? Aren't our lives valuable? How long will it take before the small, individual voices of the people supporting us will be heard? People like Sister Sarah Clarke, the Irish nun who is campaigning fiercely along with our families, my ever faithful solicitor Alastair, who continues to work for free, and the two English journalists, Ros Franey and Grant McKee, who made the documentaries about us.

I'm only now beginning to understand how much some people have been doing for us, and yet, even still, the world doesn't want to know about us. It must be easier to be outraged about injustices in other countries than to look at your own doorstep.

I'm scared sometimes now. Will anyone ever listen? By the time they do, it may be too late.

One day Gerry comes in laughing, telling me he has a funny story. A song has been written about us and the Birmingham Six. It's by The Pogues, whose lead singer, Shane MacGowan, has been a legend in the Irish music scene since he released 'Fairytale of New York'. And now he's written a song about us. It may not be Wembley, but at least someone gives a fuck enough to write a song about us. And the British government care enough to ban it. I won't hear the lyrics until much later, and eventually I'll get to meet Shane and thank him for his words. Shane's sister, Siobhan, has been campaigning for us too. He'll never know how much his words mean to us at a time when we wonder if anyone even remembers we're here.

But they're still doing time
For being Irish in the wrong place
And at the wrong time ...

The Wolfe Tones write a song for us too, pleading for our release:

Release them now and let them go
And justice will be done

This is keeping me going. It helps lift me out of the fog for a few moments. Keeps me alive.

Finally, things are moving. We hear that more people are joining the campaign for our release. Ros Franey has made some really influential people listen. Since 1986 she has been speaking to Lord Devlin, a Law Lord, about the detail of our case. And even though she isn't a legal expert herself, Ros has made one of the country's most experienced legal experts realise that it was wrong for the Court of Appeal to consider bits of evidence here and there by putting themselves in the place of a jury. Realise that we deserve a proper appeal.

Now Lord Devlin and Lord Scarman are taking note. Cardinal Hume makes a deputation, asking for the case to go back to the Court of Appeal, but Home Secretary Douglas Hurd refuses to listen to it. In response, Lords Devlin and Scarman write a piece that is published in *The Times*. It outlines the sequence of events from our trial to our appeal and up to the current day. The crux of their argument is that the Court of Appeal 'tried' the new evidence from the Balcombe Street men when it had no entitlement in law to try facts. It should have sent the case back for retrial by a jury. The impact of their opinion piece is huge, finally persuading Hurd to stand up to Thatcher. This is momentous, although, as ever, the wheels of justice turn slowly.

Since their documentaries and book about us, Ros Franey and Grant McKee have come to see Gerry and me a few times. They've also been to see Carole, so they bring us news about her. Carole rarely writes, but it's easier that way. Since her last visit a few years ago we've had an unspoken agreement that we can't torment ourselves and each other. But I love hearing anything about her and hold onto tiny bits of information to digest in the wee hours, when all is silent.

I write a rare letter to Ros, to thank her for the books and tapes and postcards she's been sending me. This warm, educated woman who barely knows me believes in me and has dedicated her life to getting us released. I barely know the words to write to her and I'm terrified I'll seem uneducated and uninteresting to someone like her. But Gerry's been writing to her a lot and I don't want her to think I'm ungrateful. So I put pen to paper a couple of times and pray that she won't think badly of my letters.

Number 462183
Name Armstrong
HM Prison Gartree
Market Harborough
Leics LE16 7RP

20/10/88

Dear Ros,

Just a few lines to let you know that I am keeping alright, and also that I got the book. It is very good, better than the first one. It is more easier to read and understand than Robert's was. I enjoy it very much …

I think you already know about them. Gerry also said that it was great. He is keeping alright. I still have not heard from Carole yet. I am hoping she is keeping alright. Still no news from Hurd yet? I suppose that it will be after Christmas before we hear anything, knowing him. They just keep dragging it out. I will be glad to know where we stand when he does say something.

How are you keeping, alright I hope. I got your postcard. Tell Grant that I was asking about him. I also got the tape you sent. Thank you very much for everything that you and Grant have done and are doing for us.

We will get there in the end, because they can't keep hiding the facts that we are innocent. I hope that you and Grant can get to visit me again sometime.

I will close for now, sorry about the letter being so short. Hope to hear from you soon.

All the best. God Bless.

Paddy

I want to tell Ros how she and Grant remind me how much English people care about us. People like them, Robert Kee, Chris Mullin and, of course, Alastair. Infinitely more than the Irish Government, which has done almost nothing to help us.

Thankfully, we have the support of some Belfast politicians, like Gerry Fitt, who has been one of our greatest advocates along with Cardinal Hume and Sister Sarah Clarke. In reality, though, there's a very small group campaigning for us. We need as many voices as we can get on our side. It's all going too slowly.

In January 1989 Douglas Hurd refers our case back to the Court of Appeal. Finally. The hearing is still a year away, so I try not to think about it. It will all be a shambles anyway – the usual pretence of a fair trial. We know this from our last appeal and from the failed Birmingham Six appeal. Gerry's more excited than me and at times I feel like he knows more than he's letting on. I don't know yet that his solicitor, Gareth Peirce, has found some key witnesses, including one whom the police interviewed years before and hid. Gareth found this witness's statement in a file with a wee note attached to it: *Not to be shown to the defence.* Yet another thing to add to the evidence mounting up against the Crown.

Meantime, Avon and Somerset Constabulary have been going through the new evidence. We don't know if it will amount to anything, but most likely they'll just try to cover up the mistakes of the last crowd. I expect nothing. No chance of disappointment that way.

And then one day I'm in the workshop when a screw calls me. *Come on, Armstrong. Get your things. You've to go to London.* I ask why, but he's being cagey. *Your appeal. I don't know much about it.* There's something wrong, I know it. Our appeal's not for months. I try to ask him more questions, but he just keeps telling me to pack my things. I want to cry. Carole is supposed to visit me in the next few days, and now this. I've only seen her once in the last few years, but since the campaign to have our case reopened has started to gain momentum she's more hopeful.

I don't want to go with the screw. I can't take a new prison. With no Ronnie or Gerry or Paddy Hill or any of the boys who look out for me. And no decent screws who know or care that I'm innocent, like Mick Haynes or the governor. I'm not sure I can take another place. I'm pretty sure I can't. I wouldn't survive it.

I go into reception and Gerry is standing there looking as scared as me. They offer us a cigarette, which makes me more suspicious. Within minutes we're in the armoured van and I watch Gartree disappear into the distance. I have no idea what's going on.

The van leaves the motorway and sure enough we're going into London. Apart from a brief visit there, I haven't been near the place since the appeal.

Twelve long years ago. The cars fly by us. Far more than I've ever seen before. So many new makes and models. It's unbelievable.

The van is moving through London now. Gerry's shouting. *Hey, Paddy, look - we're in Kilburn!* I'm pressed up against the window, the screw handcuffed to me, and now Gerry and me are shouting at each other. *Look, it's the betting shops we used to go, pubs, streets. There's Kilburn High Road and, look, there's the Memphis Belle. Only it's got a new name – it's the Bridge Tavern.*

It's all the same and yet so very different. It's a bit much to take in. The world didn't stand still during the 14 years we've been locked up. Who knows what it will look like by the time we get out in 20 years – after they reject our appeal again.

When the van crosses the Thames we realise that it's not Wormwood Scrubs we're headed for – it has to be Brixton or Wandsworth. Most likely Wandsworth. My hands are shaking again, in a way they haven't done in years. Not this badly. Oh, please, no. I can't take that place again. Gerry's trying to reassure me. *No, Paddy, it can't be there. It's not a remand prison. There's no facilities for solicitors there if it's about our appeal.* I can't stop shaking. *Jesus, Gerry, they don't care about that stuff. Nobody cares if we can see our solicitors or not.*

But I'm wrong and Gerry's right, thank God. We pull up to HMP Brixton and I realise that I've been holding my breath since London Bridge. Within minutes the two of us find ourselves dumped in reception with no screws around us. When one arrives, he smiles. Gerry and I look at each other, alarmed. Does he know who we are? It's just him. The other screws have disappeared. It feels weird to be in a room without a group of them around us. The screw tells us he can get us something to eat and now we're really nervous. When have they ever cared about us being hungry? Then he takes us to a cell. Together. In 15 years I've never shared a cell and now I'm in with a man I'm meant to have bombed all these pubs with. What's going on?

We sit there quietly. In a while the screw comes back and offers us a smoke. We're both inhaling silently, lost in our own thoughts. I don't like it when they take Gerry off out of the cell. Leaving me alone. *To process your belongings*, they say. But I know otherwise. They've left the door of the cell open, but I've no interest in going onto the wing. Someone will jump me. I'm going to wait until Gerry gets back and then we can go out together. Just sit against the wall behind the door, Paddy, and watch. Wait for it to open. If they're going to come in, they won't surprise you.

I'm looking at my hands and noticing how much they're shaking when I overhear two other prisoners talking outside on the wing.

Did you hear? They're letting the Guildford Four out.

Yeah, I did. Innocent, innit?

I'm on my feet before I know it, tearing open the door. *What's that you said?*

You wot?

What did you just say? About the Guildford Four getting out? I'm one of them. What are you talking about?

Wow, well done, man. You're getting out.

We're not. I've heard nothing.

Well, it was on the lunchtime news, mate, so they must know. You're going to be released.

I run outside, looking for Gerry, and then I hear his voice from a cell. He's with Freddie Foreman, a fella we met on remand in Brixton before. The radio is on and the four o'clock news has just started. I'm standing in the doorway. Can't move.

In a surprise move this morning the Director of Public Prosecutions has announced that the Guildford Four are to be released on Thursday.

I feel dizzy and lean on the wall.

At an emergency session of the Court of Appeal, set for Thursday morning, the court will be told that the Crown will no longer sustain the convictions of the Four, who were convicted in 1975 of terrorist offences …

I don't remember moving, but I must have because I'm falling into
Gerry's arms, or maybe he's falling into mine. We're crying, shaking, and I
don't know who's holding who up.

We've two days to put in until Thursday. Not 20 years. Two more days in
prison. That's all.

~

And now it's our last day in prison. After the initial elation, I'm petrified.
Gerry and I talk for hours. We're both restless. His family have come to see
him with his solicitor, and Alastair has come to see me. He's not sure yet
where my family are, but he's hoping they'll be able to come.

Paul Hill was brought here today, so now it's the three of us. Everyone
except Carole. I wonder what she's thinking. How she's feeling. If someone
is with her. For this interminable night I'm lying on my prison bed, for the
last time maybe. Gerry's asleep beside me, but my head is racing as I stare at
the filthy ceiling from my filthy mattress. Thinking about what I saw from
the window of the van on the way here. A different world. A place that I
don't understand and that won't understand me. How will we adjust? What
will I do? Where will I go?

I want to go back to Gartree. That's it, I'm not going outside. I want to go
back to Ronnie and the boys. To the garden party. To screws who give a shit.
Just another couple of years. I'll go when I'm ready. When Ronnie gets out.
When I've had time to adjust. I'm not ready.

And then I think of Carole again. Will she be there in the Old Bailey
tomorrow? Are we all getting out? Jesus, I realise, if this is true, we'll both
be out. I can hug her, kiss her, hold her. Maybe it isn't too late for us. Jesus
Christ! I don't care about Gartree – I'm getting out of here if it kills me.

~

On our final day as inmates in HMP Brixton they strip-search us. Twice.
Handcuff us to screws. Surround us with officers. Feed us the usual

lukewarm lumps of food. And then hand us back our 15-year-old clothes. Gerry's sister has brought him new ones. I only have my flares and platform shoes and I put them on. Paul and Gerry take the piss out of me. Tell me I look like Elton John. Gerry gives me a pair of his shoes and I put them on with the flares. I don't care.

They take us in the van to the Old Bailey. There's security helicopters overhead but it's different this time. We'll be leaving it again soon and not in a prison van. When I see Carole, she's a different girl from the one who visited me in Gartree a few months earlier. Her eyes are alive. She hugs me tight. She hugs us all. Even Paul. And somehow the bad feeling is gone. This nightmare is nearly over.

Walking up to the dock, we hear them before we see them. The crowd. Up in the gallery. The excitement is like nothing I've ever seen before. So completely different from the last time we were here. And there they are. Mammy and Josephine and Eileen and Harriet. We're holding carnations and I'm looking at them. And I just want to get up to them. To hold my wee sister.

It lasts for about an hour. The counsel for the Crown, Roy Amlot QC, talks about our confessions, and mine in particular, and that of Paul Hill. On and on. Carole keeps nudging me. Why are they taking so long to read out the verdict? They're reading out this new evidence. I'm trying to catch it all, but there's so much to take in. They talk about how our interrogations were not recorded contemporaneously as the police had always sworn. How various drafts of statements and notes have been found, proving that the confessions were concocted. A complete fabrication. Amlot finishes by saying that the verdicts are unsafe and that the Crown no longer wishes to seek to sustain them. I don't quite know what it means, but I think it means the original verdict doesn't hold up. It's only after our QCs speak that Lord Lane, the Lord Chief Justice, utters the word I do understand: *Quashed.*

As the judges sit there, stony-faced, knowing this is a very bad day for the British justice system, there's an immediate eruption in the court – cheering, shouting, crying, hugging and flowers being thrown up into the air. This is unusual in a court, Chris Mullin tells me later. We all jump up too, Gerry, myself and Paul, while Carole almost collapses into my arms, sobbing like she's in pain. I'm holding her and for that I'm grateful, because if I wasn't I think I'd be on the ground. Within minutes they're ushering us downstairs, back to the cells. Gerry's going crazy. He's marching ahead. *I'm going out the front*, he's shouting. *Let me out the front. The way I came in.* The screws are trying to stop him, but they can't.

Paul is being held. He is still a convicted prisoner because of the murder charge related to Brian Shaw. I'll later hear that he was transferred back home to a Belfast prison, where he'll remain until his appeal against that conviction is heard and he's cleared. I'm looking at Carole and at Gerry's back. He's already far ahead, demanding to be let out the front. I look back at Carole. *Come on, let's go with Gerry.* She says, *No, Paddy, I want to go out the back.* I can see that she really doesn't want to have to deal with the crowds that will inevitably be out the front. The press, who have treated us so badly. And I don't blame her. But I would love to go out the front. Out to my family. Don't leave her, Paddy – go with her. Take her arm. She came in here because she knew you. Don't let her walk out the back alone. I'll do what I have to do today. *Come on, Carole. Let's go out the back.*

When Gerry has long since gone, Alastair brings a car around the back and tells me to get into it. Carole's taken into another. We pull out and into a maelstrom outside the Old Bailey. I have no idea what is in store for us. No idea how we will get through this. But whether we like it or not, we are about to start our lives again.

CHAPTER EIGHT

I'm navigating my way down freedom's road …
(John Mellencamp)

T he weak autumn sun has made its way in through a tiny gap where
the curtains don't quite meet. I squeeze my eyes shut and turn away,
pulling the covers tighter around me. Then I open my eyes, just for a
moment. I don't see a grey wall. I see an immaculately white wall. My eyes
shoot open, and I remember …

~

We're tearing through the streets of London. Alastair's driving and there's
another man in the car with us. Alastair introduces him to me. *This is a
friend of Jim MacKeith.* I nod. *Nice to meet you.* I can't remember who Jim
MacKeith is. I barely know my own name at the moment. I'm going to stay
with this man, MacKeith's friend, for a couple of days, they explain. Until
the press have gone. They won't give up easily.

It all sounds a bit far-fetched at first – until it starts. Instead of my
usual entourage of armed guards, policemen with handcuffs, armoured
trucks and sirens, there's high-powered motorbikes and revving cars
following us, taking every corner at breakneck speed so they don't lose us.
There's cameras flashing whenever they get close enough to the dark glass
concealing me from the world and people stopping on the street to stare.

This isn't really how I imagined freedom.

Alastair's driving us around and around. *We need to get rid of them,* he's
saying. I nod like I do this kind of thing every day. *We'll just keep driving*

around for a while and hopefully we'll have lost the few on our tail by the time
we get there.

I'm trying to focus on what they're telling me, but it's hard not to be
distracted by the world outside. It's the first time I've seen everything so
clearly. In such sharp focus. Normally it's from the barred window of a
speeding van, mostly along motorways, my hand firmly cuffed to the wrist
of a screw. Now there's just thin glass between me and the people walking
along the streets of central London. People in suits, women with children,
all stopping, wondering who's in the car. They probably think I'm someone
famous. A rock star maybe. Apparently we're famous now. Hopefully for the
right reasons this time. No more signs, please. *Hang the IRA.*

Focus, Paddy. Alastair is speaking. *On the next bend we're going to*
slow down. And then you're both going to jump out as I slow down. Do you
understand? You'll jump out and I'll keep driving so they don't realise you're
gone and they'll keep following me.

He seems to be saying that we're both going to jump from the car. Me
and this man. While it's moving. Is he joking? *I'll slow down and you'll have*
enough time to jump and then you'll run from the car and in through the door
of a flat. The door will be open – someone will be waiting for you both. He's
serious. I'm not even free an hour and they're going to kill me. I nod. *No*
problem. Like I do this every day too. He's looking at me through the rear-
view mirror. *It's okay. You'll be safe.* It's like he can read my mind. Nod. I
have to trust him. *We're nearly there now. So you're going to run. Can you do*
that? Nod again. *Yes, I think I can. If they realise you're out and they see where*
you go, you'll be hounded night and day. It'll be over in seconds and they'll be
gone. I'll see you later.

Wait. I've just realised that Alastair isn't coming with me. He's going to
distract the media and I'll be in this flat with the other man. What will I do?
What will I say to him?

And now the car is slowing down, just as he said. *Go now, Paddy – quick*
– jump out before I speed up again. Take care. We literally dive from the car
and it keeps going without us, the motorbike chasing it. We're like two
stuntmen in one of those films. It's the first time in 15 years that I've been

on the outside. A free man. I could go anywhere I like, do anything. I'm in the middle of a residential street in the centre of London, on a Thursday afternoon. But all I have is the few pounds from my last wage packet and the bus ticket they gave me when they released me. What's supposed to happen now? What did they say? And then I see the open door and my fellow-stuntman is pushing me towards it. Before I know it, I'm in a kitchen with a complete stranger. .

This way, Paddy. He closes the door. *Delighted to have you here. Are you okay?* I don't know what to say. *Yes. Great, thanks.* Smile. He's a friend of Dr Jim MacKeith, he tells me again. I'm obviously meant to know who that is, but I can't remember. I nod in what I think is a knowing way. *Jim is a consultant forensic psychiatrist who works with people like yourself ...* he trails off. There's a woman hovering about too. They're both smiling and I feel sorry for them. I can tell they're terrified about saying the wrong thing. *Your family will be over in a while,* he adds. *The press will be following them too, so they'll have to wait until they're gone before they can come here.*

I sit down in his kitchen. It's really clean and bright. I feel dirty by comparison in my 15-year-old flares and ill-fitting, borrowed shoes. *Tea, coffee? Or maybe a beer?* I nod. Beer. He opens an enormous fridge, the likes of which I've never seen in a house, and takes out a bottle. A real beer. When he opens it, the bubbles rush to the surface. My first in 15 years. I take a gulp and almost splutter in shock. It's cold and really strong and full of gas. I'd forgotten. He smiles. I don't want to continue, but I'm hoping it might take the edge off things. Take it easy, Paddy. No rush. I must be closing my eyes, because when he speaks I'm surprised. I'd forgotten he was there.

He's told me their names several times now – he can obviously see that I'm not taking it in. He's a director – makes TV ads. *Of course. That's brilliant. I never thought about who made them.* Two days ago I was in Gartree, in the workshop, thinking about how I could get the money together to buy some tobacco and maybe some hash and now I'm here, in a stranger's kitchen, talking about TV ads. Shake my head and then realise they're looking at me. Wonder where Ronnie is. Wonder where they've taken Carole and Gerry.

The woman shows me to the bathroom. When I catch a glimpse of myself in the cleanest mirror I've seen in years, I stand there for the longest time. Maybe five minutes, maybe an hour, rubbing my jaw and wondering who this old man is. I splash water on my face and then finger the skin on my cheek and then wash it again furiously, trying to bring some life to my ashen skin and ringed, tired eyes.

When I come out the TV is on. The evening news comes on and I find myself looking at my younger self. The photo they took of me in the police station all those years ago in Guildford. Guildford … There's footage of us leaving the courthouse in cars. Me just a few hours ago. And then Gerry's standing outside the Old Bailey, his arms around his sisters, talking to a crowd of people, and builders hanging out of a site just behind them. *I've been in prison 15 years for something I didn't do – for something I didn't know anything about. A totally innocent man. I watched my father die in a British prison for something he didn't do. He is innocent. The Maguires is innocent. Let's hope the Birmingham Six is next to be freed …*

The crowd are shouting and the builders are banging their helmets. I feel slightly removed from it. Like this isn't my life he's describing. I'll watch it many more times before I can really process it. And then I'll realise he did us proud. And I know Giuseppe will be up there, watching. I'd like to have been there. Wish I could have said something. Or do I? Could I have done it? What would I have said? I don't have Gerry's eloquence or his fire, but maybe I could have said something to thank Alastair, Ros and Grant and everyone who helped us. And mention my mammy and my sisters. I'll wonder about this over the years, but deep down I know I did the right thing. I wouldn't change it if I could do it again – I'd still walk out the back door with Carole.

There are a lot of noises outside. The slightest sound makes me start. Cars, trucks, voices, music. *Centre of London,* the TV ad man tells me, *it's like that day and night. Don't worry, you're safe. Nobody will find you here.* I'm hoping he means the press and not the police. I can deal with anything except being rearrested. I don't ask, in case I don't like the answer.

I glance at the clock again. If I were in Gartree, I'd be in the workshop. Don't know what to be doing with myself so I light cigarettes and smoke them one after the other. Have another beer. May as well, since I might wake up in a cell any moment to the distant sounds of people shouting outside on the wing. And if that did happen, would it be so bad? Now that I've seen the outside world, I'm confused. Most prisoners get a chance to prepare for getting out. How to cope in the outside – shopping and money and getting work and paying bills. Not us. *Here's your clothes, a bus ticket. Off you go now – get on with your life.* I feel like I've been dropped in a foreign country and can't speak the language.

I'm sitting here, in this strange flat, one eye always on the door. And then there are voices nearby. High-pitched sounds, getting closer. There's a rapping on the door and I jump up automatically. Which way can I run? Suddenly there they are in front of me. Mammy. Eileen. Eileen's children. Jim, her husband. And Josephine. I'm trying to hug them all without getting too emotional. Keep it together, Paddy.

I look at Josephine properly and pull her onto my knee. My wee sister. I keep looking at her. Finally I speak. *Why did you never come to visit me? Why didn't you come for all those years?* She can't look at me. I can just about make out her voice through her tears. *I'm sorry, I'm sorry.* Keep hugging her. Don't want to let her go. She's wriggling. Tells me later how strange it was. With Daddy and me gone, she's not used to people hugging her. She looks so big, my wee sister. Feel like my heart is going to break out of my chest.

But something's not right. She isn't the girl I remember with young skin and an innocence in her eyes. She must be in her twenties now. *No, Paddy, you've been in 15 years. I turned 30 in August, two months ago.* One day she was 16 and now my wee sister is a 30-year-old woman and I just can't take it in. I want to howl now that I see it for myself – they stole my baby sister and replaced her with this woman. I'll get to know her all over again, but I'll never get back the years we lost in between. Never saw her grow up. Can't think of that now. Stop, Paddy. Don't be upsetting everyone. Just look happy. They need you to be strong now.

Our Eileen is talking now. Her children, now 15 and 13, look a bit bewildered. What do you say to this strange man you've never met? I'm smiling at them, saying God knows what. *Lovely to meet you at last* – what do you say to nephews you don't know? I've only ever met them in the visiting room with a screw watching us. Now here we all are outside, and it's mind-blowing.

Sitting around, we either all talk at once or there's silence. I ask Mammy how she heard the news. Did she get a letter or a phone call from someone in London? Alastair, perhaps? I'll find out later that Alastair was only told just hours before we were released, leaving him very little time to arrange everything. And he had no way of letting Mammy know because she doesn't have a phone. While he tried to figure out how to contact her, she ended up hearing the news on the Belfast grapevine.

It all comes out in a rush. Mammy and Josephine are out on Tuesday morning, pension day, until just before lunchtime. Just two days ago. They've just been to the post office to pick up Mammy's pension and then to the local shops. They're just coming home, Mammy pulling her wee trolley with her bits and pieces inside. She takes the lift to the top floor of the Divis flats but Josephine won't get into it – she's claustrophobic. *I'll walk*, she says, even though Mammy already knows this. (She wasn't like this when I went to prison. I wonder what else I don't know about her – what other things have changed. What other collateral damage has there been in my family?)

Mammy gets out of the lift on the top floor and there's a big group waiting on the balcony near our flat. *Your Paddy's coming home*, they shout to her. *He's getting out Thursday, Eileen. It was on the news.* Josephine arrives up the stairs to hear this. She won't believe it and walks into the flat. *He is, Eileen, our Michael heard it and he ran in to tell me. They're letting them all out on Thursday. They're all getting out.*

Mammy won't believe it either. *You're joking*, she says. She'd have been told, surely. *They wouldn't let us find out like that, would they? Go in and put on the one o'clock news, Josephine – it'll be on again.* She runs into the house and turns on the radio, her hand shaking. When the news finally comes on it's like 15 years ago all over again, hearing my fate on the national news. Around the same time as Gerry and I are dancing around our cell in Brixton, Mammy and Josephine are standing there in the kitchen. Josephine's squealing and Mammy is crying. *Paddy's getting out!*

The doorbell rings continually all day long. All evening. And into the next day. Journalists. All the local newspapers. People who condemned or ignored us for all those years we were rotting away in a cell. Mammy will refuse to talk to them. *Go away. We're not talking to you. You never wanted to know anything about them and now they're out you just want to jump on the bandwagon. Away on now.* They all leave with their tails between their legs.

And then a nice wee man from a TV station comes, she tells me, delighted. *From that there programme 'The Time, the Place'. Do you know the one, Paddy?* I don't. *Ach, you do. It's got that man, Mike Scott, on it.* I shake my head. *No, Mammy, we don't get that one over here in Gartree.* She says, *You must surely. Isn't it English, Josephine?* She nods. I say, *Well, we can't watch it, because we have to work here at that time. I go to work every morning here and only get a break for lunchtime. You can't be watching TV here.* I catch myself. I'm not in Gartree now. Gartree is there and I'm here. In London. Free. Jesus, I keep forgetting.

Mammy says, *So the man from TV says that if we go on their show, they'll get us to London. 'We'll fly you over there as soon as possible, Mrs Armstrong. Take you to the airport, pick you up at the other end. Put you and your daughter up in a big hotel for a few days. Whatever you need. We'll look after it all. Take you to the Old Bailey for when they get out. You'll be able to see your son as soon as he's released. We just need to interview you.'*

Mammy agrees. She won't let on to the TV man, but she's delighted – it's the only way they can afford to go at such short notice. With Eileen living in Scotland now, going to London is expensive. The TV company will arrange the plane tickets, hotel, taxis – all the things they wouldn't be able to do in this state. And so a day later she and Josephine are taken to Belfast Airport to be flown to London. The only problem is Josephine's claustrophobia. She's terrified of flying. But she says she's not missing this, so my petrified baby sister agrees to get on that plane.

It's the last flight to London on Wednesday night – the night before our release – and there's only a few people on the plane, Josephine tells me. *And when they saw how scared I was, Paddy, they gave me all these wee bottles of vodka. To calm me down. And the next thing I know they're bringing me into the cockpit and I'm sitting with the pilot, a set of headphones on. It was fantastic, Paddy – I watched him land the plane.* And when she says that, I hear my wee sister again.

When they get into Heathrow there's a boy holding a big sign: *ARMSTRONG.* He has Irish family, Mammy tells me. Everyone in the airport is looking at us, and Mammy looks at Josephine and the crowd and announces in a loud voice, *Well, it's not every day you win the pools,* and the two of them leave the airport laughing. They laugh now as they tell me the story. I'd forgotten how funny my mammy can be. How much she used to make us all laugh. And how long it's been since I saw her at ease, joking and laughing.

We were interviewed in the back of a white stretch limousine driving through London, Josephine tells me proudly. *And in the hotel that night. And reading the papers in the hotel this morning, and on our way to the court.* My mammy and sister in a limousine and hotel!

They tried to go in the front door of the Old Bailey, but they weren't let. Josephine says, *We were sent around to the side entrance, Paddy. Police wouldn't even look at us. Mammy is furious about it.* They met Eileen, who'd come down from Scotland and was going to stay with her friend, Lily. They wouldn't let Eileen's husband or children in. *We tried to get downstairs, but they wouldn't let us – put us all the way up there in the gallery, Paddy.* I nod, remembering. I saw them there. *Police everywhere in that place. They searched us every time we wanted to go to the toilet, Paddy, and then searched us again when we were coming back.* I should be used to this after what Mammy would go through to visit me in prison, but it still infuriates me. Do anything to me, but not to my mother or my sisters.

Every time Mammy moved, a peeler told her to stay still, Josephine tells me indignantly. I'm not at all surprised, but I'm angry on their behalf. Josephine is so busy looking at me and Carole and Gerry and Paul, she doesn't hear the judge say the word. *Quashed.* All she sees is the carnations go up in the air. My sister Eileen is trying to climb over the balcony, to get down to us. It all sounds quite funny as they describe it to me.

And then they're standing outside waiting. For me. Only I've gone. So instead they watch Gerry speaking. *The cameras were in our face,* Josephine giggles. *I pushed one so hard he nearly went in front of a bus. Could have been you getting out of prison and me going in.* They hide inside a café, but the press finds them again and they can't get out until a group of schoolboys shields them from the cameras and they run outside to Alastair's waiting car to go to their hotel. Whenever they want to leave the hotel, the hotel manager sneaks them out the back into a taxi, and even still they're chased across London until they manage to get away.

And now they're here, in front of me, and after an hour I feel weak and shaky. Not used to this. So many questions, so much to take in. Too many people. All looking at me. Expectantly. It's too much. My chest is tightening and I feel like I can't breathe. Alastair looks at me. *Do you need some sleep, Paddy?* I nod. They look at me. *Are you coming with us?* I don't know how to tell them that I need to be alone. Don't want to hurt them. Mammy can see it in my eyes and looks a bit hurt. I don't know what to say – I want to make her happy, proud. And I know she just wants her son back after all these years, but I'm scared what I'll do or say if I can't be alone soon. Feel like I'm about to shut down any moment. Alastair explains that this is very normal. We can meet again in a day or two. He's going to bring me down to his house in Guildford when things settle down, and they can come too. We can all have some time together in his house. We all nod like we know what we're talking about. Like we've done this before.

~

Wondering how long I'll have to wait here. Looking at this wall. Put the bed back up. Make it. Straighten it. Sit down again on the bed. Wonder where exactly I am. Walk around. Watch the door. Just in case. I'm afraid to look out the window in case anyone sees me. Sit down, Paddy. Relax. Someone

will be here soon. Just wait there. They'll tell you what to do next. Bit
hungry now. I know instinctively it's after breakfast time. Should be in the
workshop by now. Bit of banter. Slagging the screws. Wonder what I'll do
today. Wonder what I'll do the rest of my life. The rest of my life.

$$\sim$$

I woke up in Brixton this morning and now I'm going to bed in a bedroom
with curtains, a thick duvet and pillow, clean walls and the gentle light of a
lamp. *Just make yourself comfortable, Paddy. You know where the bathroom is.*
I nod, trying to take it all in.

I sit on the bed and leap back up again. It's really soft. I sit back down
again, really gently this time. As if it might break under me. I climb in and
pull the covers up to my chin. Close my eyes …

It's dark and everything is so quiet. Trying to focus on something, but
there's nothing to lull me to sleep. No sound of talking or shouting or
distant footsteps. No radio or record player. No bright bulb in the corner of
the room. Nothing. Lie on my side. On my back. My front. Throw away the
pillow. Take off some clothes. Still can't get comfortable. I heave the heavy
blanket off me, push it to the end of the bed. Still uncomfortable. And then I
realise. It's too soft. Creep out of bed. Check the door's closed. Don't want to
look crazy. Drag the mattress gently onto the ground. Just on the floor. No
springs under it. Just the mattress. Much better. Think I can sleep this way.

The weak autumn sun has made its way in through a tiny gap where the
curtains don't quite meet. I squeeze my eyes shut and turn away, pulling the
covers tighter around me. Then I open my eyes, just for a moment. I don't
see a grey wall. I see an immaculately white wall. My eyes shoot open, and I
remember …

I sit on the bed for an hour, or maybe two, when there's a knock on the
door. Finally. A head pokes around the corner. It's the ad man's wife. Just
seeing I'm okay. Will I be coming down soon, she's wondering. *There's
breakfast downstairs, Paddy. Just come down when you're ready. Take a shower.
There's a clean towel, shampoo and anything else you need in the bathroom.*

Alastair left some clothes for you. He thinks they should fit. I nod. I'm touched. He's a great man. Always thinking of me. *Thank you very much. Thanks for everything.* Be polite. Don't say nothing stupid. Don't tell them you didn't realise you could open the door. They'll think you're an eejit. *Aye, that's great, thanks. I'll be right out.*

I'll sit for many mornings waiting for the door to be opened. Forgetting. Waiting for someone to give me permission to come out. These habits won't leave me easily, or even willingly.

I stand under the hot jets of the shower, head down, eyes closed. I can't see the tears for the water, but I can taste their saltiness. I'm waiting for a bang at the door, an obscenity that never comes. It's so strange to be alone in a bathroom. When I finally get out, I'm amazed at the towel, its soft fibres like new skin on a baby. Like our Josephine when she was tiny. And I'm going to see her again soon. I put on the clothes Alastair left me. I feel so clean and new.

I come out for breakfast, but I have to go back to my room shortly after. I sit in there, trying to get myself together. One hour, two hours, three hours. My family arrive and coax me out. They stay for a while again and when they leave I go back to my room, close the curtains and get into the bed and stare at the shapes on the ceiling, trying to block out the noise in my head. Just need to sleep. *Alastair will come on Saturday to take you to his house, when he's not being followed.* I nod. *That's great. Thanks very much.* Pull the mattress back onto the floor. Lie there looking at the carpet, the wallpaper. Sleep, Paddy. Just relax and fall asleep, for God's sake. Wish I had my music here. Someone to shout to through the wall. Some familiar sounds, even. Not strange voices or trucks or cars beeping. Something simple, like footsteps on concrete, keys jangling, the sound of the flap of the cell door opening and closing again. Some fella singing with his headphones on. Anything. Anything familiar. But there's nothing at all.

～

I can do this. Work out the cost of the train. Pay for a ticket. Find the right platform. Cross the road. Avoid getting run over. Find my way about. Alastair nods. If he's not sure, he doesn't say anything. He always lets me make my own mistakes. Except getting run over. He's saved me more than once from walking in front of a car. There's just so many of them now. And they go so fast.

~

Alastair has come to get me from Jim MacKeith's friend's flat. Day three of freedom. *I'm taking you to my house,* he says. *While you get your head together. Unless you'd prefer to go home. Home? Where? To Belfast. Belfast? No. Not Belfast. Not yet.* Shake my head.

Maybe it should be strange that I've agreed to go to Guildford, but somehow it seems okay because I'm going with Alastair. I'll go anywhere he takes me. I owe him everything. Trust him with my life. He'll look after me because right now I know I can't.

He lives a little bit out of the town, with his girlfriend. The marriage he was in when we met first, 15 years ago, ended. Because of me. Because of us. *Sorry,* I say, when I realise. *Not your fault, Paddy. Don't worry yourself about that.* He's so direct and kind. I've never mixed with people like this before. Educated and so well spoken. But I'm comfortable around him. He understands what I've been through better than almost anyone else, except maybe Gerry, Carole and Paul.

Mammy and Josephine and Eileen come to Alastair's house and we have dinner. For the first time I sit down to eat at a proper table. With glasses and condiments and even a tablecloth. Even three days after my release the metal fork feels so alien in my hand. After using plastic for all these years, it's so solid and heavy. And luxurious. I stare more at the metal than at the food I'm eating. They gave me a ham sandwich for lunch the other day and when I lifted my knife and fork to cut it, everyone started laughing. *You don't need to use cutlery with a sandwich, Paddy.* I turn crimson. *It's okay,* they add. *There's a lot of things for you to get used to. Don't worry about it.* But there's a tightness in my chest. If I can't handle a basic meal, how will I survive around strangers in other, more complex situations?

Some pudding, Paddy. Someone hands me a plate with a thick wedge of cake, the likes of which I haven't seen since my childhood, and even then it was rare enough. I spoon a piece into my mouth and my tastebuds almost explode. It's so rich and sugary and soft. Nothing like the dry currant cake we used to make in prison sometimes. My eyes are watering in shock. I start giggling and everyone looks at me. I can't help it. I spoon another mouthful in and my eyes roll back. They all realise the source of my delight as I'm starting to shovel chunks of the cake into my mouth. *Did you not get cake in prison?* I don't even bother to clear my mouth to answer and instead raise my eyebrow. Are you joking? Someone has put another slice on my plate and I keep going. They start laughing, and I'm laughing too. There's bits flying out of my mouth. I'm like a monkey in a zoo again, but this time it's okay.

We're sitting down on another night, for another meal, and I'm told we're having lobster. *Do you remember, Paddy? When I asked you what you wanted when you got out of prison, you said lobster.* I can just about remember now, but I didn't think it would ever happen. They show me this big squirming shellfish. *It's alive? You have to cook it that way.* Put it into a pot of boiling water. I'm trying not to show the horror on my face. A pot of boiling water. Boiling water and sugar. And there he is – that tortured face. A body flailing and writhing in agony. His eyes looking up at me in horror. Pleading. *Do you want to put the lobster into the water, Paddy?*

NO! Eh, no, thank you. Take it easy, Paddy. Relax. They've gone to the trouble of doing this for me. *You go ahead and do it. I'll just watch.*

Are you okay, Paddy?

Yes. It sounds lovely. And it is. *The flavour is incredible,* I tell them all as we sit around together. But just looking at that enormous pot of boiling water takes me back there in a flash. And I can't help thinking of that scarred face and the man with fear in his eyes. The indelible mark I've left on another man's life.

Even this dining experience is exhausting. Normally I try not to eat with others. I'm too self-conscious and it's just too alien to be around other people at mealtimes. I'm used to eating alone in a cell with just myself for company. I'm comfortable that way now. But I don't want to be rude when people have gone to such trouble. The rest of the time I find ways around it. Whenever Alastair's working or if he's out at mealtimes, I let on that I'm not hungry so they just leave me some for later. Then I have mine when everyone has left. A pattern that will stay with me for life.

∼

I'm a 39-year-old man, 40 in a few months, and I'm scared of everyone. Trying to look like I do this all the time. Wait until everyone gets on the train and when I see that it's not too full, I get on. Find an empty seat. Facing the door. Always face the door, Paddy – nobody can take you by surprise. Hands cover your head if anyone tries anything.

Every time a ticket inspector gets on, I start to shake. Hand him my ticket before he's even reached me. He's looking at me curiously and I'm trying to smile. Look people in the eye, Paddy, don't look down. People aren't going to hurt you. We practised all this.

Train is quiet. People reading papers, books, sleeping. Nobody seems to be looking at me yet. Not like in Guildford. Nobody says anything there, but I know from their stares: not everyone believes that we're innocent. *Got out on a technicality*, they're saying. That's what a lot of powerful people have been whispering. And of course people believe them. Now on the train I'm okay. Keep my back to the wall so I can watch everyone in the carriage. No surprises.

∼

That first Saturday night, after everyone has left, we sit in Alastair's kitchen talking. *What will happen now?* I wonder. *Can we get those policemen who hit us?*

I certainly hope so, Paddy. I want Dirty Harry to pay for what he did to you.

Dirty Harry. Suddenly I'm back there. In that room. Looking at the pictures on the wall. The window just over there. Five of them towering over me, shouting all at once. Question after question. *Just fucking tell the truth. Tell us the truth now or we'll make you sorry. Just fucking tell us what happened, you murdering bastard ...*

Alastair's still talking, but I can barely hear him. *We have them now. Everyone knows they lied. That they beat you.* Yes, they beat me. They beat me. And kicked me. And spat, and punched. And threatened and mocked. Those fucking bastards.

He's still talking somewhere in the background. *We won't let them away with this, Paddy. There are laws against it. We have enough evidence to put them away. They'll try to wriggle out of it, but we'll do our best. Get justice for you.*

Dirty Harry is getting closer and closer. *Throw him out the window ... out the window ... out the window ... out the window.*

The bastards, I say quietly.

Yes, they are, he agrees, *they are bastards.* And suddenly it's like someone has peeled off a filter from my eyes. It wasn't me – it was them. I did nothing wrong. I was made confess. I was intimidated and tortured and forced into confessing. I did nothing wrong whatsoever. I never killed no-one, never hurt no-one. All I did was get stoned and act the eejit. Suddenly it's like I'm propelled from my chair and I'm kicking the wall. Screaming at the top of my lungs.

The bastards! The fucking bastards!

I don't know how long I cry and kick. Somehow Alastair manages to move me from the kitchen, get me upstairs to my room. Away from his girlfriend's children. I barely remember it, but now he's cradling me in his arms. He isn't trying to stop me or even calm me. Just letting me scream and kick and roar and wail.

And I am screaming. Screaming myself hoarse. *Those fucking lying bastards! What they did to me. They took my life!*

On and on I kick and scream. I want to feel some pain. Hurt myself.

Anything to stop this torture. Why hasn't the pain gone now that I'm free? Why can't someone cut it out? On and on and on I roar at the wall. Kick the shadow that could be Dirty Harry. Leave marks and holes in the wall that will shock me the next day when I've calmed down. And Alastair will just smile and tell me not to worry. *Totally normal, Paddy. Got to get it out. This is a safe place.*

The neighbours call the police, Alastair tells me years later. When they come he has to explain it to them and they leave quietly. Nodding. After a couple of hours I'm like one of those wind-up toys that's slowing down before it stops completely, rooted to the spot, liable to fall over at any moment. Alastair wraps his arms around my back, supporting my limp and shaky body. Puts me in my bed, pulls the covers over me and turns out the light. I don't hear him close the door and for the next few days all I can do is sleep, wake, eat and sleep again.

~

London. I look around. How did I live here before? It's so big and loud and busy. People everywhere. Cars. Buses. Taxis. Overwhelming noise and smells. Breathe, Paddy. Remember what those two psychiatrists said. *You can cope. You can do this …*

~

A few days after my release Alastair tells me that Ros Franey and Grant McKee, the journalists, want to come to see me. They want to interview me. All of us. To make one last documentary. This time to talk about how we are feeling. What it's like being out. I agree. They've been so good to us, I'd do anything for them.

It's so good to see them, and for the first time ever we're not in a room in the prison. We talk for a few hours and then they ask if I want to go for a walk. They'll film me walking through the forest. That sounds lovely. I'm walking along and suddenly someone jumps out. I jump. Quick, Paddy – get down low. Lift your hands. Always protect your head. And then I stop. It's Carole. There in the flesh. In front of me. In her own clothes. A white top. Blue jeans. Fresh clean skin. Sweet smelling hair. Her eyes bright. Looking straight into mine. I put my arms around her, and try to swallow the tears but all I can taste are hers and mine, mingling on my face.

They film us walking through the forest together. I put my arm around her. They ask me what the future holds and I blush. *I don't know. We've not been together for a long time. She's changed, I've probably changed. We'll have to see. But I hope we can make a go of it*, I tell them. *God, I hope so.*

Later, we sit together on the couch in Alastair's house. Everyone else is out and we're alone. I can barely think, sitting so close to her. Calm down, Paddy. Just take your time. She's not going anywhere. She's telling me a story. How she put an ice cream into a microwave. Thinking it was a freezer. We're laughing about all the ridiculous, scary and hilarious things that have happened to us over the last week.

She's looking at me and it's intoxicating. She's leaning closer now and I don't know if she feels what I feel, but I have to find out. I shuffle closer and we're laughing again. I'm teasing her about something, wondering how to do this. I feel like a schoolboy who's got 10 minutes before his ma gets home. Suddenly we're kissing and it's like electric shocks are exploding in my mouth. Her fingers are wound around the back of my head, playing with my hair. I'm holding her and I want to pull her so close that I won't know where she ends and I begin. I can't believe she's here with me and there's nobody here to stop us, to stare at us, to pull us apart. I pull back and look at her face and she's still young and beautiful. I feel old and worn down but then she smiles, and I'm 24 again.

~

I spend more than six months in Guildford and have intensive counselling sessions with two men who specialise in helping people suffering from trauma, like men who've been to war. Or falsely imprisoned. Alastair organised it all and now I'm like a child getting ready to leave home. His bag

on his back. I've made it to London and now I'm standing in the middle of
Waterloo Station, looking around. Gerry rang and said I should come up
some time, so here I am. But I've no idea how to find him. He doesn't even
know I'm coming.

So many people. All going somewhere. To work. Home. Meet friends.
They all look like they have a purpose. And there's me. Like a stone in the
midst of this busy stream. Look at my watch. Still not used to wearing one
after 15 years without it. Mine was taken off me and it was one of the few
humane things they did. If I'd had one in there, I'd have slung it out the
window and myself after it, because I'd have been checking it every five
minutes.

It's three o'clock. What would I be doing if I were in Gartree now?
On exercise, maybe. Or talking to one of the boys. Or sitting in my cell
wondering when I'll get out of this place. The irony isn't lost on me that I'm
standing here, in the middle of London, thinking about sitting in a cell and
wishing I was free. It's a funny thing, freedom. I've thought about it every
single day for the last 15 years, missed it, craved it, nearly died for it. And
now that I have it, I've no idea what to do with it.

~

Alastair gives his girlfriend money and asks her to take me clothes shopping.
I pick up a pair of jeans. *How much are they? Fifty pounds*, the fella working
in the shop says. *Fifty pounds? I've never spent fifty pounds on anything in my
life. They used to be a fiver. Have you been living in a timewarp or something?*
he asks, laughing. I laugh along with him. He has no idea.

One of the first shops I go into alone is a newsagent. I need some
tobacco. The first time I try to go in there's too many people inside so I
leave. I walk up and down the street, still too afraid to cross it. I glance
through the window again and when it's empty I go inside. There's a
counter in front of me lined with chocolate bars in all different colours and
sizes. That's what I think they are, anyway. Thick blocks wrapped in shiny
paper with names I've never seen before. Twix. Mars. Toffee Crisp. Dairy

Milk. I'm riveted – there's at least a hundred different types of them. Shelf after shelf of bright packaging. I stand there for about 15 minutes and the man behind the counter looks at me nervously. In the end I leave without buying anything.

When I finally decide to go back and pick out what I want, he has to give me several bags for all the bars of chocolate I've bought – it comes to £20. I'm still struggling with the money. Even though we changed from shillings to pence in 1971, when I first arrived in London, I never got used to it because I never had any money. Up until last week, I was getting paid £4.50 a week in prison, and most of it had to go on tea and other things, so I'd only ever end up with a tiny amount. Now I have to deal with pound coins and I can't get my head around them.

I get nervous every time I have to buy anything. I've no idea how much to hand over and I'm terrified of giving too little and exposing myself as stupid. In the end I find the best thing to do is to use a new £20 note to pay for everything – even if it's less than £1 to buy a bar of chocolate or a tin of coke. And every evening I come home to Alastair with a pocket full of coins. When he realises what's happening, he laughs and takes the coins away and gives me £20 notes again.

Everyone keeps asking me about the money and I can understand their curiosity – I'd be wondering too. But what's money going to do? It won't give me 15 years back. Won't stop me from panicking every time I see a police car or running out of a shop because there's too many people. It won't prevent me from fearing that people will recognise me, that they'll think I did kill them people and they'll hurt me. It won't stop me from drinking a bottle a vodka a day when I move out of Alastair's. In fact, it'll just make me drink more because I can afford to.

Alastair explains it to me. *The British government have given us some money. Enough to live on for a while, Paddy, while they do their psychological and medical assessments of the impact of your experiences.* Alastair also arranges for us to do controlled interviews and we've been paid for them. But it's all a bit much to take in. I went into prison with the clothes on my back and about a pound in my pocket and now I have £75,000.

Alastair isn't happy with the final arrangement – he wants an estimate of the final award and for me and Carole to be paid interest on that. That way, we'd have received a regular income instead of a big lump sum. But things aren't done that way. Instead an independent QC assesses the damages – taking into account the medical and psychological assessments as well. No final figure can be set until all those assessments are in, which may take years. So in the meantime we are given an interim payment, exactly the sort of big money Alastair doesn't want us to have in our pockets. Once we accept the payment, we can't get state benefits – that's the deal. Only later on will I realise how right Alastair was to be worried.

So for now I'm a 39-year-old man with more money than I could count, but I'm so confused by all the notes and coins that I've no idea how to manage it.

The shrinks I've been seeing want me to go out every day. *Just a little at a time. As often as you can.* But every time I do, I nearly get killed. Alastair has had to grab me so many times. Cars and motorbikes just come out of nowhere. So fast. Sometimes I wait so long and lose my nerve that I just go back the way I came. Other times I just run across and hope for the best. I want to go back to London soon, but how can I when I can't cross the road without nearly getting killed? At the age of 39, I'm like our two-year-old Gertie all those years ago, innocent and a huge danger to myself.

The shrinks make me do these role-plays. How to deal with everyday situations. Coping with conflict. They send me into a fake shop to complain about something and film me. *Remember to stay calm,* they warn. *Even when someone gets annoyed with you, don't be scared, don't react.* The girl refuses to take back the jeans I'm supposed to be returning. The first time we do it I get very nervous when she raises her voice. Immediately defensive. After years in prison, of constantly watching your back, waiting for someone to attack, it's actually very difficult. But I do it again and again until they're happy. I'm making great progress, they reassure me.

·

I'm out with a few mates I've met in Guildford. Fall out of the pub at closing time. Wee bit shaky. Might have had one too many. *C'mon, Paddy.* There's a police car coming towards us. Bright light on the top of the car is blinding. Coming towards us. Put your head down, Paddy. Oh, Jesus, it's stopping in front of us. *Get in,* my friends tell me. *Come on, Paddy. In.* No! *I'm not bloody getting in there. Take your hands off me. Leave me alone, you fucking bastards. I'm not getting in.* They're trying to pull me now. Can't let them get me in. Can't go back to prison. Kill myself first. They'll do me again. I know they want to get me. Plant my feet on the ground. Won't. Fucking. Move. *Paddy, c'mon, for fuck's sake, it's freezing. We have to go home.* No! *I'm not getting into no police car. It's not a police car, you idiot – it's a fucking taxi. Look.* A taxi. They slag me about it the next day. *Fuck, Paddy, we couldn't move you. You're bloody stronger than you look, mate. Five of us couldn't get you into that car.* They're wrong. I'm not strong. Not physically anyway. But my will is – and there's no way I'm going back to prison. Fifty men couldn't have got me into that car.

This isn't how I pictured life after my release. Knew it would be hard, but never thought it would be so lonely. I was hoping Carole and I could have made a go of it after that night in Alastair's house. It felt good then. Felt like we had a chance. Just needed a bit of time to sort our heads out and then we could meet up, spend some time together. Maybe get our own place and then, if things worked out, get married. I really thought it would happen, those first few weeks. Hoped. Thought she would get in touch when she had a bit of time, but she hasn't yet and I don't want to push it. Anyway, I'm in too much of a mess right now. I'll wait a bit longer, until I feel a bit better. Sort it out then.

I go back to Gartree. Take the train all the way there. I need to see my friends. I call Mick Haynes when I get there. My old friend from the garden party. He takes me out to see his hawks and into his home, like an old friend. Just two men talking over a cup of coffee. So beautifully ordinary. I can't believe it.

I go back to the prison, as a visitor. Sit on the opposite side of the table this time. They give me a terrible slagging. *You're back, Armstrong. Do you want your old cell?* I laugh. *Yeah, right. I'm a free man. I get to leave whenever I want.* I don't tell them about the loneliness. How hard it is to fill my days. How much I miss the routine of prison life. The PO sees me. *Oi, Armstrong! You owe me three hundred quid. I know it was you who nicked those cigarettes out of the shop. I don't know how you did it, but I know it was you.* He's grinning. I'm happy to see him too.

Ronnie and Paddy Hill hug me before we sit down in the visiting room. Tell me all about how the prison went crazy when they heard we'd been released. I miss them so much, but I can't say that. They're still locked up in here and would give their right arm to be out. So I chat away and laugh when they tell me about the two-day party I missed after Gerry and me left. *I can't believe I missed my own leaving party. Bloody typical.* And then visiting time is up and I have to go and get the train back to Guildford. My new life.

The truth is, I need to get out of Guildford. Can't live like this, looking over my shoulder. Wondering if Surrey Police will come after me again. Lost and lonely. So it's time to go. But where? And with who? Can't face going back to Belfast and all my friends are in prison, except Gerry. He rang me recently and told me to come up and stay with him. In London. Need to stand on my own two feet. So that's what I'm doing. I'm going to see Gerry.

~

I'm standing on the platform, nearly paralysed with confusion and indecision. How the hell am I going to find Gerry in a city this big, this busy? And then I remember – Gareth Peirce. Her office is in London. She'll know where I can find him.

Walk into her office, ready to ask her where Gerry is, and suddenly he's there in front of me. A big grin on his face. *Paddy, fuck! What about you? Gerry!* I'm so happy to see him. Emotional. Didn't expect to be. We hug like brothers. *I was just in seeing Gareth, but I'm finished now. Pint? Definitely. Let's go.*

I'm staying with Gerry in his place. He's writing a book. Paul's writing one too. I'd like to do that one day. But not yet. I just want to have a normal life. Not a 'go to work, come home, pay the bills' kind of life, which is most people's kind of normal. That will come one day, maybe. For now, I just want to be young again. Do the kinds of things I was enjoying in 1974 when my life was so abruptly interrupted – go out, meet people, go to the pub and the bookies. Just a bit of fun.

Gerry's a bit of a celebrity since he spoke outside the Old Bailey. The papers love him, the women love him, everybody wants a piece of Gerry. He's so friendly, funny, likeable and charismatic. We do a few talks, although that's more his thing than mine. I just want a bit of peace. We go to gigs, nightclubs, meet famous people, some gorgeous women. It's like being in Hollywood.

We go back to Ireland – Belfast, Dublin. Gerry always has an entourage and it's good craic. Lot of parties, lot of drink, lot of women. I go and see my family. They want me to come home to live in Belfast, but I can't. It'll always have a place in my heart, but it's different now. The first time I go back it's amazing. We're heroes in West Belfast. Everyone wants to buy me pints. I spend the week in the pub. Unbelievable.

But it's exhausting too, and after almost 20 years away I feel disconnected from everything. Rootless. And fucking petrified. Constantly looking over my shoulder for some RUC fella or Protestant kid who thinks he's a hard man, who wants to give me a hiding, or worse. There's even people in Belfast who think we got off on a technicality. I can't live in fear, so I can never go home to Belfast. Back to my dear mammy. My sister. My friends. My comfort zone. They took my home from me.

I like going to Dublin, though, because it's so different from Belfast. Gerry introduces me to Pat Mulryan, who he was in prison with. He's a Dub who spent years in prison for being a member of an ASU. Pat and I hit it off instantly. He's a true friend to me from the day I meet him. People who haven't been to prison think it's a bit strange that I would willingly associate with ex-IRA men. *Don't you hate them?* Of course I don't. They fought for their beliefs. They did what I could never, would never do, but they did it to get Catholics their rights. Their right to housing, to jobs, to equality. I think some people think that makes me an IRA man too, but most Catholics in West Belfast who grew up when I did, who knew what it was like to be a second-class citizen, probably feel the same way. We didn't all resort to violence, but we understood why some men and women did.

Pat Mulryan and I are firm friends. I'm closer to him even than to Gerry now. He's warm and, even though we party together, he's got his feet on the ground. When his wife gets pregnant, he asks me to be godfather. I'm over the moon because, while I'd like to have my own wee girl, it's too late for that now, so this is probably as close as I'll ever get to fatherhood. My goddaughter is named Sorcha – a beautiful girl, born in 1990. The first time I see her in the hospital she's in a little yellow Babygro, so I nickname her Mellow Yellow, after one of my favourite songs.

I watch Pat cradling his tiny baby girl and I realise I'll never be a father. I really thought it might happen for Carole and me. Thought we had a chance that night in Alastair's. If I'd known it was our last time together, I might have held her a bit tighter. A little bit longer. Inhaled the scent of her clean hair one last time. I waited too long. I let her go without a fight. And now it's too late. She's engaged. To an Irish fella she's known since before she went to prison. Gone. The girl I fell in love with. The woman I wanted to marry. The one I hoped would be the mother of my children. All gone.

I've to go to America, says Gerry one day. *I've to meet my book agent. Do you want to come?* I don't need to be asked twice. I'd go anywhere in the morning. *You'll need a new passport fast, though, Paddy.* He takes me down to the passport office and I queue up. The man behind the desk shakes his head. I'll need a load of paperwork. This form signed and that thing done. It'll take weeks. I'm terrible at this sort of stuff. *Looks like I won't be coming with you, Gerry. Not sure I can get it all together on time.* As we're leaving we bump into a man I know who works there. Some sort of official. *Gerry, Paddy, what are you two doing here?* I say, *Trying to get a passport, but no luck. Hold on*, he says. Brings us in the back. The following day I'm holding a new passport. USA, here we come!

We land in the Big Apple and I can't believe it. I thought London was big, but this is unbelievable. Gerry goes to see his book agent in New York. We meet this other Irish fella, John, and party for a few days. He's a good-looking fella, the spitting image of Mel Gibson. And a real chancer. He used to work in a bar in Boston, he tells us. On a Tuesday night it would be packed with women. Free in for them. *I'd come out with the pockets full of money. Other barmen would come and just watch me,* he'd boast. Some nights he'd check himself into a really expensive hotel and the next morning he'd let a few cockroaches out of a box and then go downstairs and complain to the management and get the room for free. A complete chancer but a gas man.

Gerry has to be in LA in just over a week's time. *Come on with me, boys. Let's drive there.* Seems like a great idea to me. We can see the whole country. Me and John agree. Why not? I don't actually have a licence but Alastair made me take some driving lessons in Guildford, so I'm happy to give it a go. We hire a car and away we go. We look at the map and see the Blue Ridge Mountains. We'll go that way – south and then west. Easy. Shouldn't take too long. Be there for dinner. We're driving and driving and still driving, but we're not there yet. Stop in this one-horse town in Virginia. There's a restaurant, garage, hotel and shop. And barely a soul around. We're in the restaurant, ordering food. The waitress asks where we're from and we say Belfast. She smiles vacantly. *It's in Ireland. You know Ireland?* She smiles again, but shakes her head. *It's … never mind. It's shit anyway. I'm thinking you haven't heard of the Guildford Four then, have you?* Gerry says. *Gee, I'm sorry, I haven't. What is it?* she asks. *Don't worry, love. It's shit too.* We laugh. He's a funny man Gerry.

It's been at least seven hours and still no sign of these mountains. *Where in the name of God are you taking us, Gerry? Don't worry, it's really close – look.* He shows us the map. When we get there, we discover we've covered 700 miles. Jesus Christ, and we're still on the East Coast! We have to get all the way over there. How far's LA then? We stop this fella wearing a chequered shirt. Like something that stepped off the set of *MacGyver*. He looks us up and down. *From here to LA?* Pauses for at least a minute, staring into the distance and then eyeballs us and drawls. *Well, I'd say that would be about 2,000 miles. Maybe more. You sure got a lot of driving to do, fellas.* He laughs and stares at us again. We look at each other. What'll we do? We've only got a few days. *Well, we can't abandon the hire car in the middle of the country – we have to get it to LA. Anyway, I can't see any airports around here. Right, then, looks like we're driving there – all 2,000 miles. It'll be good craic.* Like fuck it will. The man shakes his head as we walk off with tears running down our faces we're laughing so much.

We take turns at the wheel so we can sleep while we move. Finally those driving lessons are coming in handy. State after state – they all blur into one another until, finally, we arrive. Gerry's agent tells us he's going to take us to a restaurant. We turn up and the fella at the door looks us up and down for a few long minutes. He's not even subtle about it. I know what's coming. He's going to tell us, *Sorry, I can't let you in.* I don't care – the place looks a bit too posh for me anyway. He sashays off and disappears. When he returns a few minutes later he's carrying shirts and jackets. Immaculately clean. Like they've just come out of a shop. *If you'd like to put these on, gentlemen, I think you'll find you'll be more comfortable.* Gerry, John and I look at each other, collapse into a fit of giggles and then head into the toilet to get dressed up like we're going to a funeral. We scrub up all right, though.

We're invited to go to see Billy Connolly filming *Head of the Class* at some studios so we drive into the car park and up to near where the set is. Gerry sees a free spot and puts the car into it. The director's spot, it turns out, but nobody says anything. Billy hugs us warmly like we're old friends, and within minutes it feels like we are. He takes us to one of his shows that night and welcomes us from the stage. To go from Gartree to here in a year is very hard to take in.

We spend a few days in LA, meeting all these famous people, touring around, and then Gerry tells us he has to go back to New York quickly. *You'll have to drive back without me, fellas – I'm going to have to fly.* Myself and John have only a few days to get there before my flight home. We drive non-stop. Fourteen hours a day, taking turns at the wheel, stopping only to eat in McDonald's. Barely sleeping. But even still, it's incredible. The colours are like nothing I've seen before. After years of the same scenery – grey walls, grey bars, even I was grey – it's like breathing in sweet, pure air after you've been underwater for too long.

∼

There's a knock on the door of my flat in Largs. Something a bit aggressive about it. My antenna is up. This massive fella is standing there. Shaved head. Tight T-shirt to show off his six-pack. *I'm looking for Paddy. Is he here?* I've never seen him before. Definitely not a friend of mine. Pause. *He's not here. He's away for a couple of days. I'll tell him you were looking for him.* He cocks his head, looks at me for a moment. Thinking. *Just tell him a friend called. I'll come back another night.* I close the door. Shit.

∼

We're not long back from our American road trip when the news filters through: the Birmingham Six are getting out. Paddy Hill, Gerry Hunter and all the other boys are getting out. I can't wait to see Paddy, and when I do it's like the two years have just disappeared. I'd forgotten how funny and direct he is. It's like we saw each other only a few weeks ago.

We all party together for a few weeks, but I'm drinking a bottle of vodka a day these days More sometimes. It's hard to stop. It numbs things. Comfortably numb again. Some things never change, it seems. Only it's getting harder to recover from the hangovers. I'm 41 – I can't live like this. Need a break from this big, lonely city where people look through you like a pane of glass, recoil slightly if you smile or nod at them. Can't stay in this soulless place. So where, then, if not London and not Belfast?

Nowhere feels right. It's like being homeless. But not like in the 1970s homeless. This is different, and so much worse. Because even though I've more money than I could have hoped for, even though I've gone from waiting outside a café in London for a day's work to never needing to work again, and even though I had to move into a London squat when I was homeless and jobless before, I never, ever felt like this. Because even when I hadn't a penny or barely a pocket to put it into if I did, even then I felt more at home in a dilapidated house in Linstead Street with a load of hippies cooking and philosophising together than I feel anywhere now, with all this money. So I keep drinking.

I still go back and forth to see Pat Mulryan's family in Dublin, but it's not my home. I decide to take the train up to see our Eileen and Jim in Scotland. And their kids. It's good to see them, but I can't settle around too many people. I *want* to be there but it's like my body doesn't. Chest gets all tight. Don't panic. Stay calm. It's okay. Just go outside for a bit.

I need to go to the beach. Breathe in the sea air. Get away from the smog and the noise and the people. That will help. So I jump on a train for the day. I'll find somewhere nice along the way. On the train line there's a stop called Largs – a seaside town not far from Glasgow. I don't know anything about it, but I decide to get off there. I'm only off the train and already I feel like I can breathe again. It reminds me of Bangor. A promenade along the beach. A funfair. Nice pubs. Friendly people. Feels like a small place. People don't look through you here. They talk to you in the pub, in the street. For the first time in months I don't feel panicked or paranoid. I wish I could settle here. Just leave the world behind and set up here … And then I realise. I *can* set up here. Why can't I? There's nothing tying me to London or Belfast or anywhere, in fact. I can live wherever I want. I have the money. Why not?

For the first time in my entire life I've taken control. I find a flat to rent and move in. On my own at last. In a town where I can live peacefully. And soon enough a few friends. Everyone knows me. For a quiet seaside town you could drink every night of the week here, and every day in some cases. I do. So many friends. People are very kind. I know some take advantage of me, but I don't mind. I have lots and they don't. And I'm having a fantastic time. This is the place for me.

I meet a man who says he sells apartments. *Next to nothing. It's a drop in the ocean, Paddy, but a great investment for £20,000.* I give him the little money I have, but that's it. The rest of it's gone. Waiting for the next payment from the British government. I ring Alastair. He sends me enough for the deposit. *Get a loan from a bank, Paddy. It's a tiny amount and they can see you have the savings. Pay it back over a few years. Okay, I'll do that.* And now I have my own place in Largs.

I get on great with one of the men I know from the pub. I've been working in his shop a wee bit. It's great craic. Gives me a place to go every day. I'm just helping him out, though. Don't need any more money. *Okay, Paddy, that's great.* And then he has a great idea. *We should set up a business together, Paddy.* Yes. That's what I'd like. A business. I could live here and have my own business. I'll phone my solicitor, because he has the rest of my money. Alastair asks for paperwork from the man, and all this business stuff I don't understand. He sends it to Alastair, but when I ring him to ask if he can send the money he says no. *The figures don't make sense, Paddy. I don't like it. Don't do it.* I agree. Avoid the man for a while and then, when I bump into him, tell him I can't do it. He barely speaks to me after that. It gives me more time in the bookies at least, now I'm not helping out in his shop.

Alastair puts his girlfriend Pat on the phone one day. They've been together since a few months after I got out of prison. They'll get married in time. From the day I met her, Pat has always had words of wisdom for me. Like a mother hen, but sometimes I don't listen to her like I should. *Be careful, my love,* she cautions me gently on the phone. *Don't give all your money away. You need to spend it wisely or it'll run out faster than you think. Yes, you're right, Pat, I know. It has to last you a long time. Okay, Pat, you're right. I'll be more careful.* She and Alastair are like my surrogate parents.

It's great living somewhere as small as Largs because, even when I don't have money, people will give me credit. There's a bookie here. He's a nice man. He lets me spend whatever I want. I try to keep the bets low, but sometimes when there's good odds on a sure thing, when I know I'll win, I up the ante a bit. Spend a few grand. I've lost a few times, so I just need to win it back. Don't really want to tell Alastair. I know what he'll say. So I've talked to the bookie. Told him the money is coming. He's given me more credit. I'll win this time …

My money is gone. Can you give me a bit more credit? There's a sure thing running today, 40/1.

How much do you want?

Two hundred.

No problem, Paddy – I know you're good for it. But I'll need some of it soon. You owe me a bit now. The fella who sells the hash is the same. *Just pay me back when you have it next month, Paddy. Let me know if you need any more.*

And suddenly, over the months, I've racked up a few grand in debt. Can't tell Alastair. He won't give me the money anyway. The fellas I owe are starting to look for their money.

Aye, my solicitor is sending it to me in a few weeks. Is that okay? Just hang on and you'll have it all.

No problem, Paddy. I can give you a tiny bit more then, if you promise it's on the way.

Still haven't worked out how I'm going to pay these boys. Starting to feel the pressure. They're coming round to see me some days. I've told them it's complicated. Lot of bank things. But they know I'm good for it. Starting to panic, but there's no-one I can ask. Can't tell Alastair. He'll be so disappointed. I hate letting him down. Sort it out yourself, Paddy. You're a man. You can't keep running to Alastair and Pat. Stand on your own two feet.

I have to ring Alastair – ask him for some money to pay off these men. Don't tell him I'm scared, but I think he knows. *How can you have spent that much, Paddy? You had seventy-five thousand pounds.* He's saddened, but not surprised. He knows me. I have lots of money but my friends don't. I like to look after them. When anybody tells me a sob story, I can't ignore it. Buy drinks and whatever they need. And I can't give to one but not another fella. I've more than I could ever spend and what's the point in holding onto it? Plenty more where it came from.

I know I've disappointed him, but he doesn't get angry. *We'll sort it out, Paddy, but we'll do it our way, not theirs. Make an arrangement with them. You can pay them off over time.* It's nearly worse, knowing I've let him down. *Paddy, people are taking advantage of you. You have to be careful. You may never be able to work. You need an income for life.*

I know, Alastair. You're right.

So he suggests that he pays me a regular allowance. *Enough to live off,* *Paddy. What do you think?*

He's right. I have to make this last. We agree on it.

I look out from behind the curtains of my flat. He's gone – driven off in a car. I don't have much time. There's a sports bag under my bed. Look around. Don't need much. A few clothes and my passport. Fiddling with the zip on the bag. Hands are shaking so much I can't close it. Fuck, have to get out of here. If he realises I was lying and comes back, he'll kill me. Less than five minutes after he leaves, I'm gone. Sports bag over my shoulder and I'm up the street.

My mate opens the door. *Fuck, Paddy, what's wrong? What's all the* *hammering about? Have to get out of here now. Can you drive me to the* *station?* He takes one look at me and grabs his keys. *Some boys,* I tell him. *They're after me. Have to get out. You sure? This is Largs, Paddy – not Belfast.* *I know, but I owe them money. They'll come and beat the shit out of me. But* *what about your place? I don't care. Fuck it. They can have it. Sure I might* *come back another time.*

I've no intention of ever coming back here. Don't look back, Paddy – keep moving.

An hour later I have a ticket in my hand and I'm jumping on a train. Not sure where it's going. Don't care. Look around again. Nobody saw me. How the hell do I get myself into these messes? Time to start again. Back to London until I work out what to do.

~

It's 1993 and they're making a film about Gerry's life. And about us. Filming is starting in a few weeks. Gerry and I are consultants on the film, along with Pat Mulryan. Jim Sheridan is directing it and we're going to tell him all about prison, work with Daniel Day-Lewis, help him learn how to do the accent. And I'll get to live in Dublin, in an apartment they'll pay for. First, though, I'm going to India.

It's Gerry's idea. *Let's go to Goa, Paddy.* Some of the boys in prison
had told him about it. They'd said, *It's a beautiful place, Gerry. You have to
go if you ever get out of here. Amazing people. Stunning scenery. Parties all
night long in the forest and some of the most unbelievable drugs you've ever
experienced in your life.* He's never forgotten. *We're out now, Paddy – let's do
it. Before the filming starts.*

Within days we have our tickets and we're ready to go again. Nothing
holding us back. Gerry's travel agent has booked us into this hotel. When we
get there, we can see that it's a honeymoon place. We crack up laughing – we
look like a couple. We get out of there and go in search of a party and the
drugs we've been dreaming of. In the middle of the jungle, this fella runs
up to us. *Paddy, Gerry, what the fuck are you doing here?* It's a fella we were
in Gartree with. *Jesus, it's so good to see you both.* He came here when he
got out. Stays most of the year and then leaves when the monsoon season
comes. *Fucking unbelievable weed here, boys. Come on.*

We hire a man to drive us around. It's like being a rock star. He waits
outside bars for hours even though we tell him to go home. *No problem, my
friends.* He waggles his head. *I can sleep here. You go and enjoy. I'll be waiting.*
We party non-stop for two weeks. Nighttimes in the jungle, dancing, going
wild; daytimes, sleeping on the beach. In the middle of these thick forests
there's wee women making tea and food. When it gets really dark they
smear oil onto the palm trees and light them like massive torches. There's
a full moon one night and you can barely see five yards ahead for all the
half-naked people dancing and wandering around. Sometimes, often at the
most unexpected moments, I remember Ronnie and the other boys back in
Gartree and I wonder if I was ever really there. But I was. And as sweet as it is
to be here, it was robbed from me. Should have been doing this 15 years ago
instead of now. I'm old now – 43, for fuck's sake. I was robbed of so many
opportunities to travel, to meet new people, to discover new tastes and smells
and sights. I should be settled down by now. Fucking bastards. Still, this is
good now. Forget all that, Paddy. Life is for living. Dance the night away.

When we touch down in Dublin once again and start filming *In the Name of the Father*, my life transforms. Dublin is magic. It's a city, but not a big one. And even though it's smaller than London, it's still cool. It's in Ireland, but it's not Belfast. And the music scene is brilliant. Perfect.

Working on a film set is unbelievable. We're like superstars. Especially Gerry. Daniel Day-Lewis follows us around, listening to us talking. Trying to copy us. A true method actor. Jim takes us to Kilmainham Gaol, where he's filming the prison scenes, shows us the sets, asks us if that's how it would look in prison. It's unnerving going into a prison. Tiny cells. Cold corridors. Grey concrete landings. Steel and bars everywhere. The first time we go in, Gerry and I look at one another. Jesus. One day I go into a cell to look at something and the door slams. One of the fellas on the set decides to lock me in. Leave me there for a few minutes. *Just for the craic, Paddy. Were you scared?* Hide the sweat patches under the arms of my T-shirt. *Fuck off! It'll take more to break me than that, you cheeky hooligan.*

We've discovered Dublin's trendiest spot, Lillie's Bordello. A very exclusive nightclub for any superstar who's knocking around Dublin, this is where we go with the crew most nights. I wear my leather jacket and fisherman's hat. My ponytail swinging around the back of my neck. They put us in the Library Bar, the most exclusive section of the club, and we sit at a table surrounded by women and film stars. It's becoming more normal now, but sometimes, when I remember that a few short years ago I was on a prison wing or in solitary confinement, it's hard to accept how my life has changed. From the ridiculous to the sublime.

On Sunday afternoons, as we come down from whatever we've had the night before, Pat Mulryan and I listen to music in Café de Luxe, drinking coffee and vodka with Pete Postlethwaite and Dublin's most famous drag queen, Mr Pussy. If my friends in Belfast or my sisters could see me now, their jaws would drop.

I meet a woman from South Africa on the set. Jill. She's a make-up artist. Gorgeous-looking. We party together, and before long she's going out with me. I've never had this much attention from women in my life. She takes me to South Africa to meet her family after the film wraps. We travel all around

and I fall in love with the country and the people. They welcome me like a
long-lost son. But I'm too unreliable for her. Always breaking my promises,
she tells me. So we break up and I keep going. Keep moving, Paddy.

While I'm in Dublin, working on the film, there's three policemen going
into the dock: Dirty Harry (Vernon Attwell), Thomas Style and John
Donaldson. Going in front of the Old Bailey. They're up for conspiracy to
pervert the course of justice. In other words, for fabricating my confession,
lying, wrecking our lives.

Our Eileen says they should have to do the rest of our sentence when
they get found guilty. The remaining 20 years that we'd have done if they'd
had their way.

At the beginning of the month-long trial I'm not as angry as I was. Of
course I want them to be punished for what they've done, but day by day I
feel less resentful. They have to be punished, yes, but even when they are it
won't give me back my life. It won't ever erase the torment we went through.
That we're still going through. More than anything, I know what hatred
does to people. I've seen it. Eats away at them. Destroys them. I can't live like
that.

Their solicitor tells the court that they asked me to appear as a witness.
The court is told that a witness summons was issued but ignored by me.
It's not true. No-one approached me or Alastair about this – no letter, no
summons, nothing. Alastair checked with the court office and no summons
had been served. In order to give evidence in court, you have to have
submitted a statement. I never made a statement about their case. After
checking it all out, Alastair advises me not to attend. I'm happy to agree,
because I know that he's always acting in my best interests, unlike almost
anyone in the Home Office or anywhere else in the British judicial system.

When the case comes to court, it's clear that they intend to try me all
over again. Although all three defendants are allowed to make opening
statements (a highly unusual occurrence), they later refuse to give evidence,
which means they can never be cross-examined. So they never have to offer
any reason whatsoever for the existence of the rough, typed notes. And so,

unsurprisingly, after a month-long trial, they're cleared of all charges. Not one of them will ever do any time for their part in ruining my life. They've been cleared, in spite of so much evidence, while we were found guilty with none.

I'm at once shocked by and yet, more tellingly, resigned to the verdict. I've been expecting this. Why would they convict three of their own? It could open the floodgates to others being prosecuted. I realise it was a whitewash from start to finish. Why did they even bother to go through the motions?

I just want to forget it all, but Alastair doesn't. He's incensed. For the first time since I decided I would let go of all anger, I feel that deep hurt and resentment bubbling up again. As predictable as it was, it's also so unfair. Alastair speaks to the press, indignant and to the point. *The only chance the police had to be acquitted was to put Armstrong and Conlon on trial. That's what they have done. It's been a nonsense of a criminal trial. It is a con-trick, a dirty, lousy con-trick. It is an attempt to rewrite history, an attempt to reconvict the Four.*

When the film comes out, life becomes even more hectic. Now everyone in Ireland knows who we are, if they hadn't heard about us at the time of our release. The attention is intense at times, but it's all so positive and I'm constantly moved by people's kindness. Strangers come up and tell us how they marched for us, prayed for our release and cried when it finally happened. Hug us. Hold our hands. It's incredible. I never knew this while I was in prison. They tried to tell me, but I couldn't take it in. For a long time I didn't really believe that anyone cared except my family and Alastair. And now I'm humbled on a daily basis by the stories people tell me about marching with my face on a placard.

Now that the film is over, Gerry has decided to leave Dublin. He's had enough and wants to go home to Belfast, to be with his family and to do more advocacy work. This is where he'll spend the rest of his life, in between travelling all over the world to fight for the rights of prisoners. He and Paddy Joe Hill will campaign relentlessly.

This is where Gerry and I must go our separate ways. I can't go back to Belfast. Dublin *is* my home. I like it here. It's a place I think I can settle in. And I have some really good friends, especially Pat Mulryan. He introduces me to his friend Paddy Reilly, a genius entrepreneur who makes his fortune from aerial photos. So there's Pat, Paddy and me. The Three Musketeers.

Living in 1990s Dublin is everything I could ever hope for, just what I was searching for when I was released. So cosmopolitan, it's a smaller, friendlier, less anonymous London. With the film over, I fall into an easy routine. Bookies in the morning. A bit of TV in the afternoon. Few drinks at night with Pat Mulryan and Paddy Reilly. We start our nights in JJ Smyth's or the International Bar, both blues bars with live music, and finish up in Lillie's chatting with people like Jean-Claude Van Damme or whoever is in Dublin at the time. I'm drinking less these days. It's getting harder and harder to bounce back the morning after. I'm 45, just six years shy of the age my dad was when he died. I move in with Pat and his wife. Pat is good to me. Watches out for me. When I get myself into a bit of debt again with a few troublemakers, he sorts them out and they disappear. He's a straight-talker.

Paddy, what are these?

He's holding some of my betting slips.

Found these in the bin.

Right.

Are you fucking crazy, Paddy? Five grand on one accumulator?

It was only that one time.

I found loads of them.

Oh, right …

Jesus, Paddy, cop on! You could buy a house with the money. Get a four-bedroom place up the road for £80,000. Rent it out. You'd still have money left to live on and an income.

Yeah, that's a good idea

Seriously, Paddy. You'll have nothing left in a year if you keep going like this.

I know. Sorry.

Don't say sorry; it's not my money. I'm just thinking of you.

Feck it, thought I'd thrown them away. Thought I had a few sure things. Put a few grand on a horse or two. Lost it. I'll stop it. I promise.

He rings Alastair, but he doesn't tell me that. *He's out of control, Alastair. Spending a fortune. Watch how much you give him. He's going to spend it all. He'll have nothing left.* And he's right – I've spent most of what I've been given so far. And so Alastair checks every penny now.

It's great craic living with Pat and his wife, Caroline. They give me a terrible slagging sometimes. Tell me I have a different woman every week. I suppose I'm looking for the right one, but it's just not happening. *You're looking in the wrong places,* one friend suggests. Maybe I am. But where else do you go to meet someone? I have to accept that it's probably too late for me now. I'm 45. This is my life, and I need to accept it.

CHAPTER NINE

*Perhaps love is like the ocean … the memory of love will
bring you home …
(John Denver)*

'm waiting. It feels like a year, but it's only been about 10 minutes. And
she's not even late yet. I'm early. As usual. Don't let me down. Please don't
let me down.

~

It's a Saturday night in Dublin, early summer 1996, and I'm upstairs in the
International Bar, waiting for a gig to start. There's a woman sitting across
the way and she's gorgeous – a petite blonde with a gorgeous big smile. Must
be 10 or 15 years younger than me. Out of my league maybe. But there's no
wedding ring on her finger and no man by her side. Just her and a couple of
women from what I can see.

It's one of those tiny rooms that I like to go to for a bit of live music. A
narrow, smoke-filled and slightly grimy room with a bar off in the corner, a
few grubby couches down each side and some rickety tables in the middle.
It's a far cry from the trendy Lillie's with superstars propping up the bar.
This is the kind of place you can just go to and listen to good music.

I swore off women after Jill, but looking at this woman I think my mind
could be quickly changed. As usual I'm in a pair of jeans, black leather
jacket and of course my trademark now-faded fisherman's hat. It's like my
uniform these days, but it's a lot more comfortable than prison browns. I'm
comfortable. My hair is still long and so my ponytail is swinging out the
back. I think I'm pretty cool. Nothing to lose. And so I'm going to be cheeky

and sit beside her. Have to sit somewhere, so it may as well be beside a good-looking woman.

I'm trying to think of something interesting to say when she asks me for a light. As I light her cigarette I introduce myself. *I'm Paddy Armstrong. From the Guildford Four.* It's shameless, really, but I have to be able to get something good out of that ordeal. It does the job – her eyes widen and I can see that she's intrigued. She's heard about us, she says. I ask her if she's seen the film, but she shakes her head apologetically. She'll tell me later that she knew very little about us, as her father died the year of our release and she had a difficult time coming to terms with his death.

Her name is Caroline. Scarily close to Carole, I think. From Portlaoise. Her mammy lives near the prison, I discover later. And she's a music teacher in a school. I can't believe I'm chatting up a teacher. Or that she's so good-looking. She points in the direction of the band. *That's my brother up there,* she tells me. I look over. *Sure, I know him. I've met him a few times.* They're a musical family – most of her siblings play a brass instrument, as there was a local brass band when she was growing up; she plays trombone. I shake my head in wonder. She's some woman. I can't play anything except cards. A good-looking schoolteacher in her thirties who plays the trombone. I can't believe my luck meeting her.

We chat and it's such easy conversation. For a clever woman she's so down-to-earth and funny and kind. And I think she likes me. I get talking to her friends. One of them, Sheila, is a petite and funny Scottish woman whom I warm to immediately. It's a big night, they tell me, both Caroline and one of their other colleagues are celebrating their birthdays. *Happy birthday*, I say, but I feel like it's my birthday after meeting her.

The band has started to play and she goes back to her friends, turning to me every so often. I normally love watching this band, but all I can think about is how to get her to keep talking to me. *Let me make you dinner,* I'm saying. *I can make a great curry.* I don't mention that everything I know about cooking I learned in prison. She doesn't say no, which I take as a good sign. I give her my number. As we walk down the stairs at the end of the night, she turns to me. Gives me a schoolteacher stare and tells me, as blunt as you like, that she has two questions. I nod. *Away you go.* And so she asks, *Have you ever been in the IRA and have you ever held a gun?* I shake my head to both questions. Assure her. Which is kind of the truth. I've definitely never been in the IRA. I haven't really held a gun. Someone showed me one when I was younger and I might have had it in my hand. But I don't think that counts. Either way, I'm not telling her that. She smiles.

But she doesn't call. Not that week or the next. I'm around Dublin most of the summer and hope that one day I'll come in and she'll have rung. But nothing. Not in July and not in August. She comes back into my head when I least expect it – her smile, her laugh, her lovely soft accent. I go back to the International, but she's not there. The lovely Caroline has disappeared. I really thought she liked me. But I know her brother's band so I make it my business to go and see them again. She can't hide for ever.

~

There's a ripple through the crowd and without looking I know she's there. Everyone turns to look at her. But she's looking at me. And I'm looking back at her. Coming towards me. So slowly. She's nervous. I am too. I'd throw up if I had anything in my stomach. But there's that smile in her eyes and I know everything will be okay. It's times like these that I wait for something to go wrong. Could this be my life? Because I can't believe it. Could my luck really be turning around?

~

A couple of months after I meet the beautiful Caroline, I hear that the same band are playing again. This time at Midnight at the Olympia, a late-night event in Dame Street. *We're going,* I tell Pat Mulryan. It's not a question and he doesn't bother to argue. I'm rarely this focused or motivated, so he knows this is important. *You're my back-up. If she's there, I have to talk to her.*

We get a seat near the back and I'm looking around. It's a big place, but she has to be here somewhere, surely. I'm scanning the crowd. I have to see her again. And then I see her. Up nearer the front. She's there again with her friend Sheila and a few others. No man with her, at least. I nudge Pat Mulryan. I'm not losing that woman again. But I'm still wondering why she never rang. We got on so well that night – did I read the signals wrong? I can't go down to her. *Maybe she lost your number, Paddy.* Yeah, or maybe she didn't fancy me. Only one way to find out …

I send Pat down. Too nervous to go myself. *Ask her to come and sit with me. Don't let me down.* He goes off grinning and I sit, sick with anticipation. And within minutes he's back and I can barely look. But he's smiling and there she is with him, Caroline, smiling. I look at her and she sits down beside me. That's it – I'm hopelessly in love.

I quiz her eventually. *Why did you never ring? You broke my heart.* She laughs and makes a joke but confesses that when she told her brother that she'd met me and wanted to see me again, he'd warned her off me. *Be careful, Caroline – Paddy's great, he's a gentleman, but he's probably up to his eyes in drugs. You're a schoolteacher. You don't want to get into that scene. You could jeopardise your career.* And being a country woman who is far more responsible than me, she took her brother's advice.

Besides, she adds, *I didn't know you. What if you'd put something into my food?*

I look at her in shock. *Like what?*

Hash, maybe.

Jesus, I'd never do that.

I can't believe her brother's a garda. *Yes*, she says, *and another is a detective.* Jesus, policemen just follow me everywhere. What am I getting myself into? But I don't care. This is it. She's the woman I want. And she seems to want me.

Suddenly it's a month later and we've been together every single evening. But she's very independent. She doesn't need to own me. She has lots of friends and she goes to work during the day while I see my friends. I have to have my own space and this isn't a problem for her. But at night she comes home to me or I go to see her.

As the weeks go on I find myself thinking about her constantly during the day, looking forward to seeing her again. She's such a contradiction. Outgoing, funny, up for a bit of craic, loves music, gigs and going out. I'm the total opposite of anyone she's gone out with before, but she's enjoying the change. She loves to party. Just like me. But she's so responsible. Gets up every morning, gets ready, goes to work, pays the bills. Hard-working and clean-living. Different from me. And yet we're so comfortable in each other's company. I love it.

Her friends welcome me into their group. I feel like I've known them for ever. And just like that I feel like I belong somewhere, for the first time in many, many years. More than 20, I calculate. Since I left Belfast, really. I still party, but now I have Caroline by my side. We go out to gigs, to Lillie's, to pubs. Everywhere. And one day I find I haven't been home in weeks, so we decide I'll move in with her. When I turn up at her flat with my plastic bag she looks down at it. She doesn't ask me if that's all I have.

I'm home at last.

~

She's getting closer and I realise this is it. A new start. The beginning of a new chapter for me. Everyone is looking and I know that, without a shadow of a doubt, this is what I want. My life will change completely when this happens, but I have no idea just how much.

~

Will you come to Portlaoise? she says one day. *Come and meet my family.* I'm not sure what to say. *It's a good sign,* Pat Mulryan is telling me. *Means she's serious, Paddy. A woman wouldn't take you down there if she wasn't mad about you. Just go and charm them, because this Caroline is a once-in-a-lifetime woman.* Pat loves her. Says she's the best thing that ever happened to me. Everyone does. I nod. I know. I'm not losing this one. But I'm very nervous. Her two brothers are gardaí. All very intelligent people. And they live beside a prison in the middle of the countryside. Just the idea of being so close to one makes me nervous.

Driving down, we have the music blaring. A Tom Waits CD we play all the time. 'Shiver Me Timbers' is playing in the background and we're chatting. This album reminds me of my squatting days in London, before prison. But I'm not sad thinking about it, listening to it here with Caroline. And as we're driving through the midlands, I see it. Portlaoise Prison. Of all the places she could come from, the love of my life is from a town with one of the biggest prisons in the country, full of IRA men.

It's a strange experience, seeing this prison. I'm acutely aware that I'm on the other side of the wall now, but I could so easily be in there instead of out here. Sean Kinsella, the OC of the IRA when I was in Gartree, is in there, I've heard. He and lots of other men I was in prison with. But while I know that a lot of the men in there did kill people, there's innocent men in there too. Men who did nothing except be in the wrong place at the wrong time. Like me. And so it doesn't give me that much comfort knowing that I'm out here, just fear. Even after seven years out, I always default to a position of fear and suspicion. Wondering if they could ever try to throw me back in.

And even though I know how lucky I am to be out, and even though we've just driven past a prison where there's men locked up, all I can think about is how scared I am meeting Caroline's family for the first time. It's a big day. Caroline has six siblings and most of them will be there – and her mammy. *Call her Maureen*, Caroline tells me. My legs are shaking a tiny bit. Terrified they'll hate me. What if they think I'm guilty – an IRA man who got off on a technicality? So there I am, walking into the living room, smiling and praying I'll make a good first impression, when her brother-in-law Liam jumps up to meet me and sticks out his hand. *What about ye, Armstrong?* he says in a thick, fake Belfast accent. We both crack up laughing. And that's it, the ice is broken and my nerves dissipate. They don't hate me. They don't think that I'm a bad influence on Caroline. They seem to be happy to have me there.

Within months I'll be referring to Maureen as Mother. And she really is like a second mother to me. She tells Caroline that I'm a gentleman. *A good upbringing,* she says. *Never curses.* I'm glad she never heard me in prison – I ended up swearing like a sailor. You had to in there, but I realised early on that you can't speak like that around most people on the outside, unless you're on a building site.

As the months tick on I can't believe that I haven't messed it up yet. Even though she's a responsible schoolteacher, Caroline is very laid-back. She doesn't suffer fools gladly, but she doesn't try to tell me what to do. She knows that I need time to myself. To be alone sometimes. To see my friends. She has no problem with that.

We go partying a lot. All my favourite places. To Lillie's. To the International. To JJ Smyth's. We go out with lots of different people. Pat Mulryan and his wife Caroline. My good friend Paddy Reilly. Me and my Caroline. And sometimes Pat Shortt. It turns out that he has a wife named Caroline, too. We all get on famously. It's like a Paddy Irishman joke with three Carolines thrown in, just like me and the two Paddys back in the pub all those years ago in London. My life is full of Paddys, Pats, Caroles and Carolines.

One Friday night in late 1997 we go to Lillie's and meet Howard Marks, the convicted cannabis smuggler. He was on *The Late Late Show,* talking about his new book, *Mr Nice.* He's a funny, charming man and we laugh until the small hours. We've all had a wee drink, but now it's time to go home. I want to talk to him more about prison. He does too.

I'm staying at the Mont Clare Hotel, he says. *Come and see me in there tomorrow before I go. We'll have a smoke in my room. I don't fly out until late.*

I'll take you to the airport, I insist.

Well, that would be great.

I'll come in earlier, we can have a chat and then we'll drive you there.

When I wake up I realise that I've offered Howard Marks a lift to the aiport today – I can't let him down. One problem: I don't have a driving licence. Although I drove in America, I never got my licence, so I've never bothered to get a car. I get a friend to drive me into town, and before I know it I'm sitting in a hotel room in the Mont Clare, getting stoned. We're comparing notes on prisons; the funny and scary moments. He's telling me about US and Spanish prisons, and I'm telling him about the British ones. It's so good to talk about it with someone who understands. I don't do this often any more. It's like a language you haven't spoken in so long that you think you've forgotten it. But as soon as you hear it, it all comes back and you start jabbering away like a native.

Howard stops suddenly and looks at his watch. *Fuck. My plane is going soon. We better go.* He stubs out the joint we've been sharing. I help him throw his clothes into his bag and within minutes we're back in the car and my friend's driving us through Dublin city centre and out to the northside, to the airport. Howard's in the back and I can see he's relit and is finishing the joint. I can see my friend wrinkling his nose and then looking through the rear-view mirror. He doesn't say anything, but I know he's worried. He's an upstanding citizen and there we are, driving through the centre of Dublin with one of the world's biggest convicts smoking hash in the back of the new car. My friend is too polite to say anything; instead he frantically opens all the windows of his car to get rid of the smell. I'm pretty scared too. All I need is to get into trouble in Dublin, a city that I love. This is the first time I've lived in a city and never been arrested. Howard's finished his joint and is smiling that famous Mr Nice smile that puts everyone at ease. I can see my friend relax. After we drop Howard off, my friend looks at me. *Jesus, Paddy!* I nod. *I know.*

After a few months with Caroline I've been thinking that I want to do something really special for her. Knock her off her feet. Take her to Paris, I decide. The city of love. Show her the places I saw when I was doing the film promotions. *I'm taking you next week,* I say. She doesn't say anything. She doesn't believe me. She knows that sometimes I make promises and don't keep them. I always mean to keep them, but things just seem to go wrong. But this time I mean it. I want to take her there for the weekend, to a lovely hotel, to the Hard Rock Café. Go to the Eiffel Tower. Show her how much she means to me. She's so strong, and yet so gentle and soft in other ways. She looks out for me so much. I want to look after this amazing woman and show her what she means to me. *Just keep next Friday free,* I tell her. *We're going.*

She doesn't mention it again and I mean to organise it, but somehow things get out of control again and my monthly pay from Alastair is all gone. No money left. And even if I did have any left, I realise that I have no idea how to go about booking flights and hotels and all that. Gerry always did it for us when we were going away. So I say nothing and hope she's forgotten. Two weeks have passed. She doesn't say a word and neither do I. But I feel bad. I'm going to leave it for a while, but I *will* take her there.

~

I turn to her and take her hand. The music is still playing softly. I'm glad we're facing this way. I couldn't look at everyone looking at us. I'd probably do something silly, like laugh or make a funny face. I've promised her I won't do that. *You look lovely*, she says, smiling nervously. I look amazing? No, she looks amazing. Radiant and elegant and everything I ever wanted. I can't believe I'm standing beside a woman like this. There's a silence and we begin.

~

Within a few months of meeting Caroline my world feels like it's done a 180-degree turn. I still do some of the same things. Act the hooligan sometimes. Get stoned. Maybe something harder occasionally. Drink too much Guinness. Gamble a bit more than I should. The problem is that it costs a fair bit of money to live this kind of lifestyle, so the monthly allowance Alastair gives me is often gone within days. Some nights I go out and hope I'll meet someone who'll buy me a pint. It's one of the benefits of being so well-known. And I usually do meet someone, but there's months when I'm really stuck. One day Caroline's at work and I'm looking for something and I find a stack of money under some towels. Six hundred pounds. Caroline must be saving it, I think. I'll take it and then put it back when I get my next pay from Alastair. Just a couple of weeks and it'll be back. She'll never even know.

Within a week the money's gone. I can barely even remember what I spent it on. Partying and cigarettes and a few bets. Dublin is so bloody expensive, I think to myself. And then one day Caroline comes home and starts looking around for something. *Paddy, I can't find the rent money. Six hundred pounds. I know I left it here. Have you seen it?* I improvise. *I paid the landlady,* I say. *She came around when you were at work.* She looks relieved and I feel bad, but then she never needs to know. I just need enough time to get the money from Alastair and then I'll pay the rent. Our landlady is a nice woman – she won't say anything if it's a couple of weeks late.

I'm holding out until the money comes through, but then, typically, just my luck, Caroline bumps into our landlady one afternoon and the rent issue comes up. Caroline's furious. *Mortified, Paddy, absolutely mortified.* I don't know what to say to her. I say nothing – it's best that way. Just look down. What can I say? *I know I'm a fool. Sorry. I won't do it again.* What if I lose her? I'll never forgive myself. But she doesn't dump me. She knows I don't mean badly and that I won't do it again. And she'll find a better hiding-place next time because she knows sometimes the temptation is too great. From then on I give her most of my money and she gives it to me as I need it. We have an unspoken agreement that she'll give me what I need and no more. She knows me like Alastair.

Almost a year has passed since I met Caroline and we're still partying, but closer to home now. We have a local, the Fingal. It's a pub facing the Clontarf seafront, full of decent, ordinary people who are always ready for a chat and a bit of craic. Just like back home in Belfast, or in Kilburn, something I haven't had for a very long time. No stars or champagne. Just pints and conversation and football. I love it.

I mention the prospect of getting married to Caroline, but I know she thinks I don't mean it. Another thing I'll never mention again. But I do and I will. So a year, to the month, after the night we first got together we're sitting at the bar in the Fingal. Our usual spot. I have a pint and Caroline has a glass of lager. There's a few people we know here, and I decide, this is it. Before I know it, I'm down on one of my arthritic, 47-year-old knees, looking up at her. *Will you marry me, Caroline?* And before I get a chance to get nervous, she's nodding. *Yes.* Others are clapping, congratulating us. She's going to marry me. I can't believe my luck. This is all I've ever wanted, but I never thought this day would come. I have the love of an amazing woman and she's going to marry me. I ring my mammy and she's over the moon. She's met Caroline and loves her. Everyone in my family does.

The next day we drive around Dublin looking for a ring. We've a tiny budget, £100. And then we find a jeweller's not far from home. Caroline puts it on her finger and that's it. We set a date for six months later – March 1998. So it only took me 47 years to get a girl down the aisle. Later than I ever would have thought, but well worth the wait. We've six months to plan it, so I ring Alastair and tell him I'm getting married. I'll need money for the wedding. He agrees. I start inviting people. Caroline gives me invitations and I hand them out to our friends. The problem is, I've forgotten who I even gave them to by the time I get home. *Who, Paddy? We need to keep a list of who is coming. You know our friend Caroline, the one with red hair? Or, He lives beside the woman with the baby. You know him? No, Paddy, I don't. Look, how many have you given out? I don't know. Sorry, I know so many people. I'm terrible with names.* She's going to kill me before I even marry her. *Sure they'll RSVP and then we'll know,* I reason. *Don't be worrying, Caroline.*

I ask Pat Mulryan to be my best man and he agrees. Paddy Reilly is one of the groomsmen. The Three Musketeers together again. Her brother will give her away, and two of her sisters, Katherine and Fiona, will be the bridesmaids. My godchild, Sorcha, and her little sister Caoimhe will be our flowergirls. Our page boy is my friend Noel Brazil's nephew Paul, a tiny wee fella with blond hair. I want a wee boy like him.

I tell Caroline I want to take her to Paris for our honeymoon. I said I would. She's never mentioned that long-postponed trip I promised her a couple of years ago. She never makes me feel bad. She knows I mean well. But this time it's really happening. We find the best hotel in Paris and book it. Five nights in a suite in Le Royal Monceau, £735 a night. For five nights. That's six months' rent, but I don't care. I want to show her everything I saw when I was there. Share it with her.

The day is getting closer and Caroline keeps asking me about the money from Alastair. *We need the money for the wedding, Paddy*. I reassure her that he will send it. *I rang him, I promise. Told him all about the wedding and he said he'd send it.* I forget to tell her that he doesn't believe me and that Caroline is supposed to ring him. So a month beforehand, when it still hasn't arrived, Caroline rings him herself. Asks if he can send it soon. Alastair is quiet for a moment and then laughs. *Well, of course I can send it. The only reason I hadn't was that I didn't believe him – I thought it was just a story he made up to get more money from his account.* He sends the money and Caroline sorts out the rest of the wedding. Pat, Alastair's wife, later tells me how relieved they are when they realise it's true. Now they know that I have someone who will be there for me, who will look out for me. Because they won't always be there. They were worried I'd be alone for ever.

March is approaching and Caroline's getting nervous. She pulls Pat Mulryan and Paddy Reilly to one side. *Now, you're looking after him the night before. You're not to go mad. I'm holding you responsible. Keep him sober. Get him home at a decent time.* They nod. They're a bit scared of her when she's like this. We all are. The real schoolteacher. *Of course. We'll make sure he's home early. It'll be fine. You can rely on us.*

My last night as a single man turns into my last morning and I haven't been home yet. I'm supposed to be staying with Pat Mulryan. Paddy Reilly comes over and so the Three Musketeers decide we have to go out for one final drink. *Last night as a free man, Paddy.* The irony of that statement isn't lost on any of us. But suddenly it's 6.00am and we're only getting home. I'm a mess. I've nothing to wear except the tux for the wedding, but that's hours away. Have to get something clean. Got. To. Get. Something. Clean. Oh. God. She'll. Kill. Me. Make my way to the apartment. Rap on the window. Her sisters are inside.

Just me, I whisper. *Sorry. Could I have … hiccup … some … clothes, please? Hiccup. Shhh. But don't. Tell. Caroline. Okay?*

They're looking at me – horror in their faces. *Jesus, Paddy, are you only just home now? Oh, my God.*

Aye … don't be … hiccup … worrying. Isn't that right, Pat? Aye. Jeans. And a shirt.

Paddy, get away from the window now. You can't see her. Go back there and we'll get you something. We'll pass it out through the window.

No problem, girls. You're looking lovely, so youse are. Hiccup.

I don't know how, but by the time I have to leave for the church I'm fine. The hair is brushed, the monkey suit is on. Tails, no less. Paddy and Pat are in theirs too. We musketeers clean up well, we agree. One for the road, boys?

And now here I am. Early as usual. Standing. Waiting. At the top of this beautiful church in Clontarf. Waiting for the woman of my dreams. Please don't let me down. She must be outside. I can hear the roar of motorbikes. People up above in Belfast can probably hear them too, it's that loud. Deep breath, Paddy. The congregation turns around. What is it? They can't see it, but outside the church are about 10 Harley-Davidsons, driven by my friends from the Fingal, Ken and the other fellas in his Harley-Davidson club. They're all on their bikes in their leathers and they've accompanied Caroline to the church, in a motorcade surrounding the car. It must have been quite the sight in the otherwise peaceful seaside town where we live. Can't believe I missed it.

I squeeze Caroline's hand as the hum in the church fades to a silence and the priest begins to speak. It's all lovely. The service. The vows. And especially the music. It's sublime. About 120 of Caroline's students have formed a choir. Alastair and Pat tell me later they didn't even realise the choir was there until they started singing and their voices descended from the balcony like something from the heavens.

I do.

I do.

And before I know it I'm slipping a ring on Caroline's finger and I'm wearing one. Married at last.

There's a church organ playing in the background that lends a solemn, pure quality to the ceremony. When one of Caroline's students, Lisa Lambe, sings the Psalm in Irish, I have goosebumps all over me. I will never forget it. This is my wedding. To Caroline. And when Bryan Hoey sings John Denver's

'Perhaps Love' with Naoise Stuart-Kelly, my beautiful new wife looking at me, I have to shake myself. It's just unbelievable. It's a bizarre mixture, this wedding. There's schoolteachers and gardaí and ex-IRA men and famous singers and solicitors and journalists and a drag queen. All in the one room. People who never knew each other until today are laughing and talking and dancing and getting drunk together, while my friend Pat Shortt joins Steve Rawson's band on his saxophone, and Brian Downey, from Thin Lizzy, plays the drums. It's like the party of my dreams – everyone we know and love in one place.

People are often surprised at the mix of my friends. *Wouldn't have thought someone of your generation, from Belfast, would have such a diverse group of friends.* But when you're in prison you realise that good people come in all shapes and sizes. Just like the bad ones. Somehow, this eclectic mix works really well. My mammy is having the time of her life, charming everyone around her. She could give any of them a run for their money, she assures them. They love her. She'll hug them like they're her sons, give them big kisses on the cheek, and she loves joking with them. *How's my toyboy?* She's still going with the rest of them until the early hours.

Pat Mulryan reads out the cards from those who couldn't make it. There's one from our old friend Shane MacGowan, the man who wrote us the song while we were in prison. Pat reads out Shane's message. *Hope this sentence is better than the last. Where's my invite, you bastard?*

Everyone laughs. He's clever and funny, but it's true. I did get one life sentence – one I signed my name to, but not willingly. And now I've signed up to another one, but very willingly. And this is one contract I want to see through to the very end. Till death do us part. There are moments during the day when I can't help thinking where I was 10 years ago, in 1988. Fading away in Gartree, facing another 20 years behind bars. And if it hadn't been for people like Alastair, Ros, Grant, Sister Sarah and the many others who campaigned for us, I would be there still, with at least 10 years left to endure. Instead I've been given a chance at another life. A life after life.

Like any good Irish wedding, someone starts a singsong and then it's 5.00am and my new wife and I have to be going to the airport soon. I have a promise to keep. When we get to the entrance of Dublin Airport, it's blocked off. Some kind of dispute. So we have to drag our bags what feels like miles. And then our flight is cancelled. Caroline looks at me and shrugs. Another ill-fated attempt to go to Paris? But I'm not giving up this time. I ring the travel agent. Fortunately, I'd invited him and his wife to our wedding; they've probably only just got into bed, as most people left the celebrations just a few hours ago. The travel agent gets on the phone and gets us on another flight out of Dublin and, miraculously, we touch down in Paris the day after our wedding.

For five days I walk around Paris holding my new wife's hand like it's an extension of my own arm. She laughs at me because I want to eat in the Hard Rock Café – the same place I went to with the crew when we were promoting *In the Name of the Father*. I'm a man of routine, I tell her. We take the Bateau Mouche down the Seine and flake out at night in our expensive hotel suite. We'll pay for our extravagance years later when the money runs out, but for now it's worth it.

∼

It's 2002 and Caroline's acting strange. She's hiding something. After four years of marriage I can read her like a book. I've known it for a while. She's not herself. But I don't press her. Whatever it is, she'll tell me in her own time.

∼

Caroline's got some news. She's pregnant. I'm going to be a daddy. I can't believe it. It seems too good to possibly be true. I want to tell the world. My mammy, my sisters, Alastair, everyone. Most of all I can't wait to tell the lads who slag me about my age. I'm 48. Who'd have thought it possible? But she won't let me say anything. *Something could go wrong.* She's right. So I say nothing.

Caroline has to go to the doctor. I'm willing it to be okay, but it isn't. I was right: if it seems too good to be true, it probably is. Caroline is stoic. I sit in our local later that day. Facing the door. Old habits die hard. I wanted a baby so much. I thought I was going to be a daddy.

~

A couple of months later and she's pregnant again. Could we really be that lucky? Waiting. Hoping. But within weeks our tiny baby is gone – its tiny heart stopped beating and it feels like mine has stopped too.

I don't say it, but it must be me. I'm almost 50. My dad only lived to see 51. You don't get to go from having nothing to having everything, Paddy. Or worse, what if this is my fault? What if it's because of the lifestyle I led? Caroline will wonder this too, but she never says it. She would never make me feel bad about myself.

~

And then, almost exactly a year after our wedding, Caroline's pregnant again. After the heartbreak of the last year I'm trying not to get my hopes up. Expect the worst. Always the best strategy. But something's different this time. I can feel it. Could this be it? Might be our last chance. I'm paranoid until we know for sure. And now she's standing there, holding a tiny picture. *There's the head and that's the arm and that's the body. It's okay. It's real …*

The doctors are happy. Caroline's happy. I'm absolutely terrified. I'll not relax until I have a baby in my arms. I'm watching Caroline like a hawk. *Mind yourself, love. Take it easy.* The weeks are flying and our baby will be here soon. We've our own house in Clontarf now, just metres from the sea. Alastair sends me the money and I pay for it in cash. Money I wouldn't have had if he hadn't reined me in. And thank God he did. Because now I have a wife, a house and, soon, a baby. I can't believe this is my life. My mammy is over the moon. She can't wait to come down after the baby is born.

Caroline and I are moving into our new home, a lovely place with a beautiful park nearby for the community. Having lived in flats for years and being used to feeling quite anonymous, we're overwhelmed by the warmth of the neighbours. Trish and John live next-door to us and immediately welcome us. I find an instant friend in Shay, Trish's father, who comes around regularly to work on their garden. We often end up down in the local pub. We love winding each other up. Until the day he dies, we'll stay firm friends.

Geraldine McKeown, a dynamic and warm person, takes Caroline under her wing. She introduces us to everyone and we are often on the receiving end of her lovely meals.

And when we order soil for the front garden, one of our neighbours, Linda (who will become a very close friend), asks her husband, George, to come up and help me. Caroline and her friends secretly call him Gorgeous George, but I'm not allowed to tell him that. People are just like that around here and I can't believe how lucky we've been to find this place. There are so many special moments, like the annual summer BBQ in the local park and the Christmas Days we spend at Ray and Pat Byrne's house. Ray is our local butcher and every year he and his wife put on a fabulous spread for their friends. Within a few months we feel like we've always lived here. This is the kind of home I haven't had since Milton Street.

In the last couple of weeks of 1999 my world changes for ever with the arrival of John – our son. And now I know that the new decade, the new millennium, is my time. Our time.

There are so many special people in our lives now that we decide to have two sets of godparents: dear Alastair and Pat; and also Caroline's friend Sheila and her husband, Stephen. Being a father is everything I'd hoped for and so much more. I thought that Caroline had changed me. And she did. But this is a whole new level again – this tiny baby has just upped the ante. He weighs only a few pounds, but already our lives, our conversations, everything revolves around him. I don't know the last time I went out partying – Lillie's is a thing of the past. Feel like I'm growing up – got all that partying out of my system.

John's only a few months old when Caroline has to go back to work. I'm going to be a house-husband, a stay-at-home dad. If you'd told me this when I was 16, or even when I was 36, that this is what I'd be doing at this age, or at any age, I'd have asked you what you were smoking. But this is my life and I love it.

The routine that a baby demands suits me down to the ground. It feels so normal. Reassuring. I get up around 5.30 every morning, do the dishes from the night before and give John a feed. When the local shop opens I take him down in his buggy and we get the paper and have a walk along the seafront. He smiles at all the women and they stop and talk to us. We come home and have some lunch and then I read the paper and do my crosswords and a few other puzzles while he sleeps. We have another wee walk in the afternoon, before I make the dinner, and then when Caroline gets home I go down and put on a placepot in the local bookies and go and see my friends for an hour in our local, the Sheds. By 10.00pm I'm asleep on the couch.

Being a man in his early fifties with a tiny baby, walking around a Dublin suburb, is a funny experience. At first people assume I'm the grandad, but even that's not the norm in 2000. When they realise I'm a stay-at-home dad and my wife is out working, everyone talks to me. It's a great way to meet people. Mothers come and talk to me, give me advice and ask for mine. I find myself talking to these women about teething and nappies and anything else that's on my mind. I'm not one for reading books and I'll never be very good on computers, so if I have a question I stop one of the mothers on the street and ask them. The Lord Mayor of Clontarf, one of Caroline's friends has nicknamed me, and I laugh. I like that. The Lord Mayor with a wee baby.

My mammy comes down at least twice a year. *I'll babysit*, she says. Only she's getting on now and I worry. What if something happened to my wee boy? And so Caroline asks Sheila to come over to keep an eye on Mammy while we go out for a drink. A babysitter for the babysitter.

Just before John turns one, Mammy comes down for my fiftieth. We have it in the Sheds, my local now, and all my Clontarf friends are there. *Your life is full of good people*, Mammy says. She's so happy to see me happy. At my party she sings her party piece, 'On the Street Where You Live' from *My Fair Lady*. Her voice is so pure and sweet. It's like being a child again, looking over at her singing. Everyone loves her. One local fella who's been having a hard time asks for her advice and she sits there and talks to him. When she passes away a few years later he still has problems, but he travels all the way to Belfast, plays a soulful tune for her on his harmonica beside the coffin and then throws it in. *Good luck, missus. Rest in peace.*

~

I should be wondering what's going on with Caroline, and I keep meaning to speak to her about it, but whenever she gets home I go out for a while. By the time I come back, we have the dinner and she's put John to bed and we're both exhausted. Tomorrow I'll ask her.

~

John is getting so big. He's a busy child and just wants to move around. It scares the hell out of me. The women in the area tell me not to worry. *They're stronger than they look. Hard to break, Paddy. Let him find his feet. He'll be grand.* Everything's *grand* in Dublin. I nod, but nothing's going to happen to my son. I go down the local hardware shop and buy yards of foam and I tape it on every corner in the house, in case he falls. Before John, I'd never really thought about how my mammy and dad must have felt when our wee Gertie was taken from them. In the blink of an eye. Now I think about her all the time.

As he gets bigger, the work does too. I've a lot of respect for housewives. I'll never hear a bad word said about them. Minding John and cleaning and doing some of the cooking is exhausting. But I'm proud of myself. I'm a 51-year-old man minding my two-year-old son. The age my dad was when he passed away. I wouldn't be anywhere else in the world. Then one day I have an epiphany: if I hadn't gone to prison, I never would have met Caroline. God knows where I'd have ended up. On the streets. Dead, maybe.

It's a very strong possibility. And then I would never have had this boy of mine. Suddenly, it's like the 15 years have almost disappeared. Not quite, but they're fading. This was the plan for me, I realise now.

I'd love another baby, but I tell Caroline that one is enough. That I've enough on my plate with one. One is perfect. What man wants to admit that he's scared? What if one is all I can ever have? I'm even older now, so it's probably too late for another one. So I tell her that I'm happy with one. *That's enough for me, Caroline. He's more than a handful.*

~

She looks at me and begins to speak. She's going to tell me something. She's nervous. I can tell. What is it? I'm scared now.

Paddy, I'm pregnant, she's saying. She's looking at me, waiting.

That's great, Caroline. I'm so happy.

I thought you'd be annoyed, she's saying.

Why would I be annoyed?

Because you're always telling me that one is enough.

No way. This is a second miracle. I hug her. *That's absolutely brilliant news.*

Just when I thought I'd won the lottery – a wife, a son, a house in a lovely, friendly area, friends, freedom – when I thought that I had it all, that I couldn't feel any more love in my heart, my baby girl comes along in July 2002. Sophie. A beautiful wee thing who I'd climb mountains for. Anything.

Caroline has to go back to work when Sophie's a few months old, and I'm going to stay at home with the kids. I tried working over the years, but I've never been able to cope. Coming out of prison at the age of 39 has made it impossible to retrain. Even dealing with money took me a couple of years to get my head around. I tried working with some friends on a gardening venture. We'd go around doing some landscape work. Except I'd always end up in the kitchen, talking to the women, drinking tea, eating their cakes and biscuits and regaling them with prison stories while the others were left to do the work. They were fit to kill me after a couple of weeks, so I quit. The reality is that I'll never work outside the home, so it suits me fine. Anyway, I want to be at home with my children.

Life is great. I can't wait to show my Sophie to Mammy. *Look at her. Isn't she gorgeous?* Mammy's due to come down a few weeks after the birth. A couple of days before Mammy's due to arrive, the phone rings early one morning. It's Mammy. She's in hospital. *Come up, Paddy.* I take the train up immediately. Caroline wants to come, but Sophie's not even a month old.

In the hospital, Mammy is hooked up to tubes and wires and everything. Her heart is leaking. She's only 76. So much life left in her. She was line dancing until a few weeks ago, but her pallor is different. *She hasn't been well,* Josephine tells me, *but she refused to go to a doctor. You know Mammy.* I do. I know exactly what she's like. I rush home again on the train that night, distraught and crying. Back to Sophie. Maybe Mammy will be okay. She'll be down again in a few weeks. But I know she won't. I just can't face it. Run away. Can't deal with this pain. It's too huge.

A few days later, and just over a month after Sophie is born, my mammy passes away. Her funeral is enormous. Men and women of all ages, from everywhere. People whose lives she touched. People I've never heard of. But they all knew her. And loved her. My friends from Dublin travel up to pay their respects. *Sorry for your loss. She was a great woman, Paddy. A lady. A beautiful voice. A real character. A gas woman. We had to come.* I'm so moved. Gerry's mammy, Sarah, and his sister, Ann, rock our month-old baby Sophie back and forth in her buggy for the whole mass and then she lays in a thick baby spacesuit in Sheila's arms at the graveside. *She looks like her granny. Can you see it, Paddy? Sure she's the spit of her. Her whole face. Especially the eyes. The eyebrows. Eileen's double. The circle of life, Paddy.* Yeah. Maybe my mammy wanted Sophie to look out for me when she was gone. That would be my mammy all right – always thinking of someone else.

~

The years are flying and my babies are growing up. John's starting school soon, so I sit him down and tell him. *I was in prison, John. Bad men put me there. But I didn't do nothing. I was innocent. Bad men put me in there, but they were wrong and then I got out.* Caroline overhears me and she's horrified. *Jesus, Paddy, when he goes to school none of the children will want to play with him. Yes, they will, Caroline, because I'm innocent and everyone knows it.* And they do. John marches in one day and tells them his dad was in prison but he was innocent, and they all just accept it. They're very proud of him. They're asking him to bring me to school and he's delighted. When she's older, Sophie will do a project about me in her school and I'll laugh – I'm a school project!

My routine is fixed for life now. I get up before 6.00am, get the kids ready and then take them out. I tell Caroline I need a double buggy so I can push them up and down the Clontarf coast, one in front of the other. To playschool. Wherever they go, I'll take them and pick them up afterwards. I wouldn't let anyone else do it. Home for lunch and then out to play. I'm in my mid-fifties, but I can run and throw a ball. Caroline gets home every afternoon. She tells me I'm spoiling them. *You won't let them do anything for themselves, Paddy.* I nod and smile and do it my way anyway. They're our miracles. My second chance at life.

CHAPTER TEN

Inside it's warm love …
(Van Morrison)

September 2016

They're all staring at it. Engrossed. They asked me to come and watch it too, but I said no. Made a wisecrack. *I've seen it already, ladies. I'm actually in it. I'll leave you to it.* But that's not really why. I can't bear to. Why invite pain and memories into my life? Ask them to overwhelm me? No, thanks.

~

February 2005

Alastair rings me. There's been an official apology from Tony Blair, on behalf of the entire British government. Alastair just heard it on the radio and investigated it, and it's true.

I can't believe it. It's only just happened but, thoughtful as ever, within a few short hours of hearing it, our neighbours Trish and John pass a bottle of champagne over the back wall to us. *We're delighted for you, Paddy. Fair play.*

We've been publicly and completely exonerated. A lot of people don't realise what a big deal this is. *Of course everybody knows you're innocent.* But that's not true. Since our release there has been a whispering campaign against us, based on claims that we're actually guilty. A lot of people doubt us because of what has been said not just by the police but also by law officers and certain judges. Alastair discussed this with Cherie Blair at a reception a couple of years ago – maybe that had an influence. Paul Hill and his wife, Courtney Kennedy-Hill, also lobbied the British government, so who knows why it happened, but at this stage it doesn't matter. It's happened!

I've wanted this for a long time, but I never thought it would come to pass. Whenever people would ask me about it, I'd play it down. Tell them that I didn't care. Which wasn't completely true. Tell them my life has moved on. Which it has. Say that I'd forgotten it all. Which of course I hadn't. Who could forget spending nearly a quarter of their life in prison? But when you say it enough times, you start to believe it yourself. A self-fulfilling prophecy – that has worked for me. Kept me sane and able to get on with my life. When this public apology finally happens I'm taken by surprise by the strength of my own emotions. By my tears. When Blair makes this apology, something changes for me. It's official now. For years there have been the doubters, the nay-sayers. *They got off on a technicality. They did it. Everybody knows.* Now, nobody can say that ever again. The British government don't make apologies lightly.

We won't get a copy of the official letter for weeks, and then only when Alastair writes to Tony Blair and tells him that we're all innocent and asks for a letter addressed to each of us. When he gets the letters, Alastair sends them out to us.

When the initial elation has worn off, I read the words more closely. In his letter, Blair mentions Gerry by name. *Gerry, Giuseppe and Annie Maguire.* Which is as it should be. But *Gerard Conlon and all the Guildford Four?* And *Giuseppe Conlon, and Annie Maguire and all of the Maguire Seven.* I'm one of the *all the Guildford Four*, but we are only *the Guildford Four* because of them. They created the infamous Guildford Four. We didn't. We have real names and identities. We're real people. Where are our names?

Caroline and I talk about it a lot. I could pursue it. Insist on getting a personalised version. But I can't obsess on it. After spending so many years in pain, I can't go back there. It's an official apology, something we have been waiting on for a long time. Something that should put an end to the whispering campaign. And now we have it. Time to move on. To celebrate. The next day we book a sun holiday in Majorca. Treat ourselves. Our first sun holiday ever as a family.

~

September 2016

They're all still engrossed in the screen. I can't see it, but I can hear it. The voices. One in particular. And like a moth drawn to the flickering light of a flame, I'm edging closer. Stand back, Paddy. You don't need this. But I can't help it. Just want to be a little bit closer. I can hear her, but I can't see her. It's so eerily familiar. After all these years. Despite my resolution to stand back I want to see her smile, her hair. One last time. But I need to be quiet. So nobody sees me.

~

November 2012

I'm a 62-year-old father of a 13- and an 11-year-old and I love it. My babies are now kind, intelligent and articulate young people. It's physically less demanding and emotionally so rewarding. Just like her dad, Sophie is a dedicated Arsenal fan. We wear our matching jerseys whenever Arsenal plays. I take her down to the Sheds and she sits with me and my friends. She's smart and funny and gentle; John is a talented musician, like Caroline, and extremely witty.

'The Lord Mayor of Clontarf' still gets up early, and when Caroline comes home after work I drop in to the local bookies. A €1 placepot. A far cry from the days when Pat Mulryan was fishing crumpled dockets for thousand-pound bets out of the bin. And even though, or perhaps because, the money is all gone, I'm happier. Much happier. Money was never going to make me happy. And it was never going to give me my life back. Only love could do that.

Most nights I drop in to the Sheds to see my friends, especially if there's an Arsenal game on. My friend Conor and I watch the matches together with the rest of the locals. I've known Conor since I moved to Clontarf. He's a fascinating man. He places no value on material things and loves nothing more than a good philosophical discussion. I love his unique perspective on everything. Conor and I can be debating the offside rule one minute and the

Iraq war the next. He'll be taken from me in a few short years, in his early sixties. For now, though, he's still one of my best mates.

I still see Pat Mulryan and Paddy Reilly occasionally. We'll always be the Three Musketeers, even though our lives and families have taken us all in different directions. Paddy lives abroad now, but when he comes home we get together and it's like all the years have melted away. We laugh about our wild days in Dublin in the 1990s, but while I sometimes miss those times, I wouldn't swap my life today for anything.

~

Even though I knew it would have to happen to one of us one day, there was never going to be a good way to hear this news. Never a good time.

It's a letter from Alastair. About Carole. She's gone. Cancer. She knew for a while, he tells me, but they kept it quiet. She's already been buried. The funeral is over. Family only. Her husband, her daughter, Louise, her mum and a few select others. When she knew she was dying, Carole gave specific instructions. *No press. No reporters. I don't want them to get any more column space from me. Keep it out of the papers.*

I'm consumed by the most powerful and raw emotions – grief and anger and denial. And, more than anything, hurt. Carole is gone and I never got to say goodbye. The woman I shared this bond with for 15 years. The woman I proposed to up on a hill as the sun was setting. The woman who went to prison because she knew me. Gone.

I really didn't see this coming. This loss. Not a romantic loss: I don't think that Carole and I could have been happy together after what we'd both been through. Too much of the same pain. Both too damaged. I'm alive because I'm with Caroline. I have my babies because of her. But somehow, while Carole was alive, it was easier to pretend that everything was okay. That she got on with her life. Which she did, until it was taken from her so soon. That, in spite of what she went through, she came out the other side. But, ultimately, she didn't. Taken in her fifties, leaving her elderly mother, a teenage daughter and a grieving husband behind – it just doesn't seem fair.

This pain is so unexpected. Just when I felt like I had moved on from all this, the memories hit me. And yet, what right do I have? She's not mine any more. I got on with my life and she got on with hers. So why do I feel so sad? I'd like to have had a chance to say goodbye. To let go of the girl who was mine for a short while.

Grief is strange. I'll think I'm okay, and then suddenly I can see her, as clear as day. I'm 24 and she's 17 and barefoot. We're wandering through the London streets in the middle of the night. She's laughing while I jump into gardens, stealing flowers for her. Holding them out to her. Carrying the box of chocolates that I slipped under my jacket in a corner shop earlier, when the owner wasn't looking. Her long hair pinned back with flowers. Her hippie bag. *Come on, Piggy. Come on. Let's go home. I'm cold.*

~

September 2016
Though nobody realises it yet, I've moved slightly from where I'm standing in the kitchen. So I can see her. And there she is. Filling the screen. Almost 27 years ago. Carole. Older than when I met her. But still young. In her bright white 1980s top. So alive. This is the interview we gave to Grant McKee and Ros Franey the week after our release.

It's like I've stepped into the screen. Time-travelled from 2016 back to 1989. There I am, walking through the forest. And she's jumping out from behind the tree, surprising me. We're hugging. And I can feel her hair. Her skin. Her breath. Brushing against me.

She's talking to the camera now: to 66-year-old me, standing in my kitchen; to her daughter, almost four years after she died; to Lisa and Maura; and to Caroline and Mary-Elaine, who have only heard stories about her but feel they know her. This voice from the past is talking to us all. She looks shell-shocked. Relieved. And tired. But still so young and very alive. And, suddenly, I am overwhelmed …

~

June 2014

The last time I saw him was in my local, almost exactly two years ago. *I'm coming to Dublin*, he said down the phone that day. The same Gerry – warm and bubbly even though, like all of us, he's had his struggles, battled his demons. *I'm coming down to see Bruce Springsteen. It would be great to see you, Paddy.* One minute he's on the phone and the next he's sitting opposite me in the Sheds. It should feel weird that my old pal is sitting here in my local; that two such distinctly different parts of my life have suddenly collided. But it doesn't. Having him here feels totally normal. We could be in London, in India or in America. Even in a prison cell in HMP Gartree. But we're not. We're in Dublin in the summer of 2012.

He looks all right. Older. Perhaps even older than me. Life's taken it out of him. A bit jaded-looking, but he's been busy. Going around talking to people. Trying to help anybody who's been falsely imprisoned. But he's tired. *You've got the right idea, Paddy*, he keeps insisting. *You've moved on with your life. You have everything. I've never been able to move on.* I nod. *But I don't have that personality, Gerry. I never could have done what you're doing. You're doing a brilliant job.* And it's true. He still has that fire in him. The passion. Should I be doing more? I'm wondering to myself. I always said that wasn't what I wanted – to be touring around doing talks – but as he's talking I think about it.

We talk about everything – about Belfast in the 1950s and 1960s, London in the 1970s, prison in the 1980s and 1990s and our travels through India and America. Sometimes we're quiet for a moment when we remember the awful times. The humiliation, the loneliness, the fear. But we don't want to dwell on that tonight. We want to laugh and celebrate a lifetime of friendship. Through thick and through thin doesn't even begin to describe our journey.

He asks about Carole. *I haven't seen her in years*, I explain. *She has a daughter*, I tell him. *Louise. Alastair keeps me up to date on her life. And Alastair tells Carole about my life. She sounds happy*, I tell Gerry. *At last.* She was lovely, we agree. Did she suffer the most, we wonder? Probably. *What happened there?* he asks me. He's never asked before. I shrug. *It was just too late.* He nods. He knows exactly what I mean.

He's concerned about Sir John May's inquiry into miscarriages of justice related to the Guilford Four and the Maguire Seven, and about the 700-plus papers tucked away in the National Archives at Kew in England. They're due to be released in January 2020. Like Alastair, Gerry has been campaigning relentlessly to have them released sooner. So the truth can come out. Or, more importantly, so that we can refute the lies that are no doubt concealed in there. The lies that the police and other members of the establishment told in that private hearing after our release.

Before I left home I asked Caroline to come around to meet Gerry, but she was too shy. Said she didn't want to intrude. She always tells me to have my time with my friends. *It's yours and Gerry's night. A time for old friends.* I didn't push her. We'll do it another time. *Yes,* she said, *we will. Next time.* I wish I'd pushed her. She does too. One of her biggest regrets, she tells me years later.

Because while we didn't know it then, and I'm sure Gerry didn't, that was the last time I'd see him alive. Our phone rings early one morning in late June 2014. Paddy Hill's crying. *Gerry's gone, Paddy. He's dead.* I'm completely taken aback. Devastated. *Cancer. Hasn't been well for a few weeks. Thought it was pneumonia but it was cancer. He only found out a few weeks ago. Ravaged him. Just months after his sixtieth birthday.*

I've barely put down the phone and I'm running upstairs to Caroline, who's still asleep. She can barely understand me through my tears. And for the days and weeks to come I can see his face everywhere. On the street. In the face of a stranger. When I close my eyes. Always when I least expect it.

The next day I walk down to get my newspaper from the local shop and there he is, staring out at me from the front pages. Gerry. His soulful eyes and warm smile. It hits me all over again as I stand silently, staring. Remembering. A woman approaches me. Another customer. She recognises me. She touches my hand softly and tells me how sorry she is. Then she hugs me. She asks me to wait. *I'll be back in a minute. Please wait,* she urges. So I do. It's a relief to just stand for a moment and do nothing. And suddenly she's back, pressing a small velvet bag into my hands. *These are from Mexico. I want you to have them.* I take them, and with that, she's gone. When I get home Caroline and I open the bag and inside are heavy, ornate, silver rosary beads. My eyes fill with water.

And now, just a few months shy of the 25th anniversary of our release, Paddy Hill and I are carrying Gerry's coffin on our shoulders out of St Peter's Cathedral, our local church off the Falls. The church where almost every child in the area made their Communion, their Confirmation, where my mammy prayed for me. We carry him out of the church, just trying to keep it together. Up to Albert Street, where his mammy lived for the 15 years we were in prison. Along the Falls Road where we used to play football, 20-a-side. Past our old childhood haunts of the 1950s and 1960s – Sylvester's, the bookies, our local pub. Through what was a battlefield from the late 1960s up to and well beyond the day we all took the boat to England. Walking through these places feels right. And the weight of the coffin on my shoulders feels right. It's a privilege to carry this man, my friend, through our hometown, to his resting-place.

But he was too young. Sixty. He spent exactly a quarter of that time in prison. And yet, despite this, I'm in awe of how much fight he had left in him. To the bitter end. In her eulogy in the church Gareth Peirce, his solicitor, describes his last days. *Struggling for oxygen, with a mask most of the time clamped to his face, he was just talking and talking and talking about the things that needed to be done, the people who were wrongly imprisoned here and in Guantánamo, in Australia – he couldn't stop talking.*

And as I cry for Gerry – my childhood friend – I'm crying also for Carole. For all of us. For everything we lost. And I think about what Billy Joel sang. '*Only the good die young.*' I think he means people like Carole and Gerry.

Just like that, my world has been tilted very slightly. Nothing is the same with my two dear friends gone. I hadn't seen either of them very much in the last 20 years, but still their absence is so painful. The feelings I've been able to so easily compartmentalise are suddenly vying for attention. Loss and grief and anger. And something else. A desire to say something. To be heard.

I've been thinking about Gerry's words as we sat in the Sheds that last evening we spent together. Telling me that I did the right thing by getting on with my life. And maybe it did hurt him, not letting it all go. But perhaps I went to the other extreme by pushing it all down. Ignoring it. Maybe there's an in-between? Talking about it enough to purge it, to heal. Maybe I need to let it out more. Especially now he and Carole are both gone. There's only two of us left to tell our story. So that the world never forgets. So that what happened to us can never happen again.

~

October 2014

If Gerry had lived just a few more months, he'd have seen the 25th anniversary of our release and the 40th anniversary of the bombing. He's gone, but I'm now doing something.

After my being very media-shy, apart from *In the Name of the Father*, the daughter of our friends JJ and Mandy, Holly Woods, makes a short film about me for college (*Life after Life*). She gets an award for it and I decide I'm going to open up more. I've agreed to let RTÉ Documentary on One make a radio programme about me. *Small Lives and Great Reputations* they'll call it, using Chris Mullin's words. Our small lives which were sacrificed for the great reputations of those policemen and judges and everybody else responsible for convicting us.

The documentary takes us back to London, to Guildford and up North to see Chris Mullin, who campaigned for us and the Birmingham Six. We leave John and Sophie in the care of Caroline's sister Fiona. Leaving our babies, even though they're teenagers now, for the first time in their entire lives. They're not too bothered; we're nervous wrecks.

I've no idea what I'm in for. The small crew, Mary-Elaine Tynan and Nicoline Greer, follow me around with a big fluffy microphone as I travel in taxis, on the tube, on the street. I didn't expect it, but I'm nervous in England. I swat the microphone away sometimes. Don't want to attract too much attention here in case people work out who I am. In case some

of them still think that we did it. You'd think that after the formal apology
from Blair I'd finally relax, but there's always a tiny part of me that worries
about what people think.

RTÉ contacted HM Prison Service in advance of our trip, requesting
permission to take me inside one of the prisons I had been in. I'd love to
do that now – only because I don't have to stay. But they refuse. *Security
measures. You can stand outside, though,* they say. We laugh at the irony. I
couldn't get out of them when I wanted to, and now when I want to get
back in I'm not allowed.

So here I am, standing with a microphone thrust into my face, gazing
up at these imposing buildings that held me captive in those early days in
prison. I only ever saw a prison from the window of a van, and even then I
was too busy being terrified to look at it. And now here I am, looking up at
these prisons that failed to break me.

Brixton – the first prison I ever went to, for a TV I never stole. Wormwood
Scrubs – where they sent me after I was sentenced. And the worst of them all:
Wandsworth. The most dismal, cold and frightening place, but I went there
voluntarily so I could see my dear old mum semi-regularly. Just standing
outside it on a cold October day gives me goosebumps.

And standing here, I find myself wondering about the men locked up
inside. Are some of them innocent, like us? Are they petrified? Do they
cry themselves to sleep at night? Lose months and weeks sometimes? At
moments like this, it's like I'm remembering somebody else's life. Seeing
somebody else's memories – a man who sewed mail bags for weeks on end,
a man who looked up at Ronnie Biggs's chair nailed to the wall and knew he
would never be able to escape, a man who shook and cried for his mammy
and his sister and his girlfriend. I can't believe I was once that man, behind
those very same walls. And now I'm here.

We take the train to Guildford. Alastair and Pat are there to meet us at
the station. Hugging them, I feel like it's been just weeks since I saw them
last, when really I've seen them only a handful of times since they came over
to Dublin to be one set of John's godparents. They look at me with such
warmth and I remember how, in my darkest and most frightened years, they

were there for me. Always with open arms and an open door or ready to talk to me on the phone. And all these years later, they still feel like surrogate parents. I look at Alastair, 40 years after I first met him. That posh, serious man who couldn't understand a word I was saying. Who never gave up on me. What a road we have both travelled.

We drive through Guildford town and Alastair points out the police station. *Police station is behind those trees, Paddy. They've grown a lot since 1974.* And, yes, there it is, crouching down behind the thick foliage. Those same trees now camouflage the window they threatened to throw me from. A lifetime ago, and yet that incident room, their faces peering down at me and the cacophony of voices shouting are so vividly etched in my memory. Alastair continues, *Well, at least you were beaten up by an Assistant Chief Constable. It wasn't an ordinary constable, was it, Mr Armstrong? … Surrey's finest.* We laugh, and for the first time in years I remember all those men, towering over me. Dirty Harry and his friends. Many are dead now. Never did I think I'd outlive them.

Wandering the streets of Guildford on the 40th anniversary of the bombings, we walk past a small, well-kept garden, on the side of the street just opposite where the Horse and Groom pub was. Pat tugs my sleeve and points. *This is called Quaker's Acre,* she tells me, *but it's become a type of remembrance garden, Paddy. The local authority put a plaque up here in memory of those who died in the Guildford bombings, so this is where Alastair and I come every year to lay a white wreath for the victims.* They want me to go in with them, but I shake my head. I don't want to tell them, but I'm nervous. What if someone were to see me? What if there's still people who think I'm guilty? What if somebody said something? But the others insist. *Come on, Paddy. You have every right to come in,* Pat says. *Your life was taken away from you for a long time. You were a victim of this bombing too.* I nod and reluctantly follow them into a small but beautifully kept garden.

We lay a wreath here every year, they tell me. *But this year, for the fortieth anniversary, there are more from the police, the army and the local authority and some from the local community and the families of those who died.* There are flowers and wreaths, with handwritten cards attached.

Alastair points to a wreath of white roses. *That's ours there. I always used to put on the card that the wreath is in memory of those who lost their lives and that it is coupled with the names of those who were wrongly convicted. But after Carole died it was coupled with the name of Carole, RIP. Then when Gerry died I added his name as well. We always wrote your names on it.* I look at Alastair's and Pat's faces and I realise they weren't just *my* surrogate parents. They loved Carole so much too. They mourn her too. *It's lovely,* I tell them. *Really beautiful.*

We wander through the garden on this grey October day, 25 years exactly since we were released and just over 40 since the sleepy town of Guildford erupted. I pay my silent tribute to the victims: to the men and women who died that night in 1974, and to Carole and Gerry. And I'm glad I came in. It feels like another tiny piece of my pain has broken off and is drifting away from me, just by being in this very special place.

We wander down Guildford's Market Street, where the Seven Stars pub used to be. Gone is the shell that was left after the bombing. It's been replaced by a trendy coffee shop with outdoor seating. As we stand there, gazing at the building, I get talking to a man and end up telling him who I am. Something I wouldn't normally do anywhere, never mind in Guildford. He's looking at the coffee shops and back at me incredulously, and for a moment I'm worried. Then he speaks and there's emotion in his voice. *I'm so sorry about what happened. It's a terrible injustice.* I tell him it's been 25 years since I got out. He shakes his head slowly and then reaches for my hand. He shakes it and looks into my eyes. *Thank you,* he says. *Thank you and good luck.*

We go back to Alastair and Pat's house – a celebration lunch. Alastair toasts us. *To our guests. To Paddy – one of the best clients I ever had.* We smile. I bet he never thought he would still be looking at this case, or at me, so many years on. It's one of the few times I sit at a table, eating with a group of people. It's nice.

Pat and I stand together and talk after lunch. She looks at me the way she always does, like she can see inside me. Past the jokes, into the heart of my pain. *You look well, Paddy. You look happy. I am, Pat. I really am. Life is good today. I'm so happy for you,* she's saying. And she really is.

And even though I don't think about my days in prison on a daily basis any more, and even though I had to leave Guildford eventually, so I could move on from it, it's good to be back. I remember the early days of my release. A full bottle of vodka some days. Stoned on others. Hiding from people. Running away. So overwhelmed and rootless. Trying to find a place I could call home. Searching. Lost. I could have ended up anywhere. Six feet under if I'd kept going the way I was. But instead I'm here now with my wife and our children are safe at home. It's good to be back – if only just to appreciate how very far I've come since I left Guildford six months after my release.

And because of this I decide that I do want to share my story. So instead of hiding away, start giving talks in schools about my experiences. I go into Caroline's school first. One student asks me what I missed the most in prison. *Sex,* I say. Caroline is fit to kill me. They're so honest, these young people. *Are you bitter?* they ask. *I'm not. Not at all. But why not? You must be. How can you not be angry, after what happened to you?* I try to explain. *Look at my life. Look at what I have. I never would have had this if I hadn't gone to prison. I could have died on the streets of London. I was living it up, but it could have gone wrong at any time. And it's not my way to be angry.*

Not everybody believes me when I say this. Some people nod, but I can tell they don't believe me. *There must be anger, resentment buried deep down,* they want to say. And maybe there is, but I don't feel it. Mostly I just feel happy and lucky. So what's the point in dwelling on it?

It's funny. Without noticing it, I went from being the fella from the Guildford Four to becoming Paddy the family man. The Lord Mayor of Clontarf. The man who loves his friends, Arsenal and his comfortable routine. It wasn't easy, in the very early days. Letting go of the bottle of vodka, the drugs, the gambling was hard, but little by little things shifted for me. Mostly when I met Caroline. Looking back on it, I can see that my life has been one of moderation and normality for many years now. My progress is something I rarely think about or celebrate, but I've come a long way. I see that when I look back. I'm comfortable in me now. Not comfortably numb like I was in prison. Just comfortable.

But with recent events it feels like my past is now clawing for attention. Between the documentaries and losing Carole and Gerry it's hard to ignore. Talking in schools has shown me that I do have something to say. That my story is different from everyone else's. We all suffered in different ways. And dealt with it differently. And where we've ended up is very different. Poor Gerry and Carole are gone. Paul went to America and I'm not sure where he is now. And I'm here.

I decide I want to write it all down, while I still have time – for the record, for my children, for history. So that what happened to us is never forgotten. And so it can never happen again. A family friend and journalist, Mary-Elaine, is helping me to research it and write it all down. For months she's been dragging the memories out of me. We walk up and down the coast of Clontarf, a microphone in my face again. We're talking, debating, arguing. I'm remembering, but it isn't always easy. Or comfortable. But she's relentless. *Come on, Paddy, tell me more about that time. No, I need more detail.* Sometimes the memories come freely, painlessly. Other times she drags them from me kicking and screaming. *Stop making jokes, Paddy, and just bloody tell me. What really happened? How did that make you feel?* It's like counselling all over again.

With all this talking and remembering, my mind is frequently filled with memories, like mini-movies. They pop into my head, often uninvited. I hate remembering those times when my life was out of control. During and after prison. At these moments it's like taking a plaster off an old sore that never really healed. But maybe now it's been exposed to a bit of fresh air, the new skin is slowly growing back. Healing.

In the process of writing the book, Mary-Elaine tracks down Lisa. My old, dear friend. The last time I saw her was around six months after we were released. Early 1990. I was drinking heavily and she was trying to create a normal life for herself. I stayed with her for a couple of weeks. I haven't seen her since then. It's hard to believe it's been so long.

Mary-Elaine gives Caroline's mobile number to Lisa. Explains that I don't have one. I did for a while but, to be honest, technology and I don't really go together. And now Lisa's on the other end of Caroline's phone.

Hi, Paddy, it's Lisa. How are you? She has a soft voice. Gentle. Warm. She sounds the same and yet so different. Grown up. Together. But bubbly and easy to talk to. *I'm great, Lisa. It's lovely to hear your voice. Yes, it's lovely to hear yours too, Paddy.*

It's hard to believe that this is the voice of the 16-year-old who danced around our living room in Linstead Street in 1974, the runaway who drew psychedelic pictures of mushrooms and eyes, Carole's friend and my friend who, for a few months, called me *big bruvver* and who I referred to as *little sister*. I think about the same girl, still a teenager, visiting me in prison with presents and smiles, and the girl who took me in for a couple of weeks in 1990, after our release. Still young even then. She's a woman now. Almost 58. A long, long time has passed.

We chat away about everything and nothing. She tells me about her life now. I tell her about Caroline and John and Sophie. All the great things in life. And we talk about Carole and Gerry. *Can't believe it. So sad.*

I get off the phone and I think about Lisa back then. Fifteen, turning 16 at the end of summer, 1974. The same age as my son John is now. She seemed girlish but worldly to me then. Because I was a boy from Belfast who'd led a very sheltered life. We were all so young then, though we didn't know it.

That evening, Caroline calls me. There's an email for me. *Read that*, she says.

From: Lisa
To: Paddy and Caroline Armstrong
Sent: Tuesday, 26 July 2016
Subject: Re: Paddy

Hi Paddy
It was lovely speaking to you today after all these years. I always ask Alistair or Ros about you so have been quietly following your life. It is wonderful that you are in a happy marriage and have your children to focus on. I was saddened by the premature deaths of both Gerry and Carole. On the positive side I am in regular contact with Carole's daughter Louise and she is a fine young woman. She actually sent me the link for your radio interview for the 40th anniversary of Guildford. I thought you came across in it very well. Louise thought you seemed like a very nice man. I had to agree as I heard the person

that you have always been – kind and gentlemanly. Just for the record, Carole never held you responsible for her demise so if you still have those thoughts please let go of them. No doubt we all have scars from that time, but that is one burden you do not deserve to carry. God has given us all many gifts since you were all vindicated. I do hope we get to meet up in the near future Paddy as it is way overdue. It would be so nice to meet Caroline and the children. In the meantime stay well and clothed in the love of your family.

God Bless

Lisa xx

From: Paddy and Caroline Armstrong
To: Lisa
Sent: Saturday, 30 July, 2016
Subject: Re: Paddy

Dear Lisa,

I am writing on behalf of Paddy and myself - Paddy doesn't do emails!!

We were both very moved by your beautiful email and very appreciative.

Paddy was thrilled to speak to you and now mentions you nearly every day! It would be absolutely lovely to meet up with you.

You sound like a remarkable person.

Take care Lisa and many thanks again. Please God we will meet in the near future.

Love

Paddy and Caroline xxx

From: Lisa
To: Paddy and Caroline Armstrong
Sent: Friday, 5 August, 2016
Subject: Re: Paddy

Hi Paddy and Caroline

Hope you have both had a good week. I just spoke to Louise and she has agreed to come to Dublin with me. She really wants to meet you all – especially you Paddy. We are hoping to come sometime in Sept for a couple of days. The plan is to stay in a hotel near you. Are there any that you can recommend? It will be so lovely to spend time with you all.

Love Lisa xx

~

Lisa is coming in a few weeks. And she's bringing Louise. Carole's daughter.
I can't believe it. She emails again soon after to say that Maura has decided
to come too. Maura, whose mother sent her to Ireland to keep her away
from the police and who therefore couldn't be Carole's alibi at the trial.
Lisa, Louise and Maura are all coming to see us.

It's hard to take in. Caroline is more nervous than I am. I tend to deal
with emotions at the last minute. *It'll be fine, love. Don't be worrying.* But as
the days draw closer, I'm getting nervous. What if they don't like me? What
will Louise think of me? What will Lisa think of me? Have I changed? Now I
don't know how I feel about it all. Excited. Terrified.

~

They're here. Just on the other side of the frosted glass of our front door
stand Lisa, Louise and Maura. As soon as I see Louise, it's like seeing
Carole all those years ago. The same smile, identical eyes. It's a lovely sight.
Emotional.

Lisa springs forward first and hugs me. We're hugging and there's tears in
everyone's eyes. I swallow mine. Crack a joke. A house full of women again.
Like being back in Belfast. It's all a little overwhelming at first, but within
minutes we're in our kitchen chatting while Bobby, our dog, is dancing
around, just dying to get someone's attention so they might rub or tickle him.

And as in any typical Irish or English home, soon we all have a cup of tea
or coffee in our hands and we're swapping memories. Maura has newspaper
clippings she's brought to show me. I take out the photos I have of Carole
and Lisa, of myself and a few others in a London pub. We look at the grainy,
black-and-white images. How young we were. How innocent. We stay up
late talking, laughing, remembering.

After I cook breakfast for us all, Lisa, Louise and Maura go into Dublin
city centre to do some shopping. I arrange to meet them later. Because I
don't have a mobile, I usually meet people beside the Spire in O'Connell
Street. A massive, stainless-steel structure that looks like a pin: it's perfect –
even the most myopic tourist couldn't miss it.

I arrive early. As usual. And stand there beside the Spire. I wait. It's so wide at the bottom that I can't see all the way around it, so I move around the shiny steel every so often, to make sure I don't miss them. They're late. Ten minutes. Move back around to the other side of the monument. Just in case. Twenty minutes. Women – they must be shopping! Move around again. Thirty minutes. Wait until they get here, I'll give them a good telling-off. Forty-five minutes. I wander around in a circle, but now I'm not really looking any more. After an hour I stop. They're not coming. I'll go home and wait.

They arrive back at the house shortly after me. *What happened to you, Paddy? We were waiting for you. What happened to me! I was there – where were you? We waited at the Spar in O'Connell Street like you told us. Stood out in front of the shop, went inside. We couldn't find you anywhere. You couldn't have. I was there. Walked around and around it looking.* Back and forth we go. And then suddenly we realise. They're talking about the Spar – a shop. I'm talking about the Spire – a massive monument. So they stood waiting for me outside the Spar shop in O'Connell Street, just a few feet away from where I waited for them at the Spire. *It's your Belfast accent,* they say. I shake my head. *I don't have an accent. It's your English ears that need cleaning out.* We laugh and laugh.

After dinner in my house, on their second night, Mary-Elaine brings over a copy of the *First Tuesday* documentary from October 1989. Filmed by Ros and Grant the week after we got out, and broadcast just a few weeks later, it features me, Gerry, Paul and Carole. The only one we did together. I say, *You go ahead and watch it. I've seen it. I was interviewed for it and I saw it afterwards. I know exactly what happens. I don't need to see it again,* I tell them with a grin. *Away you go. I'll sit out here.* So now, packed into our living room are Caroline, Mary-Elaine, Louise, Lisa and Maura. I hear Olivia O'Leary introducing the documentary and go back into the kitchen. I can glance through the window that separates the two rooms if I want to see it. But I don't want to ...

And yet, as the voice continues talking, I find myself drifting closer and closer to the door, almost against my will. And finally, when I peek through the glass, there she is. Carole. Aged 32. Filling the screen. Looking out at me. So familiar. So real. So alive.

And as her voice continues to float from the living room to where I'm standing, just inches from the glass door, there's a sound somewhere in the distance. A high-pitched keening sound. Like an animal in pain. It's the most primal wailing and seems to come from the very core of someone's being.

It's only when I feel Caroline's arms around me that I realise this sound is coming from me. From a place that, until 10 minutes ago, I would have sworn did not exist. She sits me down and I fall against her. I feel a different set of arms around me. Lisa. Tears rolling down her cheeks, she too embraces me. Holds me up. And between them these two women who, combined, have known me for most of my life, hold me until the sobbing abates.

I don't know where the pain, the keening and all those tears came from. I would have sworn that such pain didn't exist. Not within me. But it did. It does, obviously. In all my years, since the night in Alastair's house, I've never cried like this. Crying out the pain, the fear, the loss. Mourning my life, my youth, the girl I once loved.

∼

Lisa, Louise and Maura are going home after our few days together. We sit in the Sheds, on their last day in Dublin. I'm looking at my daughter, Sophie, and then at Carole's daughter, Louise, and then back again. It's a funny feeling, seeing them here together. So strange and so lovely. I once thought Carole and I would have a child. Maybe a girl of our own. Instead we both have one, and even though Carole has passed on, both of our girls are sitting here talking to me. In the same pub where I sat with Gerry a few short years ago. It's so overwhelming at times. So precious. Life's strange twists and turns.

∼

The day after our visitors leave, Josephine has finally solved a mystery up in Belfast. After her partner, Rab, spent weeks combing through newspapers, he found an article in the *Irish News* about my sister Gertie's accident. We have a date. Josephine goes back to Milltown Cemetery and finds a kindly assistant who combs the records, and there she is. Gertrude Philomena Armstrong. Died 9 April 1957. Aged two years and ten months. Buried in a plot not far from our parents, our Gertie lies with our grandparents. It's like another loose end has been tied up. A tiny bit of peace for us all.

~

As a boy from the Lower Falls Road in Belfast, I never expected to go further than the end of my street. But I did. And although, in the end, I've found a home just a short distance down the motorway, only a hundred miles from my hometown, I've travelled a long, long way to get here. I've outlived many of my tormentors and I'm not finished living yet. I've survived.

That's not to say that I haven't been damaged. I'm not deluded. I know that I will never fully recover from my ordeal and that I'll definitely never forget it. But I don't want to. And I can't let others forget. We must never forget people like us and the Birmingham Six. If only so it can never happen again.

I am the sum of my experiences. Good and bad. My life has made me the man I am. Where would I have been had it not happened? I've wondered that many times and rarely can I imagine a positive outcome. Certainly nothing like where I have ended up. I'm just grateful to be here, in a place that feels like home, with people who are my home.

I am many things, but I'm not broken. Worn around the edges, perhaps, frayed somewhat by time and by the actions of the men who thought that my life and the lives of Carole, Gerry and Paul were dispensable. But they weren't. We fought back. It took 15 long years and the help of some incredible people, but in the end, we won.

I am many things, but I remain intact.

Unbroken.

And I have a life after life.

EPILOGUE: JANUARY 2017

Most of the documents from the May Inquiry relating to our case have yet to be released. Conducted in secret between 1989 and 1994, this inquiry was supposed to investigate how our miscarriages of justice could have happened. Instead it cleared those involved.

They didn't allow any of us four, or our solicitors, to take part in it. Nor did they consult our legal teams – only the police, Law Officers, the Director of Public Prosecutions, scientists and a handful of other contributions from those who had assisted us, like Dr James MacKeith, Professor Brian Caddy and Dr John Lloyd. In the end Alastair arranged for Carole and me to do filmed interviews with Dr MacKeith about issues relating to our confessions. It was traumatic, reliving that time, but we felt it would be worth it. And then after the interviews had been submitted to the inquiry, Sir John May decided to conduct the Guildford aspects in secret. When we later asked to see the evidence given to May, we were told it had been embargoed for 30 years – in the hope, no doubt, that we would all be dead by then. They were half right. Gerry and Carole are gone. But Paul and I are still kicking.

Some of the papers have just been released in recent months, 42 years after the bombings in Guildford, and they contain complete and utter lies. Statements designed to convict us all over again, in the media and in the court of public opinion. Alastair and I are not surprised by this, but I'm sad. Until the papers are released, we will never know the full extent of the contributions. It's only three years until the rest of the 700 papers are due to be released, on 1 January 2020. There have been rumours that they want to embargo them for up to another 40 years. If this happened, it would be 75 years after the May Inquiry before anyone could see them. By this time anybody who cares enough to refute them would be dead.

This is a frightening prospect – by doing so, they could so easily rewrite history again, in their own version. Try and convict us in the court of public opinion all over again. Alastair is still fighting this injustice on our behalf. If there is such a thing as a guardian angel, Alastair is a living example of one. He is always there. He never gives up.

God Bless the Innocent
May the Guilty
Be Brought to Justice

KEY FIGURES

This list is intended to help the reader and is limited to those who are specifically referred to in the book. A number of other people involved in this case are mentioned in the acknowledgements.

The Guildford Four
Patrick (Paddy) Armstrong
Gerard (Gerry) Conlon
Paul Hill
Carole Richardson

Paddy's family
Granny and Grandad Maxwell – grandparents on father's side
Granny Mullins – grandmother on mother's side, who lived with our family
Eileen Armstrong (Snr) – mother
John (Johnny) Armstrong – father
Harriet Armstrong – eldest sister
Eileen Armstrong (Jnr) – younger sister
Gertie Armstrong – younger sister
Josephine Armstrong – youngest sister
Jim Thompson – married to Eileen Armstrong (Jnr)
Fr Vincent McKinley – Canon of St Peter's Pro Cathedral and Parish Priest to the Armstrongs and Conlons

Paddy's Family (today)
Caroline Armstrong – wife
John Armstrong – son
Sophie Armstrong – daughter

London friends
Lisa Astin – Carole and Paddy's friend, and Carole's alibi for the night of the Guildford bombings
Maura Kelly – Carole and Lisa's friend, and Carole's alibi for the day of the Guildford bombings
Frank Johnson – Carole's alibi for the night of the Guildford bombings
Jack the Lad – the band that Carole, Lisa and Frank went to see the night of the Guildford bombings

Arrested at Algernon Road and Rondu Road
Paul Colman
Brian Anderson
John McGuinness
Sean Mullin

Robert Carlisle
Alastair Cully

Legal team
Alastair Logan – Paddy's solicitor (1974–present), Carole's solicitor (1985–2013), Gerry and Paul's solicitor (1977–1987)
Gareth Peirce – Gerry's solicitor (1987 onwards)

Experts on confessional evidence, concerned with Guildford case
Dr James MacKeith
Barrie Irving
Professor Gisli Gudjonsson

The Maguire Seven
Patrick (Giuseppe) Joseph Conlon
Anne (Annie) Maguire
Patrick (Paddy) Maguire
Vincent Maguire
'Young Patrick' Maguire
Sean Smyth
Patrick O'Neill

The Birmingham Six
Hugh Callaghan
Patrick Joseph (Paddy Joe) Hill
Gerard (Gerry) Hunter
Richard McIlkenny
William Power
John Walker

Members of IRA London Active Service Unit captured at Balcombe Street
Hugh Doherty
Joseph O'Connell
Eddie Butler
Harry Duggan

Members of IRA Active Service Units
Brendan Dowd
Sean Kinsella
Paul Norney
Stephen Nordone
Noel Gibson
Ronnie McCartney – Member of ASU and later a prison friend of Paddy's

Police

Assistant Chief Constable Christopher Rowe – in charge of Guildford investigation

Detective Chief Superintendent Walter (Wally) Simmons – Head of Surrey Criminal Investigation Department

Detective Constable Vernon Attwell

Detective Sergeant John Donaldson

Detective Chief Inspector Thomas Style

Chief Superintendent Jim Nevill (later Commander)

Detective Sergeant Peter Imbert (later Metropolitan Police Commissioner, 1987–1993)

Senior lawyers and judges involved in the case

Sir John Donaldson (later Lord Donaldson) – Guildford and Maguire trial judge

Sir Michael Havers QC, MP (later Attorney General and Lord Chancellor) – leading counsel for the prosecution in the Guildford, Maguire and Balcombe Street trials, and Guildford and Maguire appeals

Lord Eustace Roskill – appeal judge, 1977

Lord Chief Justice Lord Lane – leading appeal judge, 1989

John Leonard QC – leading counsel for Paddy Armstrong

Politicians, judges, journalists and public figures who argued for Guildford case to be re-opened

Basil Hume – Cardinal Archbishop of Westminster

Lord Roy Jenkins – Home Secretary, 1974–1976

Gerry Fitt – former MP for West Belfast

Sister Sarah Clarke – public (religious) figure

Lord Merlyn Rees – Secretary of State, Northern Ireland, 1974; Home Secretary 1976–1979

Lord Patrick Devlin – Law Lord

Lord Leslie Scarman – Law Lord

Ros Franey – journalist

Grant McKee – journalist

Chris Mullin – journalist, former MP

Other friends

Pat Logan – Alastair's wife

Pat Mulryan – Paddy's friend and best man after prison

Paddy Reilly – Paddy's friend after prison

Louise Richardson – Carole's daughter

Holly Woods – family friend and documentary maker

Sheila and Stephen Drumm – family friends

Mary-Elaine Tynan – journalist and co-author of this book

ACKNOWLEDGEMENTS

There are numerous debts of acknowledgement and gratitude. First I would like to thank my father, Johnny, my mother, Eileen (both now passed), my sisters and their families for their love and support. In particular I would like to acknowledge my sister, Eileen, and her husband, Jim, who visited me regularly in prison at great cost to themselves and their family. Eileen, Jim and my sister, Josephine, contributed much to this book in the form of memories and photographs.

I would also like to acknowledge my wife's family. Her mother, Maureen, her sisters and brothers and their families, who have welcomed me into their lives like one of their own. A particular thank you to Caroline's sister, Fiona, for her help with proofreading. Also Caroline's colleagues and friends, especially Sheila and Stephen Drumm, who always bring fun, love and laughter to our house.

Heartfelt thanks to my solicitor, Alastair Logan. Alastair originally took my case because nobody else would. He has been with me since I was arrested in 1974, working relentlessly to prove the innocence of the Guildford Four – for many years unpaid. I owe him my life. I am grateful to Alastair and his wife, Pat, for their continued love, friendship and support in the years since my release. Both have contributed hugely, in terms of their time and expertise, to the research for this book.

I thank Grant McKee and Ros Franey for their book *Time Bomb* and their powerful TV programmes, which helped to highlight our case and bring it to the public's attention. Ros has been a tremendous help in providing archive records and documents for this book.

From the beginning there were many people who believed our innocence and fought for justice. They came from different walks of life, ranging from ordinary people who marched the Falls Road holding my photograph, to journalists and members of the British Government, among others. I would like to acknowledge the whole of the Cardinal Hume Deputation, Paddy Victory, Lord Fitt, Robert Kee, Barry Irving, Sister Sarah Clarke, Father Denis Faul, Father Raymond Murray, Chris Mullin, Ludovic Kennedy, Bob Woffinden, Ronan Bennett, Sir John Biggs-Davison, Dr Brian Caddy, Irene Cockroft, Lord Devlin, John Fairley, Michael Fisher, Professor Lionel Howard, Father Vincent McKinley, Peter Newby, Frank Pocklington, Christopher Price, Merlyn Rees, Brian Rose-Smith, Gareth Pierce, Gavin Esler, David McKittrick, Tom McGurk, Jonathan Dimbleby, Peter Chippindale, David Frost, Mary Holland, Anne McHardy, Olivia O'Leary and John Willis.

To the artists who used their work to ensure that we were not forgotten: Christy Moore, The Wolfe Tones and The Pogues. In particular I am so grateful for the work of Jim Sheridan and everyone who made *In the Name of the Father* as they brought our story to an international audience.

I would like to thank the two professionals whom Alastair arranged to counsel and guide me on my release from prison: Dr James MacKeith and Professor Gisli Gudjonsson.

I acknowledge with sincere gratitude the loyalty of Lisa Astin and Frank Johnson.

I remember and am grateful for the great Falls Road community in Belfast, growing up with friends like John Hughes, Martin Molloy, Joe Keenan and Ronnie McCartney – Ronnie was later to help me through a difficult time in prison.

A special acknowledgement to the other groups who also suffered miscarriages of justice: the Maguire Seven and the Birmingham Six. My very good friend Paddy Hill of the Birmingham Six has spent his life since his release fighting for justice for others. It is with the greatest sadness that I remember Carole Richardson and Gerry Conlon, my dear friends who are no longer with us.

Thank you to our good friend, the gifted Holly Woods, for her award-winning documentary *Life after Life* and to her parents, JJ and Mandy Woods. Thank you, Holly, for inspiring the title of the book!

When I moved to Dublin in 1991 I forged new friendships that have endured, in particular Pat Mulryan and Paddy Reilly.

I would like to acknowledge my fantastic friends and neighbours in Clontarf, where I have now settled. At the centre of this great community is my local pub Connolly's (aka 'the Sheds'). The fabulous staff and friends there make it a home from home, especially for the Arsenal games!

Thank you to Gill Books for taking on my life story, in particular Conor Nagle (even though he is an Everton fan!)

A very special thank you to one person without whom this book would not have been written. She has been part of my life for the past few years. She has written articles and produced an award-winning documentary about my life for RTÉ Radio called *Small Lives and Great Reputations*. I think by now she probably knows more about me than I do! She is the gifted Mary-Elaine Tynan. I thank her for her huge talent combined with such humanity and compassion.

Finally, I would like to thank my wife, Caroline, and children, John and Sophie. You are the rocks on which I have built my 'life after life'. You are the centre of my world and make everything I went through worth waiting for.

Paddy Armstrong, January 2017

I would like to acknowledge the many people who helped and supported Paddy and me in the process of researching and writing this book over the last two years.

We both owe the biggest debt of gratitude to Ros Franey, Alastair Logan and his wife, Pat, without whom this book could not have been written. Their generosity has been so touching, and their impeccable memories and records are beyond impressive. Most of all, though, their commitment to justice is at once humbling and energising.

Thank you also to the many people who gave hours of their time to be interviewed, including Josephine Armstrong, Eileen Armstrong, Pat Mulryan, Ronnie McCartney, Lisa Astin, Maura Kelly, Louise Richardson, Ann McKernan, Chris Mullin and Sheila Drumm.

To all at Gill Books, in particular Conor Nagle, who believed in Paddy's story.

Special thanks to the staff in National Library of Ireland and especially Justin Furlong.

To my colleagues, friends and family, who have lived with this book for the last two years, in particular my sister, parents and my husband, Jason, who have read various drafts and tolerated the late nights and uncooked dinners.

To Paddy, Caroline, John and Sophie. I feel so honoured that you have trusted me with the story of your lives and am incredibly privileged to have worked so closely with you. Thank you for believing in me every step of the way and for making me feel like part of your family.

This book is for my babies, Aoibheann and Donnacha, who make me proud every single day.

Mary-Elaine Tynan, January 2017